I'LL DROWN MY BOOK

Conceptual Writing by Women

Cover: Rachel Khedoori's *Untitled (Iraq War Project)*, as shown at The Box, Los Angeles, September 11-October 24, 2009. Photo by Fredrik Nilson Studio. Originally printed in *X-tra*, (vol 12, no 3), 31. Reprinted with permission.

Acknowledgements required to be printed on this page. Note: These are repeated in the "Acknowledgements" section, alongside addition publication acknowledgements.

Selected work from *ALPHABET*, by Inger Christensen, translated by Susanna Nied, from *ALPHABET*, copyright ©1981, 2000 by Inger Christensen, Translation copyright © 2000 by Susanna Nied. Reprinted by permission of New Directions Publishing Corp.

Excerpt from *A Bibliography of the King's Book or, Eikon Basilike* from *THE NONCONFORMIST'S MEMORIAL*, copyright ©1989 by Susan Howe. Reprinted by permission of New Directions Publishing Corp.

I'll Drown My Book: Conceptual Writing By Women
FIRST EDITION

ISBN 13: 978-1-934254-33-2
ISBN 1-934254-33-9
Library of Congress Control Number: 2011945202

Text design by Janice Lee; additional design by Les Figues Press.

Copy editing: Harold Abramowitz, Heatherlie Allison, Diana Arterian, Amina Cain, Jennifer Calkins, Teresa Carmody, David Emanuel, Chris Hershey-Van Horn, Jennifer Karmin, Coco Owen, Mathew Timmons, and Emma Williams.

Special thanks to Les Figues Press interns Heatherlie Allison, Chris Hershey-Van Horn, Emily Kiernan, and Emma Williams. Thank you to Veronica Amaya, Mary Evangelista, Laida Lertxundi, Christina C. Nguyen, Tanya Rubbak, and Sari Thayer. See: http://www.kickstarter.com/projects/1359907001/ill-drown-my-book-conceptual-writing-by-women.

Finally, a very big thank you to everyone who supported this project through Kickstarter. This book is possible because of you.

Les Figues Press titles are available through:
Les Figues Press: http://www.lesfigues.com
Small Press Distribution: http://www.spdbooks.org

𝄢

LES FIGUES PRESS
Post Office Box 7736
Los Angeles, CA 90007
www.lesfigues.com

EDITED BY

CAROLINE BERGVALL
LAYNIE BROWNE
TERESA CARMODY
VANESSA PLACE

CONTENTS

2. STRUCTURE
APPROPRIATION, ERASURE, CONSTRAINT, FORMULA, PATTERN, PALIMPSEST

3. MATTER
BAROQUE, HYBRID, GENERATIVE, CORPOREAL, DISSENSUAL

4. EVENT

DOCUMENTA, INVESTIGATIVE, INTERTEXTUAL, HISTORICISM, SPECULATIVE

5. CONCLUDING REMARKS

0. INTRODUCTORY NOTES

LAYNIE BROWNE

A CONCEPTUAL ASSEMBLAGE
AN INTRODUCTION

> To work mine end upon their senses that
> This airy charm is for, I'll break my staff,
> Bury it certain fathoms in the earth,
> And deeper than did ever plummet sound
> I'll drown my book.
>
> *- Shakespeare, The Tempest, Act V Scene I, Prospero*

Looking for a title for this collection I turned first to the work of Bernadette Mayer, and found in her collection, *The Desires of Mothers to Please Others in Letters*, the title "I'll Drown My Book." The process of opening Mayer to find Shakespeare reframed seems particularly fitting in the sense that conceptual writing often involves a recasting of the familiar and the found. In Mayer's hands, the phrase "I'll Drown My Book" becomes an unthinkable yet necessary act. This combination of unthinkable, or illogical, and necessary, or obligatory, also speaks to ways that the writers in this collection seek to unhinge and re-examine previous assumptions about writing. Thinking and performance are not separate from process and presentation of works. If a book breathes it can also drown, and in the act of drowning is a willful attempt to create a book which can awake the unexpected—not for the sake of surprise, but because the undertaking was necessary for the writer in order to uproot, dismantle, reforge, remap or find new vantages and entrances to well trodden or well guarded territory.

My contemporaries for the most part have often been distinguished by their lack of camps, categories, or movements. This lack of naming has been useful and has enabled an appreciation of a wide range of practices and approaches to writing. So, why an anthology of conceptual writing by women? The term "conceptual" is being coined anew by writers and it is unthinkable that women should be written out of the project. This book began for me with the problem of the under-representation of women, particularly in key moments when movements begin to take shape and crystallize and are documented by gatherings, public events and anthologies. And while perhaps few would argue that women are not writing and publishing in this area, it is often at the stage of anthologizing that numbers start to shift so that women are not adequately represented. Juliana Spahr and Stephanie Young note in their essay "Numbers Trouble" that: "Overall, in our admittedly arbitrary selection of mixed-gender anthologies that in some way identify themselves as experimental/ postmodern/avant-garde/innovative, we found that between 1960 and 1999 women make up an average of 22% of the writers." Similarly, in the new website for VIDA (Women in Literary Arts), Amy King examines the gender distribution of several major book awards and prominent best-of lists for 2009 and finds represented 592 men and 295 women. Her historical tally is equally discouraging: 929 men and 454 women. These statistics are alarming because this lack of representation of women is in some sense invisible until we come to moments where codification starts to happen. To many then, this writing women out of the canon is invisible until after the fact. Bernadette Mayer writes: "Since women are often disenfranchised, depending on what country you live in, daughters are often thrown away. Hard to believe isn't it? But then a lot of stuff about females is."

Why the term "conceptual" now? Why not come up with a new term, one which is actually new? And yet the term "conceptual," because of its long association with visual art, merits a wider gaze than it has been given in relation to writing. In other words, it is not a term which can belong to a select few, or be defined too narrowly, at least not at this point in time. This term "conceptual writing" warrants a period of discovery and describes, as illustrated in this book, a wide proliferation of forms and approaches. This anthology is hopefully the beginning of opening such a passage of debate and conversation. The fact is, that the term "conceptual writing," for better and for worse, has thus far often been employed to describe a set of writing practices which seem, nonsensically, to preclude particular content. Not coincidentally, this content is often chosen by women. In this collection of work by women a reader may find that process and restraint driven writing is often expressive and intellectual, and that the assumption of a dualistic paradigm which claims that conceptual writing creates only ego-less works is actually another false construction. While looking at the work of women in this collection, it is evident that in conceptual writing methodologies do not dictate or predict the writing that follows, nor is methodology the only indicator of conceptual writing.

Thankfully, Vanessa Place and Rob Fitterman have written *Notes on Conceptualisms*, which, in a series of aphoristic statements and inquiries, suggests provocative possibilities for conceptual writing. In the foreword to the book Fitterman writes, "Conceptual Writing in fact, might be best defined not by the strategies used but by the expectations of the readership or *thinkership*." In a recent interview Lisa Robertson writes: "Poetry is not bound by movements, periodicities and canons. Poetry is a continuity fueled by political passion." The writers in this collection are not bound by a singular aesthetic intent, but rather by practices which, when considered side by side, form a mosaic of possibilities which resonate as a whole, perhaps because of a commitment to common concerns which span many practices, languages and cultures. To summarize these concerns in a comprehensive way is not practical, but I would venture to say that in all of these works collective thinking is primary, reader participation is requisite, the "I" when present is often an assemblage of voices, and process is often primary and integrative. The unknown and investigative are also common impulses. This writing does not attempt to create neatly drawn solutions, commentary or speakers, but rather to experiment not for the sake of experimentation but with the desire to reveal something previously obscured. This work may revolt from the notion that writing must follow certain strictures, and reclaims the possibility of writing as a unique field of freedom (which allows the reader to experience how, paradoxically, formal restraints in writing often yield freedom). Writers may attempt to strike out or illuminate what has come before through various means, and either approach suggests a re-examination of the possible. M. NourbeSe Philip writes in her book *Zong!* of the devastating story of the slave ship, "There is no telling this story; it must be told." Thus her work is a re-entering of history, making use of legal documents to retell or "untell." Rachel Zolf writes in her multi-lingual work on the Israel/Palestine conflict, "Loss has made a tenuous we." This "tenuous we" is an apt description of this assemblage, or the notion of conceptual writing, which is still evolving.

In terms of the organization of the book, though each piece may employ various techniques and approaches, we have attempted to place works in the category which is most dominantly displayed in the piece. We have chosen terms for classification with the intent to encourage inquiry rather than to stipulate. A note on omissions: it has been our editorial intent to make room for many lesser known and younger writers by not including many antecedents who have made tremendous contributions to conceptual writing but have also been central in previous movements. This is not to say that their work is not conceptual. It is not possible to name all of the writers whose work has been essential to the development of conceptual writing, but a few who come immediately to mind are: Anne-Marie Albiach, Mei-Mei Berssenbrugge, Nicole Brossard, Danielle Collobert, Lyn Hejinian, Carla Harryman, Alice Notley, Leslie Scalapino and Monique Wittig. Additionally, some writers we asked for work declined to submit because they did not consider their work conceptual. We asked all contributors to write a brief statement defining conceptual writing in relation to their own writing processes. These statements are as various as our contributors and often reveal much about how writers have been influenced by conceptual thinking in various fields.

I call this book an assemblage because its contributors are not all of like mind, content, process or opinion as to where their own work stands. This assemblage is focused mostly on work which is being written *now* and in which there is a timelessness and timeliness, like Bernadette Mayer's early experiments or her current project represented here in her *Helen of Troy* excerpt, which propose new ways of seeing a form such as epic or a character such as Helen. Mayer writes in her selection in this anthology: "Meeting these Helens is seeing a part of history that wouldn't exist, wouldn't have to exist either, if I weren't doing this; there are lots of people and things, including books, that are already there but being alive is different maybe." "Being alive," from a writerly perspective, necessitates that within this open assemblage or field argument may abound. This suspended or "drowned" book-in-print is merely a snapshot. This anthology is not intended to cement, but instead to collect, to document and to pry open the term "Conceptual" for a deeper examination. We do not seek to split and separate, but to provoke a greater, more expansive and rigorous "thinkership."

References

Amy King, "'Best of 2009' and 'Historical Count'," *VIDA: Women in Literary Arts*, http://vidaweb.org/best-of-2009.

Place, Vanessa, Robert Fitterman, *Notes on Conceptualisms* (Brooklyn: Ugly Ducking Presse, 2009).

Sina Queryas, "All sides now: a correspondence with Lisa Robertson," *Harriet*, http://www.poetryfoundation.org/harriet/2010/03/on-rs-boat-

Spahr, Juliana & Stephanie Young, "Numbers Trouble," *Chicago Review* 53:2/3, Autumn 2007.

CAROLINE BERGVALL

THE CONCEPTUAL TWIST
A FOREWORD

There is a phrase by Kathy Acker that emphasizes a strict causal connection between her existential dilemma as a female writer and the poetic methodology that emerges from it. She writes: "I was unspeakable so I ran into the language of others." This sentence summarizes both her feminist stance and her writing methodology. Acker famously proposed a literary mode which only exists through other texts. It twists itself through other texts. The writer conceives of writing as a collated and plagiarized multiplicity. Cultural pillaging provides a poetic trajectory that negates the original authorial voice. The uniqueness of the work is its lack of uniqueness, its negativity. It exists as a mode of textual appropriation, a process of shadowing and transference. This poetic strategy falls in line with broad notions of conceptual practice. Something like Walter Benjamin meets Sherrie Levine. Simultaneously, it is conceived as a salutary way to escape an abject subjectivity: "I was unspeakable." Textual plagiarism provides here a way out of a societal status quo that must silence or symptomatize the female, minoritarian or differential writer. The literary pauperism of Acker's late 20th century stance turns the longstanding translative and pragmatic aspects of literary borrowing into a question of philosophical and juridical property plots. Thieving denaturizes what it steals. Her writing quickly hits against the legally framed enclosures of the copyrighted text and the writer, taken at her words, finds herself in court.

What is being played out in the opening quote is a process of Rimbaldian dedoubling, of appropriative performance, an assimilation of voices that is close to Irigaray's tactical notion of female mimicry. One is not one self. One has not one self. One's speech is that of others. Intrinsic separation and alienation are offset by processes of accumulation and collation, performative masking and unmasking. The authorial voice multiplies its effects by explicitly acting as an empty intermediary, a ventriloquist, a mockingbird. But this bird distorts and misuses. It imagines the one-to-one as a friction, not an equation. Or as a phasmic trick, such as that seen among extreme chameleons, some insects and birds, or soldiers, who briefly take on the appearance of their environments. Once detected in the landscape, the whole tableau collapses with surprise, the image disassembles, the forest opens up, the animal goes live. Escher's interlocked labyrinthine lizards. Kara Walker's violent papercut silhouettes, "Narratives of a Negress," play against the entertaining shadow games of the form. Kathy Acker's chameleonic turn is indicative of an approach to writing that paradoxically, one could say contradictorily, establishes an explicit continuity between detached textual procedure and authorial motivation, between constricted social positioning and the not-I multiplicity of her writerly voice. It is conceptual as a matter of process and survival.

Conceptual Art as it appeared initially in the US and elsewhere, from the mid 1960s on, was a mode of working that, true to avantgardist modes, was critical of the commodified art object and of the art institutions themselves. The art machine needed further untooling. The aesthetic credos of originality and progress needed stripping right down. Nothing Duchampian mathematics could not assist with. Language and philosophical referencing, Wittgenstein notably, were brought in as work tools to disengage the art-making process and to create what Hans Haacke later called "productions of the consciousness industry." Axioms replaced the line. Ideas aimed to replace form (a full circle on the platonic simulacrum that did not escape the Art & Language group). Yet when it came to the logical next step, the all important business of stripping the artist's social identity, or even denuding artistic persona itself, investigating the artist's "authorial function" as it were, this proved largely beyond the frame. It simply reiterated on a circularity: anartist is anartist is anartist. On Kawara did play the game out, exploring the distribution of his name as an extended part of the work's aura. Collaborative groups such as Art & Language, the earlier proto-conceptual Mass Observation, the French Nouveau Roman writers, the OULIPO and later the L=A=N=G=U=A=G=E poets engaged with some of the programmatic aspects of the authorial function by resorting to collective, collated, intertextual forms and multiple narrative angles.

By and large, the artist persona found itself neither intercepted nor sabotaged by conceptual methodologies. And the narrow representation, which remains one of the mythological (in a Barthesian sense) determinants of art groups, remained unaddressed. Seen coarsely, Conceptual Art turned quickly into a small coterie of largely given, largely male, largely white art stars. The readiness with which its stratagems and indeed the artworks themselves were actually absorbed into the art system they were meaning to alter increased the unease at a time when art was all about street fighting. Here we had a question of framing, a methodological proposition, rather than a political art-life proposition. As a case in point, the term itself was briefly revived by the fanfare and ego circus of the Young British Art scene of the 1990s. Being now also essentially stripped of its investigative and critical incentive, it flatly came to represent a hodgepodge term for any non-traditional and non-expressive, performative aesthetics.

Yet, from its remainder, from its unlikely "truffles," as Gordon Matta-Clark might have designated the unexplored sewer level of conceptual art, have emerged many crucial applications. For instance, conceptual methods paired with psychoanalytic and specifically feminine investigations have provided an ideal combination to seek out the somatic, cognitive and symbolic bases for language and gender development (Mary Kelly, Susan Hiller, Bracha Ettinger, Theresa Hak Kyung Cha,...). Sociological collages, survey mappings, environmental studies by identity-conscious and politicized artists have given a twist to the "sociology at home" maxim from the British literary grouping Mass Observation of the 1930s (Adrian Piper, Martha Rosler, Ellen Gallagher, Agnes Denes, Ruth McLennan,...). Structural constraints of sounded language have released new listening techniques from art's overfunctioning speaking machine (Alvin Lucier, Bernard Heidsieck, Amanda Stewart, Christof Migone, ...). Others have each in turn examined, mimicked and re-enacted the iconic representations of power structures (Xu Bing, Jeremy Deller, Marcel Broodthaers, Hans Haacke, Andrea Fraser,...). Thus largely abandoned as a capitalized denominator, conceptual art has found its terms and limitations broadened, cross-fertilized and internationalized into an instrumental adjective denoting primarily a critical and investigative approach of language, materials, methodologies and socio-cultural situations.

The conceptual poetics collated in this collection are filled with the meandering troubles of the term itself, as much as by the suspicion many female writers have harbored for its historical umbrella and initial propensity for exclusionary models. Language manipulation and textuality being after all the native domain of writing, it makes sense to discuss conceptual writing not only in relation to its intellectual cross-pollination with contemporary language-based arts, as outlined above, but first and foremost in continuity of some literary antecedents, for whom the symbolic territory occupied by literary language had become a fraught and intensely contentious issue (schematically from de Sade to Beckett, from Nouveau Roman, Language Poetry, via Situationism, Fluxus, aspects of Lettrism, ...). Indeed, the main point of commonality is that the pieces included here all share an acute awareness of the literarity of literature, of the paratextuality of the book, of the technologies of writing, of the examination of the poetic function. There are some methodological commonalities too: An emphasis on mediation, on translation, on stylistic flexibility, even opportunism; there is a frequent reliance on research, on explicit sourcing, on palimpsestic structures, on machinic handling, on mixed media, on structural games. The deployed methodologies stage and recreate some of the many laws proposed by literary productivity, by institutional framing, by knowledge archive, by identity formation and by language acquisition. The flattening of stylistic impulse, in the narrow sense of authorial parole, and the examination of syntactic logic, narrative construction, authorial voice, intertextual polyglossia are used to investigate the creation of textual sense and release new significatory forms. To all this, one would be remiss to ignore the hidden or explicit influence of literary games, lists, rebuses, cryptography, puns and anagrams, homophonic translations, mixed code texts and constraints on verbal architextures.

One question irks, underlines, pushes at many of the pieces. It echoes the dissident emptiness expressed by Acker. How does one acknowledge social invisibilities within questions of authorial openness? How does one put a text together that depersonalizes, that disengages from personalized modes, yet manages to engage with processes of personification and identification? If literature is perceived as a mediating apparatus, a symbolic representation that highlights features of social engineering as much as of individual motivation, how does one create textual works where the authorial hold over the text is somehow distanced, perhaps neutralized, yet where the structural impact of experience, of living, of loving, of knowing, of reading are in fact recognized. Evidenced rather than evinced. How does one make conceptually-led work that does not do away, ignore, silence or mute some of the messy complications of socio-cultural belonging, but rather collects from the structure itself? The balancing act remains difficult. From research to composition through to realization and distribution, it involves radical rethinks about the codes of literature's production line. The writer finds herself necessarily, structurally destabilized by the denuding undertaking. Or she might become captive to the seductions of the stripping machine.

In my opinion, there are two principal ways, two main avenues, represented by this collection, through which conceptual poetics or, adapting Rancière, "critical poetics," largely avoid falling for production fetishism.

Firstly, there is the road of engaged disengagement. A willingness to constantly, relentlessly examine the means of one's own intentionality, positioning, assumptions, expectations. Acker exclaiming: "I sell copyright." Secondly, there is the route of engaged disengagement. A willingness to accept the laughable obsessiveness of one's intent in the face of the all-corrupting consumption machine (in economic, gluttonous and medical terms). The skillful play, the trick of showing one's hand. It is dead serious playfulness, interdependence, networked provocation, and conscious games. Games as source of perception and knowledge, as a shake-up of one's expectations, frequently locative. Responsiveness rather than competitiveness. Bliss is the gaping shirt, writes Barthes.

Games assume that one is usually, but not always, more than one. And they assume a familiarity with the rules to be played. Of course playing language and playing it against itself has provided the past century with its most important treasure troves of symptoms and revolts. Already in the 16th century a doctor had understood the value of games as a structural *mise en abyme* as well as a narrative logic. In his *Gargantua*, Rabelais lists some 217 games, from parlor games to cards to sports as well as fortune-telling devices, that are played after dinner by the young novice. Bakhtin reminds us that the first German translator of the work took the idea of translating a list, a non-exhaustive conceptual text by definition, at its word and added some 376 German games and dances to the original one. The English Thomas Urquhart added many English games in his own seminal translation. In these distended translations, it is the parasitical endlessness of associative stimuli that is arresting, the virtuoso display of a task unfaithfully executed. It is executed along the lines of structure, rather than verbal correspondence. Here a game is cheated, bent and extended while being played by the rules. The translation exercise becomes more diffuse and opaque. The calque is no longer an illusory one-to-one, but a one-to-one intercepted and recirculated via a different register (regional games, not languages). Deviation and redirection displace the expectations of translation. It is the list factor that is being translated, not the textual list. The list value is what increases in the traffic.

This anthology never underestimates the meaning of bluffing, of thieving, of surprise, of winning streaks, of the playing hand, of calling quits, of lost cards, of changed rules, of hiatus, and everything else that collapses the conceptual constrictions in on themselves and moves the text away from a morbid submission to the mechanics of rule. That is to say: the methodological flair for conceptual principles, the conceptual principles laced with practical research, the practical research undone by rebellious stamina, the rebellious stamina bullied on by engaged poetics, the engaged poetics traversed by multitudes.

1. PROCESS

CONSTRAINT
MIMICRY
MEDIATION
TRANSLATIVE
VERSIONING

KATHY ACKER

from *Great Expectations*

I RECALL MY CHILDHOOD

My father's name being Pirrip, and my Christian name Philip, my infant tongue could make of both names nothing longer or more explicit than Peter. So I called myself Peter, and came to be called Peter.

I give Pirrip as my father's family name on the authority of his tombstone and my sister—Mrs. Joe Gargery, who married the blacksmith.

On Christmas Eve 1978 my mother committed suicide and in September of 1979 my grandmother (on my mother's side) died. Ten days ago (it is now almost Christmas 1979) Terence told my fortune with the Tarot cards. This was not so much a fortune—whatever that means—but a fairly, it seems to me, precise psychic map of the present, therefore: the future.

I asked the cards about future boyfriends. This question involved the following thoughts: Would the guy who fucked me so well in France be in love with me? Will I have a new boyfriend? As Terence told me to do, I cut the cards into four piles: earth water fire air. We found my significator, April 18th, in the water or emotion fantasy pile. We opened up this pile. The first image was a fat purring human cat surrounded by the Empress and the Queen of Pentacles. This cluster, traveling through a series of other clusters that, like mirrors, kept defining or explained the first cluster more clearly—time is an almost recurring conical—led to the final unconscious image: during Christmas the whole world is rejecting a male and a female kid who are scum by birth. To the right of the scum is the Star. To the left is the card of that craftsmanship which due to hard work succeeds.

Terence told me that despite my present good luck my basic stability my contentedness with myself alongside these images, I have the image obsession I'm scum. This powerful image depends on the image of the Empress, the image I have of my mother. Before I was born, my mother hated me because my father left her (because she got pregnant?) and because my mother wanted to remain her mother's child rather than be my mother. My image of my mother is the source of my creativity. I prefer the word consciousness. To obtain a different picture of my mother, I have to forgive my mother for rejecting me and committing suicide. The picture of love, found in one of the clusters, is forgiveness that transforms need into desire.

Because I am hating my mother I am separating women into virgins or whores rather than believing I can be fertile.

I have no idea how to begin to forgive someone much less my mother. I have no idea where to begin: repression's impossible because it's stupid and I'm a materialist.

I just had the following dream:

In a large New England-ish house I am standing in a very big room on the second floor in the front of the mansion. This room is totally fascinating, but as soon as I leave it, I can't go back because it disappears. Every room in this house differs from every other room.

The day after my mother committed suicide I started to experience a frame. Within this frame time was totally circular because I was being returned to my childhood traumas totally terrifying because now these traumas are totally real: there is no buffer of memory.

There is no time; there is.

Kathy Acker (18 April 1947–30 November 1997) was an American experimental novelist, poet, playwright, and essayist influenced by feminism, punk, post-structuralism and critical theory. Among her seminal works are *Blood and Guts in High School* (1984), *Don Quixote* (1986), *Empire of the Senseless* (1988), and *In Memoriam to Identity* (1990).

OANA AVASILICHIOAEI, ERÍN MOURE

from *EXPEDITIONS of a CHIMÆRA*

ANATOMY OF TEMPERATURE

Living Proof

and so, i took the temperature of the mouth.
and so, i took the temperature of the armpit.
washing it first, patting it dry, closing
the arm to the body,
tucking the elbow where the waist is.

and so, i took the temperature of the anus,
bending my arm around my back
to do so.

churchbells rang out, it was noon.
no-one was outside on the road.

everywhere, everywhere, everywhere:
the same temperature.

(trans. from Română by___)

PS (temperature)

We transgress between *temperature, temperatură, température, temperatura*
with ease. We are misled, illusionary. Solid and breathing we enter their
temperaments only to feel a jolt, a sudden change in wind, a dissolving at
the edges. A peasant's blouse convulsively catches fire.

Dovadă vie

Şi uite-aşa, am luat temperatura gurii.
Şi uite-aşa, am luat temperatura subraţului.
Întâi l-am spălat, ştergândul uşor
apropiând mâna de corp
apăsând cotul pe brâu.

Şi uite-aşa am luat temperatura anusului
punându-mi mâna în jurul spatelui
ca să ajung.

Clopotele au sunat. Era amiază.
Afară nimeni pe stradă.

oriunde, oriunde, oriunde:
aceeaşi temperatură.

(trans. from ___ 's Engleză by ___)

PS (famished)

Noon's successors were squabbling over walnuts and lace. It was autumn, an incendiary season. I ate the letter *q*. Its one leg, dangling-lopsidedness somewhat bothersome, and that language kept forgetting to use it. To cure the ensuing stomachache, that evening I ate the letter *i*…

Diving into Life

if i whet my wings, i glow temperature through.
if i whet my wings, i glow temperature hot subsiding.
and if i intuit a spatula, an old match
lights one hand from my body
and simmers it in thick ink, a cutlet.

if i whet my wings, i glow temperature unusually.
indolent hand injured by a spatula,
where are the young?

A pot lid clatters sunlit and there's the din of a lawnmower.
Far away, nobody's foot touches a lawn.

where am i, where am i, where am i,
the temperature's crazy!

(trans. from ___'s Română by ___)

PS (inconsistency)

The season's dénouement unwittingly made her entrance as my enemy.
I battled the clocks with disheveled hair, infuriated by the steady
constancy of the act, present in every act, of translation. To take a bodily
feeling, a sensation of aliveness, a quickness in the air, the noise of a
smell, and set it down in words is to translate. From being to words. No
equivalency.

(In copying the above paragraph you will mistranslate what I mean to
say.)

The Lettuce Smeller

"just as one can have the desire to eat from the mouth of a friend..." J. D.

And thus, she lit the temperature of my mouth.
And thus, she lit my breast subtle with light.
May spilled muscatel everywhere.
The body is properly manna
ingested where the lock expired.

And thus, she lit the temperature of my anus,
her indolent hand touched a blade of shoulder
from far away.

Bells have the sound of gold. It was noon.
No one walked from the doorway into the road.

over and under, over and under, over and under:
i acquiesce to her temperature.

(trans. from ___'s Română by __, dissatisfied with the first translation ...)

PS (Celan's sky)

The roof we might have climbed like a limb. Perch of bird smiles.
Tomorrow is a flowering cloud over these ~~words~~ citadels. Tomorrow
we translate into today, then into yesterday. *Ziua de mâine e ziua de
astăzi, apoi ziua de ieri.* Once you'll speak to me wildly: where is the sky,
where?

Living Pr...

and so, i took the temperature...
and so, i took the temperat ...
washing it first, patting...
the arm to the...
tucking the elbow where the ...

and so, i took the temperature of...
bending my arm around...
to do so.

churchbells rang out...
no-one was...

everywhere...

the same...

PS. (roof)

a translation of roof, where building is text:
roof translation *n. & v.* • *n.* **1 a** the upper outside covering of a text,
usu. supported by its walls. **2 b** the top inner surface of an opening. **3**
the upper limit or highest point. **4** *literary* the area overhead, such as
the sky, heaven, etc. • *v. tr.* **1** cover with or as with a translation. **2** put
(something) on top of a translation, accidentally or intentionally. ☐

2. Thus seen, i took the temperature of the.

3. Ieri, in the present futuro

4. mijloc

5. Nimeni pe stradă. numai noi.

6. *lilas, lilas.*

Ring out the hours.

6. *liliac*: a blind bat holding up the roof of a cave
with his blind feet, or an armful of lilacs

5. On the street no one to witness the street into a
street. *(Where are we?)*

4. The middle of the story exposed like a bare belly.

3. Time kept unfolding tomorrow. *(When are we?)*

2. *The word seemed alive:* we began to pulse its
temperature.

go through the translation *informal* reach extreme or unexpected
heights. **hit the translation** *informal* become very angry. **raise the
translation** make a lot of noise inside a text. **a translation over one's
head** somewhere to live. **under one translation** in the same text. **under
a person's translation** in a person's home text.☐ **translationless** *adj.* ☐
translator *n.* a person who constructs or repairs translations.

Livid Roof

In the time of the smashed hourglass
when time's glass had shattered all clocks
its hour's shard lodged in us

time's arm bent around the roof
of time's pinnacle, tracing fresh pinnacles

till the church bells ran out of ours.
My hand on the blade of your shoulder

crests waves to
turn the hourglass over.

We could not shatter better, yet, or acquiesce

aqua, quente, water

"we ran back into the house with the table folded"
"the knives of the clocks had winnowed all the sky"
"till the roof opened, greening text where we had lain"

(transmitted from a translator…
$\qquad\qquad\qquad\qquad$ gone through the translation,
$\qquad\qquad\qquad\qquad\qquad\qquad$ irreparably)

PS Is it all about surfaces? And their shifting… sand? When you turned the water clock over, water tumbled out, soaking your shoes. Once they'd dried out, on the back balcony, the rains came. But when you turned the hourglass over, the sand stuck at the top for several hours, detaining time. It was in a film that they ran inside carrying the table, wearing white chemises and running to stay dry. The translation stole it. There was so much, so much evaporation. Surface tension in a fluid ambiance. It's hot, may I please open the window?

CURIOUSLY "MY" WRITING

When writing, do we play on the threshold of writers and audience, that old border made porous? When materialing a word's meat, do we threshold the foreign and indigenous? Content is plastic. Language even more so. Plurality wonders us into writing. Tongues migrate us across.

In the essay "Des tours de Babel," Jacques Derrida speaks of "the necessary and impossible task of translation, its necessity *as* impossibility." Translation, which is always *writing*, is impossible because there are no equivalences, only counterparts and digressions, and necessary because there are no equivalences, only counterparts and digressions.

In *Expeditions of a Chimæra*, we engage this impossibility, moving between languages of periphery and of centre to destabilize English's authority on the page. By allowing other languages' influences into a given language, we allow their rhythms, syntax, vocabularies, cultural contexts and movements to disturb and affect that language, to alter it. There's an ethos of space and body, sound, reaction to sound, to the way a word looks on the page and feels in the body in any of three languages: a *polyphonicity*. And each subjectivity—both of our two writing subjects and the multiple subjectivities that emerge in the text—is dented and moved by what is proximate to it, by Romanian and Galician, and by the unpredictability and exquisite risk of working alongside another person. In working through the unknown language, for Avasilichioaei does not understand Galician, nor Moure Romanian, there's also a beautiful paradox that blows apart conventional considerations: *Meaning happens without understanding.* And the reverse holds as well: *understanding takes place without "meaning."*

Most conceptual poetry engages its constraints passively, from above: they are set out in advance and then followed; the writing subject may not be visible *in* the text but does push down on it, "striates" it, to use a Deleuzian term. The "messy I" does not really vanish (though it may be claimed that it does); a subject still decides. In *Expeditions*, the process is active, and pushes upward: subjectivity surges up from below, from the textual material. As well, the decisions made in performing one piece inform the writing of subsequent pieces and are folded into future composition. Thus body and embodiment, inescapable factors in the aural text, impact "writing."

"Subjectivity in flux" does not describe what we do in *Expeditions*. It is more that subjectivity itself is subject to alteration and failure and denting. The pressures from above/below in the process of writing turn out to be flexible: inside and outside can change places, as they do in a fold. Rather than try to pretend we've made subjectivity vanish, we recognize that it is doubled, then doubled again—and across the folds and doublings, multiple subjectivities or "subjectivity-figures" (because we both occupy and propagate them) operate.

Here, "constraint" is not simply working with and through some work of Nichita Stănescu or Paul Celan. It is also confrontation with the subjectivity and corporeality of the other: admitting that language takes place outside "me" as an individual and that this is writing too, and is, curiously, "my" writing.

- Oana Avasilichioaei & Erín Moure

Oana Avasilichioaei is a poet and translator, living in Montréal, whose work explores history, geography, public space, textual architecture, multilingualism, translation, and textual and collaborative performance. Her books include *feria: a poempark* (Wolsak & Wynn, 2008), a translation of Romanian poet Nichita Stănescu, *Occupational Sickness* (BuschekBooks, 2006) and a collaborative work with Erín Moure, *Expeditions of a Chimæra* (BookThug, 2009). A translation of *Les Îles* by Quebecoise poet, Louise Cotnoir, was published as *The Islands* in 2011 (Wolsak & Wynn).

Erín Moure is a Montréal poet who writes mostly in English, but multilingually. Her most recent books are *O Resplandor* in 2010 and, in collaboration with Oana Avasilichioaei in 2009, *Expeditions of a Chimæra*. Moure has also translated Quebec poets Nicole Brossard (with Robert Majzels) and Louise Dupré, Galician poet Chus Pato, and Chilean poet Andrés Ajens into English, as well as Fernando Pessoa from Portuguese. Her essays on 25 years of writing practice, *My Beloved Wager*, also appeared in 2009.

LEE ANN BROWN

selected works from *PHILTRE*

WRITING IN THE DARK

> I trace
>> a score
> of notes during films

Sometimes I get excited
This is one method of composition
Scribbling in the dark
not looking down

film goes by so fast

a visual thinking
that doesn't need meaning
liquid music that explodes
that is quietly
making me feel a music
shot to shot is liquid
a pivot that connects
brings me back to the next
unfolding shadow
or color
what I notice
might be different
every time
even though it's the same film
It reminds me of a poem
I read over and over
the connections are so
that their dimensional hinges
radiate again at new angles

these notes are loaded

More interesting poems
are easier to misread

Movies wake me up
A stimulating comfort

     Notes "by nature"
      are discontinuous

          The handwriting makes it
          That's why they say "suture"

  I invite you to list

    (The Notational)

grind new philtres

         lens and potion both

    to write what I may

      not have

  I invite you to write

     in the dark

IRIDESCENT JOTTINGS

Writerless devil's tick
in a pluperfect grasp
the poet of of's inverted abyss
goes quantum on the diatonic
kaleidoscopic udder
Optical converse twists
the charged part of ten to
'heal it by language'
Bedoin arcs heal wet focus
Emptual fish stitch fragments
to phantomn Indies indices

Calendic & orangeness coldness
Geomantic law below tribe-o-lights
Multipular food stuffs
tear my incognito
pelvic smolder asunder
Vulpine archer

During a poetry reading by Will Alexander, who is "the poet of 'of'" according
to Harryette Mullen, Beyond Baroque Literary Center, Los Angeles, February
26th, 1999.

PHALLUS PHILTRE

(Phe´dre)

DEFLECTED EMO   the vocab is there

now ---------->

Phaedrus Workshop

/ **Wooster Group June 3, 2001**

Venus

Skineateles Venus

Petticoat 2

(Dickie needs to see)

Underneath the bush

"I love Orisha"

subtly pinned safety
shuttlecock nervous

Venus as

Venus as "Ump"

Twirl cock

fidget

fair skinned bird

Coordinate sad & potty

Wenus / Watching

    reminds me
        of my Desire
                grid

    live breathing

                fidget & quiver

    adjust   adroit

    wheel & brow

            gaze

    takes a while plus

    knows what's

    going on
    going on

    these kinds of dark

    Delay
                      stop it
    sync out

        Not Now,

        Palm Tree!

my mother's / Venus sickness

    like a virus

      in my

blood

fucked

by a

wheel
chair

watching TV

from the labyrinth

enema still

attended

umbilicus

"Dramatic tension?"
  Glasses with loin cloth

Sword slid into pool

sportslike

perverse to her

Delay

buzzer   wipe   ultra passive

no rules
        only material constraints

1 to 1

You have the vocab

You flatter dirt

Freedom from the mirror

Umbilical mic / moon

     pussy-sion

     cypher net icks

        (draw Beckett)

     Relentless Venus!

     Why / How does it work?

        He HATES me

mirror video scant driftwoo
no space

"this science is tight"

I let myself fall apart

blurb

We who are language sensitive with
A deep capacity for melancholy
know its good shit if we want to write during it

When Universe collide

These pieces are a part of a larger collection entitled *PHILTRE*. They are transcriptions of times when I was unpredictably moved to "write in the dark" during film, music, poetry readings, lectures... usually experiences which somehow sent me to a higher level of associative perception, where I was multiplicatively alternating through modes of silent processing, meditation, and stimulation to write. At first I didn't even recognize these works as poems. I felt them to be more gestural, notational, unrefined, expressionist, free associational kinds of writing. As time went on, I became increasingly aware that their composition was on a continuum with other compositional practices of mine which privilege writing in the continuous present moment. I look for poetry everywhere. In process, these scribblings are often "mistranslated" or "mistranscribed" (for the better I think) due to the scrawling and overwriting that occurs in the dark in the back row of a movie theatre or during a rock show. It's as though the writing helped me experience another's art more fully. As if I couldn't help it. I guess it's a kind of poetics of reception theory, a kind of associative art criticism, or a record of a trace of what was flashing by through my particular filters. I call this accumulation *PHILTRE*, which means a love potion, since it's also about the mind-body erotics of being turned on by someone else's art enactment. The project grew into my response to ATELOS' call for work written "under the sign of poetry, writing which challenges the conventional definitions of poetry."

- Lee Ann Brown

Lee Ann Brown's books include *Polyverse* (Sun & Moon), which was selected by Charles Bernstein for the New American Poetry Series, *The Sleep That Changed Everything* (Wesleyan University Press), and many collaborative works. She teaches poetry at St. John's University in New York City. She is the editor of Tender Buttons Press and co-founder of a new project for multidisciplinary poetry and performance, The French Broad Institute of Time and the River in Marshall, NC.

ANGELA CARR

selected works from *Rose Concordance*

OF ALARM AND FOUNTAINS

that i isolated and romanced this fountain
reading in the nakedness of self-contained spray
such diffuse words
how i love words
if this word is a hood
episodically thrust downward to reveal "fountains"
i recovered
the fountain is a hood
soft material fountaining
i obsessed over its advantage
i understood fashion anew
as one single movement into depths of earth
sex's humectant randomness alarmed me
i mirrored the rhetoric of employment
in this tactical handshake
we are "friends"
the sparkling stones of the fountain have scraped my palms

OF RUNNING, OF THE CORE

how running dryly from complicity
running dryly with fragile limbs
nothing runs more beautifully than instinct
no one runs more beautifully
to poverty when running yields
runners, these aspects, leaves in her hair.
can you fashion such a beautiful runner?
my heart races
it appears softly enough
presumably slows your running
the running of our voices changes nothing
how the smell runs into me
running and the smell of your body
i say running when i mean to say bodies
the bodies of our voices change nothing

how bodies dryly from complicity
bodies dryly with fragile limbs
nothing bodies more beautifully than instinct
no one bodies more beautifully
poverty for whom bodies cede
bodies, these aspects, leaves in her hair.
can you fashion such a beautiful body?
my heart races
it appears softly enough
presumably slows your body
the bodies of our voices change nothing
how the smell embodies me
bodies and the smell of you running
i say bodies when i mean to say running
the running of our voices changes nothing

OF NATURALLY

of the state all humans naturally desire knowledge
now you speak natu
unless demystified, we pity natu
fear of bodies, which he believed in natu
called belief because milk is natu
a national affectation they natu
the subjection of each natu
now you speak natu
their country and obey natu
dialecticians don't mean natu
we said devils natu
because they were pleased by them natu
husk of a word how natu
cracking is natu
natu
leaving the offices abandoned that were their fathers'
natu
Dear Son, the affection natu
is like the wind natu

natu

you have that which would please most humans natu
obedience that he natu
and blood, too, that natu

ally
ally
ally
ally
ally adopt
ally due their ruler
ally
ally (know this is the state)
ally but with pleasure
ally believed in good people
ally
ally it cracks
ally the relief of "marriage"
ally the shadow follows not the body but the cracking

ally
ally due your father
ally consumed by windmills

ally you'll see him under the surface of your old age

ally
ally gave his lover
ally conducts time

OF CRITICAL AND NAÏVE CONFUSION

let's say that in this presocial fountain we splash freely
i'd like to naively delete the deiform source
in this critically naive and
complicitous gamble with humanism
of the prefeminist fountain, gushing is essential
existence is an aromatic crease
credulous and rich secretions
and now in my hands an encyclopaedic gathering
such confusions
such praise as circulates in critically fleshy fountains
inferentially junked theologies in a pile on the floor
inferentially junked theologies collecting attributes on the floor
choosing abjection is a stance of defiance?
is this the critical substance of drank?
your art given as fleshy keepsake?

OF BETWEEN

Between the precious and the radical
Between the strategic and the tragic
Radiant and strained
Fountain is a folding fan of water.
The pressure of errant streams
massages precious togetherness open.
From the fissure clear water issues
as though from a purse
between clasps of discourses
and their embroidered surfaces

Between the institutions of pairs

The middle is a guess of worn surfaces
Between the privilege of two
Between the two of conformity
or the two of caution

if vanity is between us
as much as
we have yet to break

Between the surfaces of singing
and the surfaces of speaking
Entre tes braz trestoute nue

Still in the what happens middle of never

Still in the what middle happens of never

Still in the middle what happens of never

Still in the middle what of happens never

Still in the middle of what happens never

Still in the middle of what never happens

In still the middle of what never happens

In the still middle of what never happens

In the still of middle what never happens

In the of still middle what never happens

In of the still middle what never happens

Of in the still middle what never happens

VERTEBRAE: A STATEMENT

Two concepts are at work in my *Rose Concordance*: translation and allegory, or more specifically, the dance of terms in an allegorical mode. The process: to translate a literary concordance to the *Roman de la Rose* of Guillaume de Lorris, where lines of the medieval French poem are regrouped according to key words. In the act of translating lines that are not readily comprehensible (unless one is accustomed to reading in old French), which lines, further, are fragmented so that meaning is clearly elusive, the concept of translation itself opens. Deviations from the expected path occur; for example, adjectives turn to adverbial forms and soon become unrecognizable altogether. Only the beautifully simple concordance form remains intact, its key words like vertebrae (while the medieval matter rests peacefully).

Despite this distance, anthropomorphized concepts from the allegory emerge to deliberate their place in contemporary poetic discourse. Love, Vanity, Luxury and Reason tease amatory lyricism. Conceptualism might be their foldaway table from a forgotten generation. A proliferation of new concordances arises in the process of writing on that table; lines may be remixed, possibly endlessly. Coincidence, whether voluntary or involuntary, generates infinite possibilities.

- Angela Carr

Angela Carr's most recent book of poetry is *The Rose Concordance* (BookThug, 2009). She lives and works in Montréal. Her translation of Québécoise writer Chantal Neveu's *Coït* is forthcoming with BookThug in 2012.

MÓNICA DE LA TORRE

selected works from *All Are Welcome*
After Martin Kippenberger's *The Happy End of Franz Kafka's Amerika*

(An assortment of catalogued tables and office desks with pairs of mismatched, design-wise anachronistic chairs arranged as for job interviews—based on protagonist Karl Rossmann's with the recruiter for the Nature Theater of Oklahoma in Kafka's Amerika*—placed within a soccer field flanked by bleachers.)*

TABLE NO. 17

(A desk with a door for a top, with a hole in the middle due to a missing glass panel.)

My English is no good.

My English is not very well.

My English is ... no English.

My English is no where near perfection.

My English is not good and it is badly to heard.

My English is no frequently.

My English is no native so apologies to everyone.

I AM SHOCKINGLY UNQUALIFIED. I DON'T EVEN KNOW HOW TO TYPE, FOR EXAMPLE.

But I'll go to Oklahama

Oklahoma

Oklahama

Oklahoma

EYE EXAM

(Bather sits on a lifeguard chair. Directly across from him, a lookout stands on a small observation platform.)

BATHER:

If you can see what you can't see, does that mean you're seeing it?

LOOKOUT:

I see shapes, not edges.

BATHER:

Meaning?

LOOKOUT:

Meaning.

BATHER:

Astigmatism, you mean?

LOOKOUT:

Nothing I can't just simply ignore.

BATHER:

There you go, getting everything confused again.

LOOKOUT:

That's it; that's exactly it.

BATHER:

If you purposefully avert your gaze from something your eyes can't help but see, are you lying if you say you're not seeing it?

LOOKOUT:

I see a nesting table in the distance. Table or tables? My vision is blurry at all distances. My corneas have flat and steep areas; likewise my mind.

BATHER:

Do you trust your other senses?

LOOKOUT:

It depends on where I'm standing.

BATHER:

Do you want the job or not?

(A woman sits on an adult-size chair behind a mid-'50s modern two-person school desk. A black non-functioning geometrical lamp and a typewriter sit on the desktop.)

QWERTY

Fingering

Index finger   left hand
frfv fvrf vrff vrrf rfvf rvff frrv frfvfrfv fvrf vrff vrff vffrf frfv f (1'6")

Index finger   right hand
jujm jumj muju ummj jumm jmuj umju jujm jujm jumj muju ummj jujm j (35")

Index extended finger   right hand
hyhn hynh hnyh hynn hnyh ynnh hyhn hynh hnyh hynn hnyh hnyh hyhn h (53")

Ring finger   right hand
Lol. Olo. Llo. . lol .lol lo.l lo.l lo.o lol. olo. Llo. .lol l (32")

All fingers   both hands
The practice of shorthand is very common in business working. (15")

Copy

Be accurate. Every conscioys error you make, slows up your mental process and cuts down speed. (95 strokes, 28")

Keep your eyes on the copy. Every time you raise your etes to see if you have made an error, you lose caluable seconds examining the paper in uyour typewriter, and finding your place again on the copy. (199 stroked, 35")

Sales letters

Sales letters are of two general types. First, the letter which is actually designer to sell as service or commodity. Secondly, the adjustment letter, which sells good will. Any library has good books on handling sales correspondence. A majority of such books, howeber, are written more for executives who head departments. The result is that the busy secretary is discouraged from reading lengthy columns. The following simple and tested rules will suffice for daily office activities. The four aims of the sales letter are: attract attention: create desire: convince the mindl stimulate action. The four aims of the adjustment letter are: conciliate the reader; restate the facts; make reparation; conciliate again. To give your letters cgaracter, you should: take a personal attitude; adapt your letter to the reader's background, education or station in life; keep your temper; avoid scarcasm or witticisms; remind rather than instryct. Or, you can fgoret about these five points and summarize the principles into: "Be sincere." (1020 strokes–4', 28")

(Two office chairs with black umbrellas over them circling on a carousel surrounding a sculpture of a fried egg.)

A Theory of Distraction / The Problem of Labor

Angela found photos of *The Collection of Silence* on Flickr. Nice photo of Kim and Angela. Who posted these photos? Who's John Kelly again? Go to Dia's page announcing the event. Cute photo of Eileen. Go to her Wikipedia page. This photo not as good. Glanced the wikipage over. Return. Wait? Did it mention Holland Cotter? Were they related? He called her "a cult figure to a generation of post-punk females forming their own literary avant-garde." "Oh, that was John Kelly!" Bruce says. He tells me John Kelly is a performance artist with an amazing trajectory. Trash Brian Kim Stefans Ubu listserv email on "Processing test." "Who are you emailing?" No one. I'm typing. Go to Google books. Advanced search. Distraction + Walter Benjamin. *Selected Writings. 1935-1938.* Attempt to determine the effect of the work of art once its power of consecration has been eliminated. Parasitic existence of art based on the sacred. Fashion is an indispensable factor in the acceleration of the process of becoming worn out. Technology is an indispensable factor in the acceleration of the process of becoming worn out. The values of distraction should be defined with regard to film, just as the values of catharsis are defined with regard to tragedy. The values of distraction should be defined with regard to. Distraction and destruction as the subjective and objective sides, respectively, of one and the same process. The relation of distraction to absorption should be examined. Saw ad for Rich Maxwell's *Ads* on YouTube again. The survival of artworks should be represented from the standpoint of their struggle for existence. Their true humanity consists in their unlimited adaptability. The criterion for judging the fruitfulness of their effect is the communicability of this effect. The Greeks had only one form of (mechanical) reproduction: minting coins. They could not reproduce their artworks, so these had to be lasting. Hence: eternal art. Just as the art of the Greeks was geared toward lasting, so the art of the present is geared toward becoming worn out. Checked emails. Nothing. *The Practice of Everyday Life. La perruque* is the worker's own work disguised as work for his employer. It may be as simple a matter as a secretary's writing a love letter on "company time" or as complex as a cabinetmaker's "borrowing" a lathe to make a piece of furniture for his living room. Under different names in different countries this phenomenon is becoming more and more general, even if employers "penalize" it or "turn a blind eye" on it in order not to know about it. The worker who indulges in *la perruque* actually diverts time from the factory for work that is free, creative, and precisely not directed toward profit. Play the game of free exchange. Please read: a personal appeal from Wikipedia founder Jimmy Wales. Freeze-frame Baroque. This phrase was used to describe the work of someone whom I can't remember. Google alert on a namesake's Twitter. Deleted spam for Viagra. Deleted Facebook alert of a friend request by a stranger. Deleted Facebook alert inviting me to become a fan of a new Asian American literary journal. Deleted invitation to a 60th birthday celebration of someone who wouldn't know who I am if I showed up at her party. Deleted Facebook alert of a reply to a thread I deleted earlier today. Deleted email by UnionDocs announcing that tonight no documentaries will be screened, but that you can buy a ticket to a fictitious screening if you want to make a donation. Checked emails. Confirmed friend on Facebook. Removed tags of family photos on Facebook. Added item to list of to dos. Looked up definition of "the aughts."

(Wooden puppet seated at a table formed by laying the movable surface of a self-standing mirror horizontally.)

—Do you have any previous experience?

—Would *you* hire a former self to deal with unfinished business?

—Did you work at an office?

—I am the world's biggest procrastinator.

—What happened?

—I kept creating little tasks for myself and lost the overall picture. I got distracted. I had a surplus of energy and it turned against me.

—Define yourself.

—A catalogue of failures.

—You've got inventory?

—I'd overcompensate to make it in; invariably, I ended up working double: one for today, two for tomorrow. There was no lack of interest, though, on the contrary. Work keeps me going.

—Exaggerate your flaws. I don't know if it works for you, but it works for me.

(Person at the bullhorn screams "Goooooooooooooal!")

Consider All Are Welcome...

a form of institutional critique, for its avowed awareness of the mechanisms of inclusion and exclusion intrinsic to the project of establishing a corpus

my entry fee into the arena of competition, here a symbolic soccer field (appropriated from appropriationist Martin Kippenberger's *The Happy End of Kafka's Amerika*), in which the communal is organized in teams

a demonstration of my competence in a certain vocabulary

notation (per force immaterial) for a time-based performance on the problem of labor in all its multivocality and polyvalence

an attempt to generate a situation:

> "By adopting the point of view of enunciation, we privilege the act of speaking; according to that point of view, speaking operates within the field of a linguistic system; it effects an appropriation, or reappropriation, of language by its speakers; it establishes a present relative to a time and place."
>
> (Michel de Certeau, *The Practice of Everyday Life*)

a disavowal of totalizing views and its products, an embrace of process

a statement against *positioning* myself, which would imply an aspiration on my part to attain status within a hierarchy

a deliberate adoption of multiple, often clashing positions, resulting from my engagement with the task at hand: inclusion/exclusion ⇨ competitiveness ⇨ performativity ⇨ identity as performance ⇨ personas ⇨ multiplicity (positions, by definition, are tactical)

a sloppy, unfinished bricolage held together by a borrowed framing device, in turn framed by a borrowed framing device

a wink at the spectators on the bleachers

- Mónica de la Torre

Mónica de la Torre is the author of two books of poetry in English, *Talk Shows* and *Public Domain*, and two in Spanish, *Acúfenos* and *Sociedad Anónima*. She edited the newly released anthology of post-Latino writing *Malditos latinos, malditos sudacas: Poesía hispanoamericana Made in USA* (Billar de Lucrecia, 2010) and is a 2009 NYFA poetry fellow. A translator and essayist as well, she is senior editor at *BOMB Magazine*.

DANIELLE DUTTON

FROM *MADAME BOVARY*

Part I

Chapter II
Night came: letter, rain, countryside, time. Charles turned. Emma hurried, stood. Inevitably house came weeping. For such she went, that's why.

Chapter III
Monsieur heard "what" "through" "lost" "to" "I" "I" "almost" "eat" "happens" "brace." His trees seemed him, himself.

Chapter VIII
Emma's *décolletages* twisted red. Partner-swaying to violinist's doorways, to pale low gentleman. Spanish curtain and violin. His relief opened to ears—the lives, the doctor's plates. Near turned to from. Out it woke, in yearning.

Chapter IX
Down petered her *Corbeille* and the city came midnight. Girl Emma, pathetic sometimes, sometimes down. And everyone and ambitions (people) was further bourgeois. And she back under (arm blazing!), new from large alluring senses. In the highway. In the garden. To poke stuck waste, wept nights, was pregnant.

Part II

Chapter III

Polite morning in silent spent. A woman-like girl, her convalescence the tragedy. Noon wind weak moment to low "up" of sound (other bedroom blushed). Nurse the nothing. Nurse a peasant. Both went rapidly to hair that spent to weather, silently. There the dinner walls had nothing. Can nothing spot stopping? Boring—completely—Madame was there.

Chapter VI

April arbor among moving young: candlesticks again raised emotion. Lestiboudois swinging above. Bovary muttered catechism. In ran dinner, furiously.

Chapter VII

One shrouded brought her and he to themselves, bareheaded. One fortune surrendered to enterprise: Léon. Beside actual—whether by passion (now A) and wearing history. Many would, usually sheet gray. The corner. He applying calmly cravat strings.

Chapter VIII

She *finis* came to the puffed-thumb Emma person. Provincial and jolly, wasn't square in the rattle. The rockets candle her, then collapse.

Chapter IX

Rodolphe himself had had must the he the his he on come that on in ears (soft) a know was made. Horse and his ray out the firs follow in that into were and would between her. Again mustache spoke first: "Madonna on my grass, listen against velvet. Swelled of leaves, be distant." And him before was of sunrise. Fields fluttered his room.

PART III

Chapter III
Shipyards, tar, downstream of—stretched. They followed oars, sang sailing. Small sitting black she looked. Tell feel nothing. Chill spit.

Chapter VII
Close-fitting spineless love. Hearing hope crushed into pharmaceutical—gorged, crunched—his porcelain woman mistress. Sob, but not the gentle breast. Petticoat peasant thought of eyes on river as her story.

Chapter IX
Memories talk, twitched (with velvet), walked, sighed, pacing (to the dead), returned, called, introduced, sagged loudly—once.

A cried candle stayed to water the sigh-wreath and pharmacist-things, to shock being for someone swollen to the bedsheets.

"Selections from *Madame Bovary*" came about as I was reading *Madame Bovary* at the same time as Jackson Mac Low's *The Virginia Woolf Poems*, and in particular the series "Ridiculous in Piccadilly," which Mac Low wrote using language from Woolf's *The Waves*. I had also very recently read *The Waves*, and the conjunction of all of this caused me to wonder to what extent a particular narrative is actually lodged in words, individually and collectively, even when those words are taken out of context. So I devised a system by which to extract words from various chapters of Flaubert's book (I also had a system for how I chose which chapters to play with; both systems involved math, which is something I never can hold in my head for very long, and these systems are long forgotten). All I could add or change was punctuation.

- Danielle Dutton

Danielle Dutton is the author of *S P R A W L* (Siglio Press) and *Attempts at a Life* (Tarpaulin Sky Press). Her work has appeared in *BOMB, Harper's, A Best of Fence*, and other magazines and anthologies. She designs books at Dalkey Archive Press and edits Dorothy, a publishing project.

RENEE GLADMAN

EMERGENCE OF A FICTION

When I set out to talk about the sentence, I naturally find myself looking at the mind and how it relates to language. I try to picture the shape of my thinking pre-articulation, imagining a constellation or some other scattered array of simultaneous happenings. We think multiply, many things at the same time that are often at odds with one another, or regarding unrelated topics, or anachronistic in how they appear to us. Often a thought in the mind exists in its entirety, meaning you don't think one part of the thought and then think the next part—rather, you somehow hold the complete thing at once. Yet to write is to turn that timeless, instantly expressed (or felt) idea into an unfolding narrative, which is to break a whole (that is unbreakable in a very real way) into approximate parts. The writing we produce seems to be other than the writing we thought.

The loss of that complex arrangement of ideas—moving from the constellation to the single, progressing line of the sentence—is not the only effect of going from an interior space of thought into an external space of communication; another, more positive, consequence is the onset of a kind of semantic delay that puts a particular sheen (particular to the person writing or speaking) over the entirety of the text or speech. This delay represents the slippage between what you are trying to say (to match the picture in your mind) and what you actually do say. Articulation, then, becomes a kind of performance. And the performance is usually a success, that is, you usually do make some version of your feelings known, and this is because of the agreement held between performer and witness. To have a language is to make a pact with every other user of that language that you will, for the most part, employ its vocabulary in the agreed upon fashion; you will not wake up one morning and decide to refer to the queen-sized object on which you are lying as "notebook" instead of "bed."

But I'm still trying to set this thing up. We've recognized the moment before writing, altered ourselves subconsciously to begin translating, and now are about to step into the written word. However, there is more to marvel over. It's the shared language I mentioned above. It is how each word of our language is a story all its own, in fact, it is the root of endless stories. A language that one has inherited comes flush with narrative, stories of triumph, oppression, custom—the entire history of the speaker up to that point. Nothing has happened to any of us that has not in some way been engraved into our language. So to begin a story, "The man," is to immediately, inadvertently call up lifetimes of weight. Even the way our words relate to each other "gives off" a story. I say "The" and your mind instantly alerts you that a noun is coming. I might delay its deliverance with an adverb, but if that noun fails to appear then ultimately I will not have made sense. What excites me is this: there is a feeling I want to communicate to you. It is already at one remove because I have taken it out of its originary space—my mind—and brought it into the open. After this briefest of moments in the open, a second remove is introduced. I have to lay the feeling over a string of words that, though they represent to some degree what I want to express, are not the feeling exactly. The words I choose have their own associations, calling to my sentence meanings and textures I did not intend. And what tops off this incredible drama of just the first sentence of this provisional text about a seemingly long ago feeling, is that the very structure of the English language (or at least the way in which we are taught to practice it) requires that I express my feeling as if it were a coherent, linear story. That is, I begin with a subject, put it in action (or a negation of action), and round it off with some significant consequence. Each phase of the sentence is a cause for deep questioning, but to look at that first phase, the subject, is enough to stall one's progress through articulation. Subjectivity is a crucial assumption we make when we set out to express anything, yet it is one of our biggest mysteries. Not just who we are, what we mean to ourselves and others, but also where we come from, the history of our being in the world, which differs dramatically across race, class, gender, sexuality, and ethnicity. I really believe this. I really believe that my "I" could not possibly be the same as yours.

What I'm left is with an understanding that to write is to take a position in relation to experience and time; it is to etch, within the margins of a text, a philosophy of experience that pertains only to that moment of writing (for a different text might engender an entirely different position with relation to experience and time). This is particularly interesting in the writing of prose narrative, where the encounter that the writer is having with language as she envisions or projects characters and events into narrative space *itself* becomes a story that unfolds along the periphery of the "primary" one. That story is like a distant presence that our main character glimpses as she moves along the street, or a sensation that brushes by her, that effectively alters her trajectory. A great example of this, which I return to often, can be found in Gail Scott's first novel *Heroine*. Somewhere in the middle of a story about a woman living in Montreal in the 1980s, reflecting on her past decade of intense political engagement as she moves toward a future marked by new priorities, one comes upon this passage:

So, we're sitting in a Spanish restaurant on Park Ave. talking about how the French modernist scene is different than the English, etc. Smoking cigarettes and drinking Sangria. When suddenly I can't remember how to get to the end of a sentence. Each time I start, it's as if the memory of the past (the noun, the sentence's beginning) wipes out the present (verb). So I can no longer move forward in the words. This is so scary I run out of there around the corner to the shrink at McGill.

Here, the narrator undergoes a kind of crisis of speech, which because we are reading it, also becomes a crisis of writing. The narrator's description of attempting to move through a sentence is an event that happens external to the event of sitting in a restaurant with friends, it suggests an action "Each time I start" but doesn't present a picture, does not itself become a part of the surface we are reading. However, this inability to progress through the sentence, to get beyond "the sentence's beginning" causes a real-time response, which is fleeing the restaurant. I like what the Czech writer, Michal Ajvaz, says about "the beginning" in his novel *The Other City*:

> How could you understand anything at all, how could you utter the simplest sentence if you hadn't perfectly understood the beginning, the place where constellations are born ...

This passage not only recalls that constellation of thought I discussed earlier, but also *brings* to the sentence itself, to the first utterance, a kind of labyrinth that must be reckoned with. To be able to communicate, it seems to say, one must have a firm grasp, *a competency*, so to speak, of the place from which one speaks. What is important here is realizing that in many cases people do not at all understand "the beginning," and that this "lack" of perspective must have a profound affect on their relation to the sentences they create. And further, it's this "lack" that fuels the most wondrous of our world's fiction.

With regard to the dilemma expressed in the Scott quote, I like to treat that problem of progression as a point of departure rather than something that needs correcting, especially in the context of fiction. It is deeply pleasurable and re-affirming to me as a person in the world to read a fictional work where those derailments are incorporated into the unfolding narrative, rather than suspended or repaired through forced linearity and tidiness. In fact, the whole notion of "unfolding," of "culmination," of "beginnings and endings" must be re-considered within such environments.

The narratives I write, which appear to be the same story over and over again, where a character or "self" is projected into a (usually) urban terrain that proves difficult to cross or assimilate due to real and imagined obstacles—these narratives, I'm beginning to understand, not only ask how does a person emerge again and again, from day to day, or event to event, as a consistent, intact, recognizable being. They also ask another question that would be difficult to represent literally. That is, what is the experience of the subject as it moves through the avenues of the sentence? To address this literally, we would have to compose a text of sentences all, more or less, like this Gail Scott sentence I quoted earlier: "Each time I start, it's as if the memory of the past (the noun, the sentence's beginning) wipes out the present (verb)." Something like, "I tried to tear the noun (my destination) away from its qualities (red, some other adjectives), so I removed everything."

This would make for an interesting approach to thinking about grammar and how the parts of the sentence relate to one another, how they collude toward the making of meaning, the rendering of reality, but the hermetic nature of this interrogation would make it difficult to build a fiction. However, one does not need to go so far in the other direction that we get all story and no report of the drama of the composition. A sentence like the following from Gertrude Stein's novel, *A Novel of Thank You*, tells at least two stories: one about desire and departing, and the other about repetition and circularity. One results from the content, the surface, of the words, and the other from their interaction. She writes:

> This makes them wish and afterwards this makes them leave and afterwards this makes them leave and wish and this makes them leave and leaves and wish and afterward, this makes them wish and leave and leaves and afterward. (3)

Samuel Beckett, who has been essential to me as a writer, seemed to use the sentence as a platform for drawing out the struggles of being a person to which things happened. His sentences are burps and howls, sometimes cackles of frustration at the sheer perplexity of person-ness. The use of simple, everyday words and direct speech create a kind of front seat for the reader. One finds oneself in the realm of confession, which tends to be purposefully transparent. However, in the Beckett sentence, perception gets reorganized through the arrangement of words and the intervals devised through punctuation. What are the conditions that set up the composing of this sentence taken from his novel *The Unnamable*?

> Can it be that one day, off it goes on, that one day I simply stayed in, in where, instead of going out, in the old way, out to spend a day and night as far away as possible, it wasn't far. (287)

We've heard about difficult writers and difficult texts for a long time, but I think it would be interesting to reflect on what that modifier "difficult" means. When we decide that something doesn't make sense what are we making decisions about? Are they about the presentation of character, about how events are rendered? That is, are we saying we believe that subjectivity is something other than what is being presented, that time flows differently? Are we revolting against our progress being interrupted or against a certain ambiguity in the content? What philosophy of experience and articulation are we putting forth when we respond this way?

The conditions that cause one to stutter in the making of a sentence, that cause one to introduce ambiguities into one's text, that make one highly conscious of the order of words as a force bearing down on one's creation, these conditions also make way for the emergence of an alternative fiction. A narrative that uses the immediacy and incompleteness of the present as a generator, a sort of pressure cooker, to render its details.

References

Michal Ajvaz, *The Other City* (Champaign, London, Dublin: Dalkey Archive, 2009).

Samuel Beckett, *The Unnameable* (New York: Grove Press, 1958).

Gail Scott, *Heroine* (Toronto: Coach House, 1987).

Gertrude Stein, *A Novel of Thank You* (Champaign, London, Dublin: Dalkey Archive, 1994).

Renee Gladman is the author of six works of prose, most recently the novel *The Ravickians*, and one collection of poetry, *A Picture-Feeling*. She is the publisher for Leon Works and lives in Providence, RI, where she teaches fiction and books arts at Brown University.

JEN HOFER

SPENT NUCLEAR FUEL

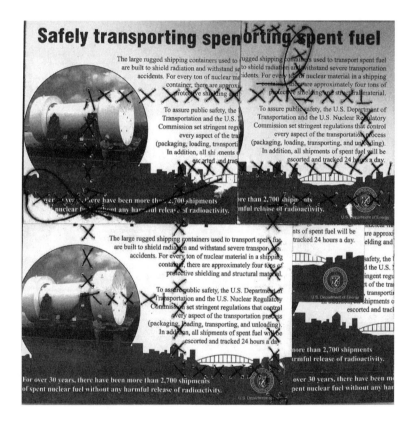

NUCLEAR ENERGY
IN THE UNITED STATES

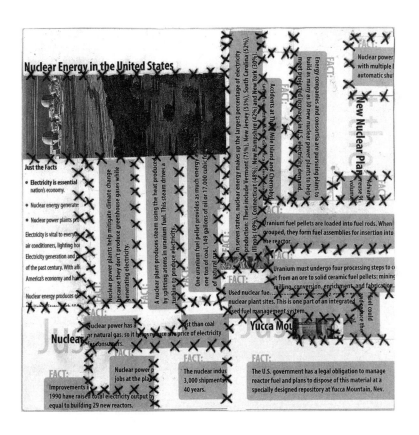

NUCLEAR ENERGY
BENEFITS THE ENVIRONMENT

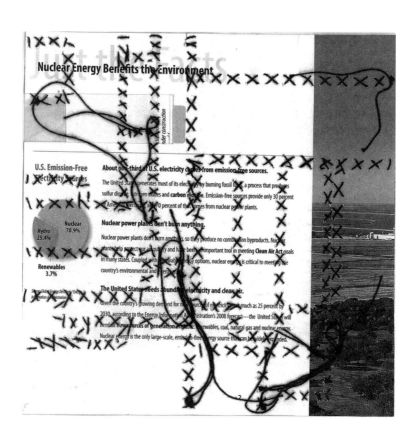

Nuclear Energy Benefits the Environment

U.S. Emission-Free Electricity Sources

About one-third of U.S. electricity comes from emission-free sources.

The United States generates most of its electricity by burning fossil fuels, a process that produces sulfur dioxide, nitrogen oxides and **carbon dioxide**. Emission-free sources provide only 30 percent of America's electricity, and 70 percent of that comes from nuclear power plants.

Nuclear 70.9%
Hydro 25.4%
Renewables 3.7%

Nuclear power plants don't burn anything.

Nuclear power plants don't burn anything, so they produce no combustion byproducts. Nuclear plants help protect our air quality and have been an important tool in meeting **Clean Air Act** goals in many states. Coupled with renewable energy options, nuclear energy is critical to meeting the country's environmental and energy needs.

The United States needs abundant electricity and clean air.

Given the country's growing demand for new sources of electricity—as much as 25 percent by 2030, according to the Energy Information Administration's 2008 forecast—the United States will need all major sources of generation available: renewables, coal, natural gas and nuclear energy. Nuclear energy is the only large-scale, emission-free energy source that can be widely expanded.

TERMS AND LIMITS

Notes Toward Further Reflection on Conceptualism in the World and in Poetry

> I have nothing to say and I am saying it, and that is poetry.
> - John Cage, *M*

The town of Goldfield, Nevada is 117 miles from the proposed nuclear waste storage repository at Yucca Mountain. In an octagonal building that may once have been a gas station, the Esmeralda County Repository Oversight Program has set up an information center about Yucca Mountain. Other than the Oversight Program's own newsletter, the entirety of the information presented comes directly from the U.S. Department of Energy and reflects uncritically the view that the creation of hazardous nuclear waste is and will be a fact of life, and that its transport and storage are completely safe and unproblematic.

When is the re-presentation of materials itself a critique? How much intervention—and of what sort—critically re-frames the materials represented so as to incite non-complacent thought?

I am not interested in setting the terms. Or I am only interested in setting the terms. Or I am only interested in unsettling the terms. Or I resist settling.

Writing that does not examine the terms doesn't ask for much from the writer or the reader. Stasis and affirmation of what already is are fairly easy to achieve; do we need writing to be another religion, institutionalizing itself all over again? Do we need to be soothed?

There is nothing new to say. The world is already there, ever changing. Change is often undocumented, or is documented by someone who is not me, or is documented by me and many others, and these varied, conflicting, overlapping accounts make up a history that may or may not matter, and may or may not extend an influence toward a future.

If you want to learn about the proposed nuclear waste storage facility at Yucca Mountain, Nevada or the transport of spent nuclear fuel pellets or the life cycles of barn swallows nesting in target ranges or how to make a home-made ice cream machine out of a drill and a coffee can, it is not my writing you need to read.

What is "need"? And if I perceive needs—my own or those of others—how am I to respond to them responsibly, respectfully, thoughtfully? Conceptually?

There is nothing new to say; I have nothing to say. I have been repurposing paper materials encountered in different types of natural history museums—thrift stores, junk shops, small local newspapers, information centers—and hand-sewing them into quilts. Hand sewing paper is a slow process; I spend many hours thinking about the ideas presented in the texts I sew, and about the spaces—natural habitats—

where these ideas reside and transit in the world. My contemplations center as much on what I don't know as on what I do. These quilts are for uncovering. Further research is necessary.

- Jen Hofer

Jen Hofer is a poet, translator, social justice interpreter, teacher, knitter, public letter-writer, and urban cyclist. Her recent and forthcoming poem sequences and translations are available through a range of autonomous small presses including: Atelos, Counterpath Press, Dusie Books, Kenning Editions, Les Figues Press, Palm Press, and Subpress. She also makes tiny books by hand at her kitchen table in Cypress Park, Los Angeles.

BERNADETTE MAYER

HELEN REZEY SESTINA

mom still lives in south troy
now everything is much more different
there aren't as many buses, there are no markets
there was a mural of gullivar in the troy library
you don't get too many people
interested in your name

corbett is helen rezey's maiden name
there's a lot of greek revival architecture in troy
named troy like ithaca & the other troys to honor the people
in greek democracies, a concept as liberal & different
as a fancy private house is from a public library
soon, in downtown troy, there'll be a co-op market

for a long time in troy, there was no market
if you lived somewhere else, would you have a different name?
what are the chances you'd go to this library?
& be a helen in a city in upstate NY named troy?
if you had your way, how would things be different?
would you prefer being the head honcho or one of the people?

politicians OFTEN BRAG ABOUT BEING A MAN OF THE PEOPLE
BUT DO YOU EVER SEE THEM AT THE MARKET?
maybe, for that to happen, you'd have to be a helen of a different troy or
a woman of a different name
in a nonexistent market in michigan where there's a troy
with a post office, some people & a library

socialism's ok for americans sometimes, e.g. the library
the post office, the schools where people
can learn about ancient troy or all the troys
even the ones without any markets
by the names of price chopper or hannford, names
that might appear in our dreams where a different

landscape or map, as it were, leads to a different
way of perceiving like books in a library

can lead you on a quest, already inherent in your name
to find the place where people, all people
freely & unworriedly go to a crowded market
whether it's in syracuse, utica, rome or troy

there's something about troy that's different
even without markets, a movie theater, a library
you still will get people interested in your name

HISTORY OF TROY, N.Y.

for howard zinn + ed sanders

i sing of arms & legs & the helens
of troy, n.y. / one could do a cartwheel /   spell out
& tap dance up a wall
another helen has a titanium knee
these are the faces
that launched a thousand ships
but wait . . . this here troy
the former farm of a guy named
van der heyden who was as pissed
as saint cyril at hypatia
that troy was called troy
+ formerly ashley's ferry, was named
troy in 1789 in a move of love of
democracy & a startling ambition
for the town to be a center of commerce
not just detachable collars & happy
chocolate. There was a mount olympus
a mount ida, an ilium café, an antique
shop called the trojan horse, the possibilities
for play (ludum) were endless + everybody
hated the hegemony of the dutch anyway
henry hudson no more discovered that river
than columbus america. If americans
were to begin to be interlopers, why not
go all the way so shamelessly troy
become troy, as good a harbor as albany
named after a british duke
who knows the thoughts of people?
who, in accounts at the time, were in the number 50

in a place where the american indians lived
& nobody owned the land, you could name
anything anything. Too bad white people
reared their ugly heads in other ways
there's still a lot of dutch names for things
creeks named kills, valatie, van everything
+ a lot of indian names – tsatsawassa
schaghticoke, shenendowa, shinnecock, schmuck
all the american indians got pushed farther & farther

west & south under the aegis of andrew jackson
because the white people wanted their land
the miami, originally from ohio, had to go to miami!

this is what the trail of tears was because
tears were shed by the natives forced to leave
their fertile ancestral lands for land
nobody in their right mind would want
the native americans were gotten drunk
to sign the pieces of paper, unknowingly
ceding the land they had no concept of owning
the u.s. govt ignored them when they could
get away with it & if you think about it
the u.s. is all about what you can get away with
the indians were mahicans & tsasawassans
like any aborigines they knew every tree & hill
or moved a lot like birds to a different hill
                              the bodies of water
that converged on this place called troy
were hudson & mohawk river, the poestenkill
and the sweet milk creek, later the erie canal
always the cohoes falls, herman melville lived there
+ uncle sam wilson who sent meat to the troops
labeled US, 'a visit from saint nick' was published
in troy, it was a stop on the underground railroad
to canada, the starchers of the detachable collars
formed one of the first women's labor unions ever
there was a musical comedy in the '30s about
the helens of troy, in 1866 the troy haymakers
played the mutuals of ny
                              for the next 150 years
troy was insatiable, the people of troy made
bells, carriages, coaches, train cars, horseshoes
nails, axes, woodstoves, paper, sand paper, cloth
the famous burden ironworks had the biggest waterwheel ever
the "niagara" of waterwheels, there were ferries
& ferris wheels everywhere. you could walk everywhere
there were butchers, bakers & candlestick makers
stores to get girdles in, hot stoves, ice cream,
waterfalls, tiny waterwheels, ruffles & swimming
there was nothing you couldn't get in troy or cohoes
the schools were emma willard, russel sage, troy u
& rpi. there were veins of iron ore & movie theaters
there was even washington park with a key to it

THE FACES THAT LAUNCHED A THOUSAND SHIPS

I think I know my name. It's not Molly or Tasha. It might be Minnie. I was born, my mother's daughter & I can prove it. Just look between my legs. Well, that doesn't prove who my mother is. Just that I'm somebody's daughter, a daughter, not a son. Even sons are mother's sons. You can be a mother of either a son or a daughter. Since women are often disenfranchised, depending on what country you live in, daughters are often thrown away. Hard to believe isn't it? But then a lot of stuff about females is. I'm glad I didn't live in a previous century. The quest for a husband would've driven me crazy & that my own identity depended on it.

The *Helens of Troy* project will result in a book and an artwork— photographs of all the Helens of Troy, New York, I can find, & poems written by me about each of them. In the midst of doing this project (I've photographed & talked to five Helens so far), I've become interested in the plight of the city of Troy. Troy here. First let me tell you the story of Hector, a dog I live with. Russell, a friend was reading the *Iliad* in Inwood park, New York when a women came up to him with a young, scruffy brown dog & said hey do you want this dog? I have to go to Troy. Meaning my troy. Or this Troy.

In high school I was regaled with stories of the Greek myths. We also read the *Aeneid*. Sometimes it seems my whole life has been setting up to do this *Helen of Troy* project.

When I moved to East Nassau, across the road from me was a Helen of Troy, now Helen Green.

Everything in Troy here has burned down in various fires. Proctor's theater, which didn't, was one of Troy's 3 or 4 movie theaters, and also a vaudeville house. Here, in the '20s or '30s was a musical comedy by a guy who wrote two of the Marx Bros. movies. The musical is about the Helens of Troy, New York. It went to B'way for a while & is apparently on microfiche in the Troy library. This Proctor's (& there were many others in surrounding cities all of which were refurbished) is owned now by RPI, who you'd think would be realistic or regular, but they want to raze it. I haven't gotten in yet to take pictures, but hope to thru one of the Helens I met. Apparently there's a mural from the Helen of Troy show. I hope that to get into Proctor's isn't as futile as the hope to be rich or even solvent.

"Maroon Muckle" is the title of my first poem about one of the Helens. Muckle's her maiden name; maroon her favorite color. Meeting these Helens is seeing a part of history that wouldn't exist, wouldn't have to exist either, if I weren't doing this; there are lots of people & things, including books, that are already there, but being alive is different maybe.

I met a Helen, born in Australia, who when her father wanted to name her Helen after Helen of Troy, her mother made her middle name Hypatia after the Greek mathematician, so she'd have intelligence as well as beauty.

She became a professor of astronomy at RPI & moved there with a guy who taught geology. Her name was Bailey & his was Bayly. I wish to have all these Helens in my backyard for a picnic.

Who are the Helens of Troy, New York that I've been able to know a little? I haven't met any hostile Helens yet, except maybe the one who said over the phone, "I'm not interested."

Pretty much the Helens are like fireflies or creeks or maple trees. The Helens are making me corny, there's a lot of sentimental stuff going on: Love of the city of Troy as a child, at Xmas even, the mother with alzheimer's who's a happy Helen, who somersaulted, then tap danced up the wall. The secrets of the Helens I'll never tell.

My plan now is to become a community activist, I'll save Proctor's theater, sell stuff from my farm to the local people and open a restaurant in the woods where I'll make free grilled cheeses for anybody who happens by. If it's a long-term hiker I'll have half-pints of ice cream ready. I'll take pictures of people eating & call it: THE FIRST COMMUNION WORK—because the free grilled cheeses are my body and my blood test, though it seems totally irrelevant to mention my upcoming venapuncture.

- Bernadette Mayer

Bernadette Mayer is the author of numerous books of poetry and prose, including: *Poetry State Forest* (New Directions, 2008), *Scarlet Tanager* (2005), *Two Haloed Mourners: Poems* (1998), *Proper Name and Other Stories* (1996), *The Desires of Mothers to Please Others in Letters* (1994), *The Bernadette Mayer Reader* (1992), *Sonnets* (1989), *Midwinter Day* (1982), *The Golden Book of Words* (1978), and *Ceremony Latin* (1964). From 1972 to 1974, Mayer and conceptual artist Vito Acconci edited the journal *0 TO 9*. With her husband, writer and publisher, Lewis Warsh, she edited United Artists Press. She has taught writing workshops at The Poetry Project at St. Mark's Church in New York City for many years and she served as the Poetry Project's director during the 1980s. Bernadette Mayer lives in East Nassau, New York.

SHARON MESMER

from *In Ordinary Time*

REVENGE

It all started when, drunk at home, I knocked over a lamp. No damage to the lamp, but the bulb had shattered and I was out of extras. Luckily, the K-Mart was only short sprint away—how easy life could be once quality and beauty were sacrificed to convenience! As I made my way across the garish agora, my hair lank and plastered to my forehead, she stamped past me in tight pants and jacket, stuffing a hot dog into her mouth, her eyes fixed on the distance, contemptuous, defiant. How many women with that same inscrutable look (but minus the hot dog) had I stared at on subways and never dared to approach? But this time something, maybe a sodden resignation to Fate, made me brave. This time, I would say something! But something that would confound her, confuse her (and hopefully reveal her low mind to her—female vulgarians need a lesson like that). Dubious manhood be damned! And so, with breath suspended like a feather on the air of failure, I uttered:

"Excuse me, but you seem to be hatching an alien doppelgänger. Oh, I'm sorry—that's your head!"

To my utter shock she stopped, turned, fixed me with her dark, suspiring eyes and … laughed! Had she actually understood? If not, she was at least playing it right, her head cocked sweetly to the side, the planes of her face reflecting the fluorescence in a way that conveyed a feeling of Alexandrine jalousies at evening. Or the daytime moon at high noon. Or maybe the frustrations of small town auto repair. Or maybe a haunted landscape of naked suburbanites smearing human waste on holy statues. My refined mind, as you can see, was reeling. And in that reeling my initiation into the Mysteries began.

What happened that night? A whirlwind of things. I remember teeth, a flushed feeling, and cheeks suffused with moonlight. The next day, still reeling, I cancelled class and ventured to collect her at the address she'd given me, which turned out to be an abandoned, half-collapsed American Can warehouse in the used car district—not what I'd expected (five-floor walk-up off a wide, dull boulevard, packed with squalling kids and sprawling grandparents). In the fashion of people of her station, I yelled up for her—no doorbell. She breezed to the door smiling and flinging a long scarf across her shoulders—also not what I'd expected: the trademark look of the Bryn Mawr mafia? No, not her! Glowing, she smelled of tuberose, and I pulled out all the stops: took her to sample freshly-made patés in the back room café of an otherwise disregarded bakery; for mussels and butter, gratis, at the Spanish-style bar of a swanky old place sequestered high above downtown where my favorite wizened waiter brought me my usual (which impressed her more than anything that day, I think); and finally, at her request, to slobber down tacos at her favorite ramshackle joint in back of the factories. I learned that she was actually educated, and had in fact finished college, although her choice of college communicated class status—alas. But to her credit her style of dress reflected an innate, intelligent embrace of fashion's temporary zeitgeist: a tight white t-shirt with black satin pants, Beatle boots (or what looked like), and of course that anomalous scarf. Her eyebrows were unplucked. She wasn't wearing rouge. She didn't need to; her complexion was clear, smooth. In fact, I became a bit obsessed with the planes of her face, and how her beauty imparted a deeper elegance to the elegant places we visited that day.

She continually surprised me, as we got to know each other over time. But at the same time, her pretentiousness started to grate: sweeping into a room, shaking Florida water onto her hand, she'd declaim some discovery concerning "text modules" (whatever that was); daubing her face and neck with white cream from a flat blue jar she'd mutter something about "creating decorum out of spiritual excrement." Her favorite gesture seemed to be waving a cigarette around her head, gleeful eyes raised, and making some grand statement about... oh, who knew (her quotes were always erroneous, but I never corrected her; after all, I wanted to sleep with her). Even the placement of objects on her dresser was designed to further the image of artistic integrity and inquiry that she was attempting to project: an Art Deco gold compact resting atop a first edition of Reisling's *Faith and Fear* (had she actually read it? I certainly hadn't); Egyptian "depilatories" (I suspected they were just drugstore cold creams) in green glass jars; and this, scribbled in lipstick on her mirror:

What I want. What I want now. What I want to devour. I'm just a little black stone, tiny little cold stone. You don't notice me, at least not right away. You may think I don't feel, because I don't say . Because I just wait. But don't be fooled. I'm watching and waiting. For you. For the right moment to destroy you. And create you anew.

Her laughable lines were as empty as the moments she felt they occupied and defined. She was a self-defined "master of moments." She had done a study: every day, every hour, every second, had its own angel. For instance, for the first twelve hours of Sunday it was Michael, Anael, Raphael, Gabriel, Cassiel, Sachiel, Samael, Michael, Anael, Raphael, Gabriel, Cassiel. And so on, in a slightly different order, for the subsequent twelve hours. And each angel embodied some emotional idea. Once, when we were in bed and watching "Columbo" she suddenly announced, "Oh—we've switched to Raphael. Can you feel it?" There were also angels of the four seasons, angels of the altitudes, angels who ruled the twenty-eight mansions of the moon, the watchers, the sixty-four angelic wardens of the seven celestial halls, and seventy amulet angels invoked at time of childbirth. She used the information to ponder her place and role in the harmony of the spheres, which seemingly shifted from moment to moment. And oh, those moments: the changes, the transformations, the little invisible victories and defeats in the arrivals and departures of thoughts... maddening intricacies! Even the slight shift of light when walking through automatic doors into a department store revealed something of Eternity to her.

I soon accepted that she occupied a realm where profound gifts and fatal flaws held sway, a place where herculean strength is demanded and only the strong survive. To merely appease the weakness one hated in oneself was not enough because it would just grow into something else, something worse. It became clear to me that she believed it was necessary to feed one's weaknesses to someone else and then devour the person because that way you were also taking into yourself what was good as well—in essence, turning every good and bad thing into one's own sustenance, thus transcending dualities.

By late September we were sleeping together. Sex with her was not what I'd guessed it would be—a roil in realms of invictive (& thus instructive) pleasure. It was less a descent into her delicious flesh than me feeling like I was staring down the length of a long industrial corridor at a pathetically decorated Christmas tree. But soon after that our denouement began, at her hands, and as expected. It didn't mean much to me. She was inconsequential. It was the experience I was interested in. I was outside pain because this was my experiment, my project.

"CONCEPTUAL" WRITING STATEMENT

I hesitate to write this because I fear that by defining what I've been doing for the last 35 years—appropriating diversely sourced material to generate language for prose and poetry—I will inadvertently switch a bare ugly light bulb on the process, thus rendering the occluded interstices which appropriation has allowed me to work within too visible. Concealing also reveals—but after the fact, and "after" is the moment where surprise and delight reside. Then again, even a bare ugly light bulb is a source of illumination.

Over the last six years, as a member of the flarf collective trolling the Interweb, I've come to realize that what I've been doing all along is just regarding the ubiquitous familiar that others have disregarded, and making that activity—and those findings—the foundation of my work. I was always an obsessive reader of myths and fairy tales, and it always struck me that the thing which ends up being the boon, or the thing that opens and closes the mysteries, is the homely familiar thing: Aridane's thread, for instance, or the evil fairy disguised as an old beggar lady. These objects/characters put things in motion, start the story off, and end it. In the case of the evil fairy, there's something unsavory in the mix, and the caution there ends up being: if only you'd really looked, none of this would've happened. But then again, therein lies the tale. To look or not to look? There's a responsibility.

I guess I've chosen to do both: utilize the ubiquitous familiar—because to not use it would be to perhaps miss something that might benefit the writing (or benefit from it)—but at the same time not look too closely at it during the process. My story "Revenge" (from *In Ordinary Time*, Hanging Loose Press, 2005) was generated primarily from press releases for readings at the Drawing Center circa 2004 and secondarily from sundry journal notes that hadn't found homes in poems. I already had a character that I'd been working with (the unnamed woman who tortures the presumptive narrator—at the end it's revealed that she is the narrator) but I hadn't found an effective way to frame her within the constraints of a traditional story where characters interact and conflict occurs. The press releases pissed me off because I found them ridiculously obscure, and then I found myself tortured by trying to figure out just why this pissed me off so much. Finally I decided to view them as pure language, to throw them in with the cast-off ideas. In doing so I developed a narrative of a woman "narrating" a man narrating her— still ridiculously obscure, but in a different way. This method is similar to my basic flarf poems: generated by taking lines from poems that went around the list via email and putting certain lines through Google, and then reconstituting them with secondary *materiae* (usually lines from the emails themselves). The difference between much of my prose and poetry is that while the prose is a solitary endeavor, the poems happen via involvement and incorporation. The poems take, usually, less than fifteen minutes, and the prose a couple of days. In that short amount of time, the light bulb—if it gets turned on at all—is a mere flicker, easily disregarded.

- Sharon Mesmer

Sharon Mesmer is a 2011 Fulbright Senior Specialist and a two-time New York Foundation for the Arts poetry fellow (1999, 2007). Her recent poetry collections are *The Virgin Formica* (Hanging Loose 2008) and *Annoying Diabetic Bitch* (Combo Books, 2008). Her fiction collections are *Ma Vie à Yonago* (in French, Hachette, 2005) and *In Ordinary Time* and *The Empty Quarter* (Hanging Loose, 2005, 2000). She is a member of the flarf collective.

HARRYETTE MULLEN

FROM *S*PERM**K*T*

Lines assemble gutter and margin. Outside and in, they straighten a place. Organize a stand. Shelve space. Square footage. Align your list or listlessness. Pushing oddly evening aisle catches the tail of an eye. Displays the cherished share. Individually wrapped singles, frozen divorced compartments, six-pack windows express themselves while women wait in family ways, all bulging baskets, squirming young. More on line in- cites the eyes. Bold names label familiar type faces. Her hand scanning throwaway lines.

With eternal welcome mates omniscient doors swing open offering temptation, redemption, thrilling confessions. The state of Grace is Monaco. A shrine in Memphis, colossal savings. A single serving after-work lives. In sanctuaries of the sublime subliminal mobius soundtrack backs spatial mnemonics, radiant stations of the crass. When you see it, you remember what you came for.

Pyramids are eroding monuments. Embalmed soup stocks the recyclable soul adrift in its newspaper boat of double coupons. Seconds decline in descent from number one, top of the heap. So this is generic life, feeding from a dented can. Devoid of colored labels, the discounted irregulars.

Just add water. That homespun incantation activates potent powders, alchemical concentrates, jars and boxes of abracadabra. Bottled water works trickling down a rainy day watering can reconstitute the shrinking dollar. A greenback garnered from a tree. At two bucks, one tender legal portrait of Saint No-Nicks stands in for clean-shaven, defunct cherry chopper. Check out this week's seasonal electric reindeer luz de vela Virgin Mary mark downs. Choose from ten brands clearly miracle H-2-0. Pure genius in a bottle. Not municipal precipitate you pay to tap, but dear rain fresh capped at spring. Cleaner than North Pole snow, or Commander in Chief's hard boiled white collars. Purer than pale saint's flow of holy beard or drops distilled from sterile virgin tears.

Aren't you glad you use petroleum? Don't wait to be told you explode.
You're not fully here until you're over there. Never let them see you
eat. You might be taken for a zoo. Raise your hand if you're sure you're
not.

S*PeRM**K*T is the word "supermarket" with some letters missing and asterisks replace the missing letters. The missing letters just happen to be U-A-R-E, so it's like "you are what you eat." This is a book about food, and everything that's in the supermarket. *S*PeRM**K*T* is sort of like your shopping list when you go to the supermarket. So, each one of the aisles that you would find and the things that you would find in the supermarket, that's how this book is organized. And it also has some nice black and white pictures that Gil Ott took himself in his local supermarket of the meat wrapped in plastic and the baked goods in that kind of plastic that I don't think they even can recycle. [...] I was thinking about domestication, about the role of women, women as consumers, women having a supposed power as consumers but also being disempowered in other ways—even as they're being appealed to. So, because of the limited images that are available in the marketplace, you know, you can't necessarily buy who you really want to be. You have to buy the available images. Then, of course, I'm dealing with a whole retrospective view of television and marketing.

- Harryette Mullen

Harryette Mullen is the author of *Trimmings, S*PeRM**K*T, Muse & Drudge, Blues Baby, Sleeping with the Dictionary*, a finalist for the National Book Award, the National Book Critics Circle Award, and the *Los Angeles Times* Book Award in poetry, and *Recyclopedia*, which received a PEN Beyond Margins Award. Mullen was the 2009 recipient of the Academy of American Poets Fellowship. Her other honors include artist grants from the Texas Institute of Letters and the Helene Wurlitzer Foundation of New Mexico, the Gertrude Stein Award in Innovative American Poetry, and a Rockefeller Fellowship from the Susan B. Anthony Institute for Women's Studies at the University of Rochester. Harryette Mullen teaches at the University of California, Los Angeles.

LAURA MULLEN

I WANDERED NETWORKS
LIKE A CLOUD

That floated o're my couch, remote
In one hand, drink in the other, a crowd
On the screen (wounded, enraged)
Fleeing the tanks beneath the leaves
Fluttering and dancing in the breeze.

Continuous as the stars that shine,
These wars, these displaced "refugees,"
Filmed in never-ending lines
Along the margins and at bay.
Ten thousand saw I at a glance,
Hurrying nowhere, like frightened ants.

The waves beside them danced; but they
Bent weeping over loved bodies:
A poet could not but be gay,
Far from such desperate company:
I gazed—and gazed—and little thought
What wealth the show to me had brought:

For oft, when on my couch I lie
In vacant or in pensive mood,
They flash upon that satellite dish
Which is the bliss of solitude;
And then my heart with pleasure fills,
To be so far from the world's ills.

CLOUD AS LONELY

And verb with the nouns, and my
Sullen heart and the bliss of
The eerily violent
Description of memory as a sort of IED
In the home entertainment center
Are you in an adjective or pensive mood
When I lie
Following me

sick of the mention of flowers the stench of flowers when

for the dead

What bailout the show had
Pronoun verb—conjunction verb—and little thought
Such a company could not be
But that the cost of this
Out-did the sparkling waves:
Waves beside them but they
Displaced the local industry
Tossing their heads

Storyboard it: do you see them casting
Their heads into the air or to each other

Just asking (do you follow)

Shadowed the man describing a live
section of landscape his pretence he'd been there
Alone the main thing

Did you see me dreaming this? (On your inward eye?)
"If you're reading this"

Oddly specific number weird syntax torqued
For the rhyme's sake along the margin of
A never-ending line
Anyway continuous as

Wither darkened number
Line about motion and location as cause
Gerund and gerund in the breeze
Preposition the noun preposition the noun
Verb location and preposition nouns
When all at once I saw a host golden

CLOUD SEEDING: FROM A JOURNAL

Head full of markers
Production of mists the history of
Who here has been truly educated
Signs on stakes wires actual
Imagined construction of
Outlines boundaries borders
Mechanically echoing
Production of proof of
Pictured where exactly
A dog when you rang the bell
The more direct route obviously
"I can read" barking
Prerecorded notes vs posted official
Warnings rain chant apologetic
The writing looked desperate
Barking mechanically
As if there wasn't any reason
The shorter route clearly
Visibly evaporating
Demarcations property lines
A silence or "pause" between
Rights of the citizen comic
Misspellings and human
Prohibitions vs dark admonitions
Repeated "Bad dog barking!"
Conjured trusty guardian
Worn itinerary of chewed shoes
Formed and vanished
Neither snow nor sleet nor dark
A voice in a cloud of suspicion
Gr-r-r-r as *of night*
Forms of literacy, who here
Has barked their shins
On something
Sound triggers an image
Seeing no obstacles truly
To open a digression breathing
Flashed on that inward eye a fanged hot
Source knuckles on the collar whitening

A barked command blinds
Who here was meant to identify with
I wandered not exactly complaining

Each lonely parasite an entry

NO VOICE

Wandered lonely as a variety of complaints in the voice of another who
had no voice

This is what I remember

Two figures by the water's edge, stopped by such beauty, one numbers

The complaints travel the body stop nowhere never stop are always

Later by an open window notebook open "This is what I remember..."

Who had no voice she said, still, but I wonder how you are

I wandered like "like" refusing the information

I wandered, realizing I hadn't mourned, and that I would still

CLOUD COVERS

"The wind seized our breath.
The Lake was rough."
- Dorothy Wordsworth: *Journals*, April 15th 1802

On April 15th, 1802 (a "threatening, misty" day), the Wordsworth siblings took a walk. Dorothy described the experience in a journal entry—an entry used by her brother in writing and revising what would become a well-known poem transforming recalled and appropriated material in significant ways. While Dorothy anthropomorphized the daffodils, she saw them as weary, and she moved through "tossed" and "reeled" to get to "danced." Her brother's famous "breeze" was a "furious" wind, in Dorothy's account, that "blew directly" to the flowers after taking a shared "breath." William, using her words in the service of his entertainment, was not breathless, though his breathing (in rhyming sestets) might seem labored to us. Perhaps most striking was the poet's decision not to include his companion in the "lonely" / solitary experience he recounts. Why must the woman be removed, why must the wind be tamed and the flowers numbered, why must their motion be legible as pleasure? These questions came to me accompanied by others: about gender and genre, appropriation and originality, and the relationship of art to life. Influenced by Picasso's variations on *Las Meninas*, my on-going examination of intertextuality became, after the aftermath of Hurricane Katrina, an exploration of voice, performance, embodiment, entitlement, and contested experience.

Part of what makes my work conceptual, as per current definitions of that term, is the application of strategies from other areas (art, music, film, criticism, etc.), for the view of the view: a way to see our seeing. But though I often start with an idea, unless and until the process itself becomes compelling the idea remains a ghost: a line in a notebook or a single example, aborted or just not (although carried out) engaging. The importance of conceptual art rests, for me, in its deep involved inquiry into repetition—that is, *time*, and memory. As I wrote this brief introduction I laughingly considered a still briefer one: "It better be 'conceptual' because otherwise it's crazy." Conceptual art stays with the implications of its project and in its refusal to 'move on' risks being seen as stuck, a stutter at the site of the traumatic....

- *Laura Mullen*

Laura Mullen is the author of five books and a Professor at Louisiana State University. Her recent books include *Murmur* (2007) and *Dark Archive*, published by the University of California Press in 2011. Composer Jason Eckardt's setting of her poems, "Undersong," performed by the International Contemporary Ensemble, is available on Mode Records.

DEBORAH RICHARDS

from *Nine Nights*

SCIENCE AND NATURE

1. The jungle is extensive and dynamic yet each tree is known
    by its girth and ability to take the weight of man (or woman)
    great ape or chimp.

2. She is so succumbed on a branch over hanging. He pulls her
    to him roughly.

3. There is a rumble in the jungle.

So far about **a fifth of the Amazonian rainforest** has been
razed completely. Another **22 per cent** has been harmed [...],
**allowing the sun to penetrate
to the forest floor drying it out.**   1

The Brazilian government has announced a huge rise in the
rate of Amazon deforestation, months after celebrating its
success in achieving a reduction. In the last five months of
2007, 3,235 sq km (1,250 sq miles) were lost.   2

Sapo is probably one of the last places on Earth to experience
virgin rainforest. It is extremely difficult to navigate through
with a temperature and humidity that make carrying a
backpack and normal thought processes extremely difficult.   3

4. She is almost natural.

5. First night.

IT'S A JUNGLE OUT THERE

1. The lions roar the crocodile plunges forward into dark water
   the scream of my love detained and snuggled.

2. The white men come looking for gold and I turn them way.
   So gung ho and I say no.

3. The black men are shaking off the monkeys.

The forest vegetation carries cholera and the tree sap
also contains certain flesh-eating micro-organisms.   3

Culture, in part, provides people with the tools
and resources to steel themselves against adversity
and convinces them not to kill themselves or others.   5

Kenya is fast becoming Africa's hottest destination for 2009,
with tourists returning in increasing numbers to a country
that seems to have shaken off its troubled image of last year,
when elections led to riots throughout the country.   7

4. I am preoccupied.   5

5. Night falls.

COMMON LANGUAGE

1. Let me grasp you girl embrace your righteous body you got going hazy reel me up reel me up let me rambunct you go wild all around me feel me feel me don't change girl...

2. To know her is to love her.

3. Now this has been emphasised...   3

Sapo is beautiful. Looking from a bird's-eye view, one can see rainforest from horizon to horizon, and it does not contain the expanse of rubber trees one is used to seeing in rural Liberia.   3

However, the latest estimates indicate that the tipping point is indeed imminent.   1

At the moment in which we must look defeat, disillusionment and discouragement in the face and work through it—a sense of the tragicomic keeps alive some sense of possibility.   5

Kenya is so buoyant that we have added a new itinerary – a Gamelands and Gorilla Safari, taking in Kenya, Uganda and Tanzania.   7

4. Time may change you.

5. Sun sets on the horizon.

EARTH THE WEEPING SORES

1.   The Afar women collect the water from the river, walk 2 miles to wash the clothes, rebuild the houses and thatch them. The visitor bends to cross the threshold.

2.   The women plait the visitor's hair. They talk about her beauty.

3.   Where does the Earth fall apart?

Gilberto Camara, of INPE, an institute that provides
satellite imaging of the area, said the rate of loss
was unprecedented for the time of year.   2

In the remote Afar depression in northern Ethiopia,
the African Continent is slowly splitting apart and a new
ocean is forming. In September 2005, a series of fissures
opened along the Afar Depression.

Over about a week, the rift pulled apart by eight metres and
dropped down by up to one metre.   4

Local people told of a series of earthquakes and how ash
darkened the air for three days.   5

4.   Some sense of hope. Some sense of agency. Some sense of resistance.

5.   Another night.

1. I wasn't the only one with a crack in my soul and mine was so beautifully carved from my vestigial life.

2. People wait; they pass by; anglers fish; nothing happens, and there is a sense of waiting, of imminence, of emptiness.   6

3. Just measure it.

Violence in Liberia has played a part in protecting this region of wilderness, as though some people were driven to living in the park the countries [sic] infrastructure was so damaged by the fighting that not much construction, the enemy of many African forests, took place.

The squatters have now been driven out but there are still people inhabiting the park, many who are looking for mineral treasures, who threaten the survival of some of the park's exotic creatures through hunting and the rainforest itself with their mining.   3

A week at the three-star Diani Sea Lodge costs £699, including flights and all-inclusive accommodation (departing 1 April), a saving of £112 on last year's price. Perhaps most surprising is that bookings are higher than before the troubles occurred.   7

4. One of life's riddles.

5. The red sun sinks beyond the trees, turning the clouds pink.   6

Each of these poems comes from a larger work entitled *Nine Nights*, which is an accumulation of sources and questions. Here is a small sample:

- Memorials on park benches
- 1930s Tarzan films
- Henri Rousseau's jungle paintings
- *Tribal Wives*, a television series
- Ethnographic tourism and Ecotours
- "Earth Song" by Michael Jackson
- "Encounter" by Czeslaw Milosz
- In the *House of My Father* 1996-7. Photograph on paper on aluminium image: 1220 x 1530 mm by Donald Rodney

My poetic practice is akin to Vito Acconci following a stranger to his door as part of an art performance. In my case, an idea catches my attention, but I don't quite follow it home—I turn instead to the neighbour, ally or cynical friend. Like Acconci I never quite know where I will end up. *Nine Nights* could be a room with books kept open by weights, photos from news sources, paintings, copies of art and literary reviews, boxes with newspaper cuttings, clips from DVDs, ephemera, etc.

The initial spark for *Nine Nights* was the brief memorials found on park benches. I tried but failed to get information on how a memorial could be commissioned at my local park. From this abortive lead, I returned to previous investigations of the imaginary jungle in film, art or literature as the place where sudden and early death is a potential that is managed successfully for the protagonist and not the indigenous people (on the whole). However, I discovered when I looked at Tarzan films again, that Tarzan is an early eco-warrior who defends and protects the jungle from the exploits of the white men who clearly hate this 'hell hole' and only stay on the promise of a fortune beyond their wildest dreams.

Then I caught part of the television series *Tribal Wives* where a woman from the United Kingdom goes to stay with the women of a tribe in a remote region in the world. The British woman experiences the physically hard and ordered life of the tribal women (e.g. The Afar women in Ethiopia) and she comes away renewed and often invigorated to settle and appreciate her life back home. Unlike on jungle reality shows such as *Survivor* and *I'm a Celebrity—Get Me Out of Here*, the tribal women are able to explain their lives and provide their own commentary on the strange ways of this outsider. An article I read in *The Guardian* newspaper investigated the increase in the controversial practice of placing large plush tourist resorts in remote regions of the world and how they encroach on the lives of the inhabitants. Often the indigenous people become part of the tourist experience, and the worry is that the tribes cannot effectively defend themselves from Western influences, disease and money.

However, the issue with my kind of trails is that it is difficult to pin them down. I have always liked "Encounter" by Czeslaw Milosz, and I have used this poem as a loose set up for *Nine Nights* in this print version. More particularly, I have made each section of *Nine Nights* a 'day' of 5 parts: brief description; events that follow one after the other; information/data (usually quotations from selected internet websites); musing/ramification; night/day end.

Here are moveable memorials that change focus and direction. Memorials that catch the attention like bunches of flowers left on the road side signal a sudden death and reminds us for a few moments of death.

Nine nights is more commonly known as the vigil that takes place when someone dies—I am not sure how common it still is in the Caribbean. Anyway, this vigil has become a resting place for the poem thus far.

- Deborah Richards

The numbers on the right side of the page in *Nine Nights* identify the following numbered internet sources. [accessed 08/18/09]

1. Corrosion doctors. <http://corrosion-doctors.org/Climate-Tipping-Points/tipping-amazon.htm>

2. BBC World News Thursday, 24 January 2008. <http://news.bbc.co.uk/1/hi/world/americas/7206165.stm>

3. World Reviewer Travel Guides.
<http://www.worldreviewer.com/travel-guides/rainforest/sapo-national-park/14374/ >
Rowan McShane is the author of the texts on pp 97,98 and 99; Kate Griffin is the author for page 101.

4. Afar Rift Consortium.<http://www.see.leeds.ac.uk/afar/ >

5. *Hope on a Tightrope: Words and Wisdom* by Cornel West. <http://www.amazon.com/Hope-Tightrope-Wisdom-Cornel-West/dp/1401921868/ref=sr_1_1?ie=UTF8&s=books&qid=1219849491&sr=8-1#reader >

6. *The Guardian* 'Stumble in the jungle' by Adrian Searle. <http://www.guardian.co.uk/culture/2005/nov/01/1>

7. *The Observer* 'Aggressive price cuts drive Kenya's recovery surprise recovery'
<http://www.guardian.co.uk/travel/2009/mar/15/kenya-travel-news>

Deborah Richards is the author of chapbooks, *Hide me from the Day* (Bootstrap Press), *parable* (Leroy Press) and the poetry collection *Last One Out* (subpress). She has work published in a number of journals including *Chain*, *XCP: Cross Cultural Poetics*, *Callaloo*, *Nocturnes* and the *Encyclopedia* anthology. She has also been published on-line at *Tarpaulin Sky* and *How2*. On her desk, Deborah has a photo of Paula Rego that inspires her to keep going. (The photo is taken from the brilliant feature on Rego: 'You punish people with drawings' *Guardian Weekend* 8/22/09).

JULIANA SPAHR

THE REMEDY

1.

After the baby was born, I was often desperate to get out of the house, to walk somewhere and be with other people. Even though I was always with the baby, I felt very much as if I was by myself. So to be near other people, I would go for long walks, carrying the baby in a sling that hung from my shoulder. On the walks, I would be near other people only for a few brief moments as I passed them by. Still, that felt like it was some sort of more to me. On these walks, if the baby started to cry I would stop and sit on a nearby bench and nurse him. Sometimes men spat at me as I did this. At first, I was not accustomed to being spat upon and when it happened I would be surprised and dismayed. But eventually I got used to it and came to expect it.

2.

I got used to the spitting. But I did not get used to having the body that got spit upon. My mind would think something like my body is once again my body. But my body was not really agreeing with this because it felt even less like it was mine. When the baby came out, something that was not me left me. However it had not left me with my former self but with a new self and I did not yet feel as if this self was mine. My body did new and often unexpected things. It was not just that my breasts now produced milk and the milk seemed to have a life of its own, spurting out across the room at moments. And it was not just that new hormones coursed through my body and made me feel new emotions, some pleasant and some not. But my brain was also different. And so when I tried to talk about my new self that did not yet feel as if it was mine, or talk from this new self, I did not know the right language. Words came out wrong. Often I said them backwards or I confused their order in sentences. Or I tried to say I feel weird and I would find myself saying I am fat. Or I mixed several languages together in one sentence.

3.

Not only did I not know the right language, I didn't really know how to fuck anymore. Nursing would send oxytocin coursing through my body, so I knew how my body might feel good. But I could no longer remember how to make oxytocin when fucking, although I did remember that fucking used to make oxytocin. I had gotten used to fucking with the baby before he was born. He took up a lot of room in the bed. He was there. It was nice. But then, after he came out, there was a hole in my self and I had not yet figured out how to fill it. I had started fucking again a month or so after the baby came out. When I had sex at first, the hole felt big, too big. The baby had only stretched a hole for a few minutes as he descended down out of the birth canal, but it was long enough to stretch out the hole, and it took several months for it to close back up. When I fucked with someone, there might at moments be something inside that hole that felt so empty, something filling it up, but I was still not whole.

4.

A few months after the baby was born, after I started fucking, I began to spit on my lover, usually when we were fucking. Even though by this time I was used to men spitting on me when I nursed, my sudden desire to spit on my lover was unexpected. I did not know what to make of it. Sometimes my lover would, exasperated, scream at me to stop spitting. But most of the time we just kept fucking, my lover sometimes dodging the spit, sometimes just lying there and putting up with it.

5.

Soon after I started spitting on my lover, I started doing sit ups. I did three sets of thirty each day. I began to masturbate regularly again. And I returned to work. My first week back at work I began importing submachine guns to Slovakia through an Egyptian arms broker named Sharif al-Masri. And also I began to collaborate with a friend on a piece of writing about a small historically unimportant plot of land. I did all of this with a hole in me. I often started my day by attempting to fill the hole by fucking with my lover. I often did three sets of thirty sit ups while my lover gave the baby breakfast. I tended to masturbate later in the day. Part of most days were spent thinking about the collaboration. My collaborator and I would often give each other assignments and usually neither of us did them, and so I usually just thought about the collaboration rather than doing it. Then often I made some phone calls to see if the weapons had arrived yet. If they had arrived someplace, like say Slovakia, I would claim that they did not meet specifications in the contract and request that al-Masri return them to the manufacturer. Day after day went like this. One day I would sell the arms to Pecos, a Guinean brokering company later linked to a series of illicit arms transfers to Liberia instead of arranging for them to be shipped back to Slovakia. Another day, after I was done masturbating, I might see about the delivery of 1,000 sub-machine guns to Liberia along two parallel tracks, one originating in Moldova and the other in Liberia. Then I would divert sub-machine guns to Liberia through an elaborate bait-and-switch scheme that spanned three continents. And at the same time, I might continue to think about how to make collaborative art and suggest to my collaborator that we make a lyrical poem and how in this poem there could be a list of all the cars that drove by the small plot of land in two minutes and how much gas was being consumed by cars as they drove by the small plot of land and that perhaps this poem would then be about both the bourgeois individualism of the lyric and the extremities of consumption that define us. And while thinking about the poem, I might masturbate with a brown, medium-sized dildo and think about my lover or sometimes the small breasts of a woman I knew and then when I came I might say my lover's name or I might say jesus. Later that day, my collaborator might email me and suggest for our collaboration that he put an ad on an internet website that said he would be at the small historically unimportant plot of land for an hour one day with a set of nunchucks and that anyone who wanted to come by and beat him up was welcome to do so and perhaps this would be about a rejection of his white and western and patriarchal privilege. I would then seek and receive permission in Moldova to charter an Il-18 airliner to another Moldovan company, MoldTransavia, and claim that the aircraft was needed as a substitute for a damaged Tupolev-154 originally scheduled to fly passengers from the UAE to Moldova. And then I would do another thirty situps, working on keeping my neck relaxed at the same time. And then when the arms arrived in UAE I would call and say that the Tu-154 had been repaired and had already flown back to Moldova with its passengers and then I would get a representative of Centrafrican Airlines, Serguei Denissenko, to give me a new contract to fly cargo (identified as "Technical Equipment") to Uganda and then on to Liberia. When my lover was inside of me I might think at that moment about the hole in my body or I might imagine that I had my lover in my chest. And after I had signed the contract and faxed it back, the Il-18 would depart for Uganda shortly afterwards. And while it flew to Uganda, I would meet my collaborator on the small historically unimportant plot of land with a few sprigs of rosemary and we would rub some of the rosemary between our fingers and sniff deeply the rosemary smells on our fingers and imagine we were the opposite of our individual genders and thus attempt to enact a reversal of the patriarchal structures that so defined our daily life. Then we would sit down in the grass on the small plot of land and write furiously from this position. And whatever my gender was at that moment, later that night when we fucked my lover would begin by putting thumbs on my nipples and cupping my breasts and while fucking, my breasts would leak milk and then the next moment ants would begin to gather in our bed, attracted by the milk. After we fucked and usually before the ants figured out that there was milk in the bed, I would get up and sign another charter contract for the Ilyushin with Centrafrican. While I signed the charter, I might imagine we had a different body, a different societal gender conditioning. And from this different societal gender conditioning, I might teach my lover about my hole, the hole that my lover kept trying to fill by sticking stuff in it. Often after we fucked together I would read to my lover the charter contract which listed a cargo of 14.5 tons, the exact weight if the plane had flown the full amount of rifles to Liberia in two separate flights, and the same routing specified in the contract with Vichi. Meanwhile, we might attempt to get inside some other skin. And I might show my lover how to put a different sort of pressure on the fleshy area right behind the front of the entrance to my hole, which the contract referred to as "the performance of several air transportations," an apparent reference to additional arms transfers and also the same name we chose for our other skin. I might show my lover how to use not only back-and-forth pressure but also side-to-side and as my lover did this, shortly after the Ilyushin arrived in Entebbe, and loaded my breasts with seven tons of sealed boxes containing 1,000 of the 2,250 sub-machine guns that the Ugandan government believed were being returned to the manufacturer in Slovakia, my collaborator and I might be able to think together about how our writing could be different. Sometimes I might say go around the entire lip of the hole as the plane headed west and arrived in Monrovia on 22 November and as we landed, we would sniff the herbs on my fingers while thinking and writing from our other skin.

INFLUENCE & ORIGINALITY

1.

I was walking along the street. I wasn't doing anything. I was looking for some action.

It was night, late at night, Times Square. The blue yellow green red white and violet neon lights were still blinking. They wouldn't stop blinking for another two hours. And it would still be dark. It's always dark on Times Square: only rats live there, rats and some of those creepy insects that only come out at night.

My name is Jacqueline Onassis.

I kept walking down the slightly wet shining street. The neon lights were blinking at me, winking, inviting hot desires I had never known existed. In one dark alleyway, seven naked women were waiting to slowly peel off my clothes. One had her tongue under my left arm. One had her hand buried in the soft flesh of my thigh. Hot. There was a woman waiting for me who's madly in love with me. In fact she can't live without me. Every waking minute of the day she sees my face, my face twice its normal size hovering in front of her eyes, my hands tangled in, pressing, messing her wet cunt hairs. She dreams that I'm wet: my thighs are pillars. Joined at the top. Water streaks down their insides. I'm so wet and anxious that sweat's pouring out of me. "Come get me," I whisper to her. "Come get me and handle me."

The street was still wet and shiny. I felt a hand lightly touch my shoulder.

I quickly turned around.

"Look," a young dark-haired man said to me, releasing his erect cock from his pants. "See what you do to me? Every moment I see you. Three nights I've been following you. Three times I had to relieve myself."

I laughed. "Didn't anyone tell you that was bad for you? You could stunt your growth doing it so much."

He didn't laugh. "When are you going to spend a whole night with me? Just one time that we could make love ..."

I laughed again. "You're too greedy. I'm a married woman with responsibilities. I must be home every night so that I see my children when I wake up in the morning."

"What would be terrible if you did not?" He pouted.

"Then I'd be remiss in the one duty that my husband demands of me," I said. "And that I would not do."

"Your husband does not care. Otherwise he would have come to see you and the children at least once these past three months," he said.

My voice went cold. "How do you know that? What my husband does or does not do is none of your business."

He sensed instantly that he had said too much. "But I love you. I am going crazy for wanting you."

I nodded slowly. Relaxing. "Then keep things in their proper perspective," I said. "And if you're going to keep playing with your cock, you'd better get to the nearest bar before a cop arrests you."

"If I do, will you suck me?"

2.

As a child in sixth grade in a North American school, won first prize in a poetry contest. In late teens and early twenties, entered New York City poetry world. At first sight everything seemed to revolve around the theme of plagiarism as the key to a renewed understanding of the literary. Then prominent Black Mountain poets, mainly male, taught or attempted to teach her that a writer becomes a writer when and only when he finds his own voice. Since wanted to be a writer, tried hard to find her own voice. Couldn't. Writer thought, all these male poets want to be the top poet, as if, since they can't be a dictator in the political realm, can be dictator of this world. Want to play. Be left alone to play. Want to be a sailor who journeys at every edge and even into the unknown. See strange sights, see. Want to focus less on the kinds of interests and beliefs formulated on the basis of identity claims and more on precarity and its differential distributions, in the hope that new coalitions might be formed. If I can't keep on seeing wonders, I'm in prison. Claustrophobia's sister to my worst nightmare: lobotomy, the total loss of perceptual power, of seeing new. Wanted to be a writer. Didn't want to be restricted to purely literary questions about originality, the cult of genius or the modern invention of the rights of the author. Wanted a series of concepts and doctrines—the beautiful soul, purity, sincerity, the abolition of the new and the persistence of the old, good faith and bad conscience, the logic of melodrama, etc.—that, in reality, can be read as responses to a question about literature and politics that stills remains open. Since couldn't find 'her voice', decided she'd first have to learn what a Black Mountain poet meant by 'his voice'. What did he do when he wrote? This world both represents and is human history, public memories and private memories turned public, the records and actualizations of human intentions. Decided, no. To hell with the Black Mountain poets even though they had taught her a lot. This understanding would situate the act of writing between the two extremes of originality, which turns out to be undesirable aside from being an illusion, and falsification, which becomes deliberate to the point of turning into an authentic duty. Later she would think about ownership and copyright. I'm constantly being given language. Since this language-world is rich and always changing, flowing, when I write, I enter a world which has complex relations and is, perhaps, illimitable. Everything as a two-way affair, about erect and sucking participation, not merely consumption. Motherhood and making love and tongues under left arms. By using words arranged by Harold Robbins attempts to close this gap between the autonomy of the text and its social and political inscription. Went out night after night to lightly touch the shoulders of others from behind and keep playing with my cock in the nearest bar. Used the exploration of the limit of misogynist discourse to explore other boundaries and borders, like that of literary ownership. I didn't create language, writer thought. I can't make language, but in this world, I can play and be played. Realized that to refuse to write "literature" but to continue writing "criticism" implies withdrawing the former from bourgeois thought but leaving the latter well anchored in it. Realized that what I call my own writing appears perhaps at times as something that I author or, indeed, own. But the terms that make up one's own writing are, from the start, outside oneself, beyond oneself in a sociality that has no single author (and that radically contests the notion of authorship itself). Decided that since what she wanted to do was just to write, not to find her own voice, could and would write by using anyone's voice, anyone's text, whatever materials she wanted to use. By way of a new practice of storytelling to try and demonstrate the fallacy of these oppositions, together with others such as the one between commitment and vanguardism, such would finally have been the ambitious project made possible by the idea of plagiarism—all this, it seems, without having to exceed the limits of the literary itself, with everything this notion promises or threatens to convey. Had a dream while waking that was running with animals. Wild horses, leopards, red fox, kangaroos, mountain lions, wild dogs. Running over rolling hills. Was able to keep up with the animals and they accepted her. Pleaded come get me and handle me and then build a bottom-up, participatory structure to society and culture, rather than a top-down, closed, proprietary structure. Realized that if we are to make broader social and political claims about rights of protection and entitlements to persistence and flourishing, we will first have to be supported by a new written ontology, one that implies the rethinking of precariousness, vulnerability, injurability, interdependency, exposure, bodily persistence, desire, work and the claims of language and social belonging. Claimed from now on she would read only things that have come from somewhere else, which would be easy because everything written comes from somewhere else because everything is written in language, one of the most open source open content tools ever. All the while, she continued to use language to write, had to use language to write, and so continued to contribute, discuss, annotate, critique, improve, improvise, remix, mutate, and add yet more ingredients that she could not own, things that are beautiful, revolutionary, and irretrievable.

- Juliana Spahr

Juliana Spahr wrote "The Remedy" for *Army of Lovers,* a collaboration with David Buuck. "Influence & Originality" was written for a panel called "Influence & Originality" at Goddard College.

CECILIA VICUÑA

FROM *INSTAN*

b

ι

ə

ə

instan

ᴠ

s

i

ə   l

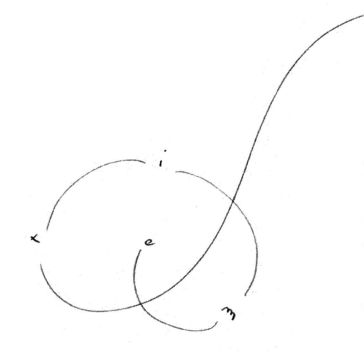

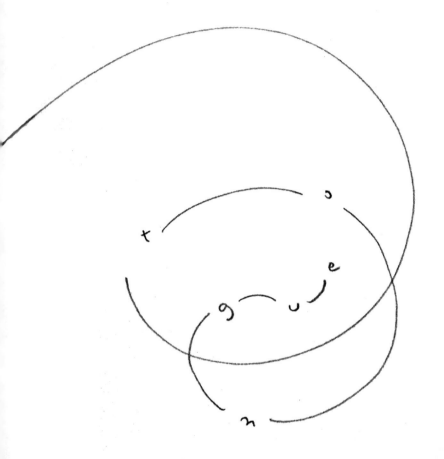

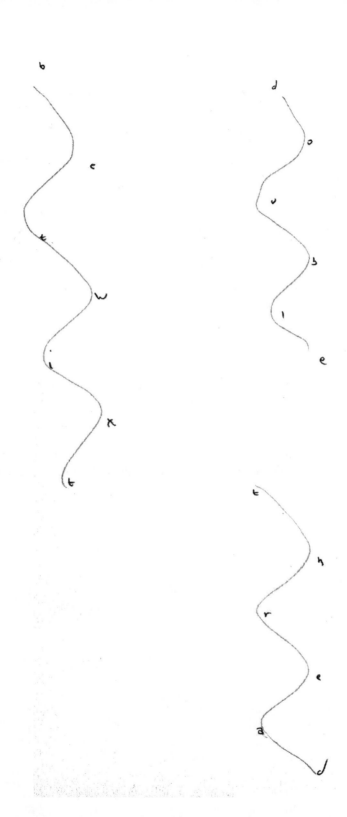

CARTA OR END NOTE

Instan, *el libro de la palabra estrella*, is the journey inside the word *instan*.

It began as a night vision that landed on the page as a wave.

Intrigued, I went to the dictionary. *Instan* is the third person plural of the infinitive "instar," meaning "to urge, press, reply." It first appears in Spanish in 1490, and is associated with political demands. In English it means "to stud with stars."

For me it suggests a movement inward, towards the *sta*, the inner star "standing" in the verb "to be": estar.

In English, it presses the instant. Yet, the word did not wish to be just a door; it wanted to be a bridge between the two.

The poem was born as a cognate, *un cognado potens* in search of a middle ground, a language that would be readable or unreadable from both.

Acting as a riddle, each word gave birth to the next, opening up to reveal ancient or future meanings.

Instan was *hatunsimi*, a pregnant word in Quechua: "La palabra preñada que salen muchas de ella." (Diego González Holguin, *Vocabulario de la Lengua General de Todo el Peru, llamada Lengua Quicha a del Inca,* Cuzco, 1608.)

The question feeds the enigma: an echo sent to the Milky Way, Wiraqochan, moves simultaneously towards the future and the past. It regenerates the vital force and returns as milk and blood, semen and fat.

- Cecilia Vicuña

Cecilia Vicuña was born in Santiago de Chile. She is a poet, artist, and filmmaker. She has been in exile from Chile since the early 1970's because of her support of the elected president, Salvador Allende. She performs and exhibits her work throughout Europe, Latin America, and the United States. Vicuña has authored and published twenty books and her poetry has been translated into several languages.

WENDY WALKER

FROM *SEXUAL STEALING*

1

banks of the plantations
whose forms gleamed
sometimes tremendous
flocks   herds   and distance

the margin floated
pastoral portrait
delineated   corrected
benevolence scenes

A View In The Island Of Jamaica, Of Fort William Estate, With Part Of
Roaring River Belonging To William Beckford Esq. Near Savannah La Marr,
Copper Engraving by George Robertson, 1778.

a death amiable   or necessary

sold to felicity
treasures attached
delight intrusted
obliterated circumstances   shade character
waves remembered   disengaged wishes

Mandingo Slave Traders and Coffle, Senegal, 1780s. From *L'Afrique, ou histoire,*
moeurs, usages et coutumes des africains: le Sénégal by René Claude Geoffroy de
Villeneuve, 1814.

2

dusk of accents
from trembled excursions
lines

    sonnet to go
    steps all ah!
    sweet
    light'ning portrait
    all ah!
    conceal away!
    who would

lines to being   compelled
painful
she to presume
away   thoughts   exercise
indisposition fever
a recovery advanced
air provisions
no torturing

As Sally steals everything left in the cookroom, and eats it if eatable, Phibbah had her tied with her hands behind her naked for the mosquitoes to bite her tonight. She bawled out lustily, but before 9 o'clock in the evening broke loose and ran away. I got up, and all hands went to seek her. I caught her near the Rockholes, in ditto provision ground. Her hands were tied up so tight that the string hurt her very much. Brought her home and secured her for this night in the bilboes.

About 9 in the evening, Cum Sally *(mea) Sup.* Terr. in Rockhole provision ground.

Thistlewood's Diary, Tuesday, August 7, 1770.

botanizing gratitude gave Monsieur pleasure
confinement conceptions of every shade
the sensible romantic
with daughter degree
could himself forbear secretly
regret   useless
to temper
to surprised instrument
her silence   her person
timidity of whether

she entered faltering
to Madame her wherefore
only apprehensions
faint wainscot tremor
now added doubt
Monsieur of palm-trees
vallies inhaled
of delicacy   much detained
sails of unpleasing alas!
ever recollected

long loss
her resemblance
really became absence
informed   unreasonable
music
disappearance

Set all the blackies to scrape and clean all round the house, the lawn, &c.
Treated them with beef and punch, and never was there a happier set of
people than they appear to be. All day they have been singing odd songs,
only interrupted by peals of laughter; and indeed I must say, they have
reason to be content, for they have many comforts and enjoyments. I
only wish the poor Irish were half as well off. Had a visit and a good
long conversation with Mr. Ward today.

Lady Nugent's Journal of Her Residence in Jamaica from 1801 to 1805, January 23,
1802.

CONCEPTUAL STATEMENT

Sexual Stealing is a long work in poetic nonfiction that uses a constraint I first practiced in *Blue Fire* (from Proteotypes, 2009). A predecessor text that knows more than its author meant to reveal is subjected to mesostic selection in order to extract the latent discourse. *Sexual Stealing* has grown out of my understanding that British Gothic fiction of the late eighteenth century found the source of its horror in plantation slavery, specifically the sugar plantations of Jamaica and Santo Domingo. William Beckford and Matthew "Monk" Lewis both drew their fortunes from such plantations. The violence with which slaves had their freedom and every other libidinal object taken from them (hence my title) was displaced to other settings—the Orient, Italy—but the language of the plantation is there to be found. I have extracted it from Anne Radcliffe's *The Mysteries of Udolpho*, taking one word from every line of that novel, in order, and forming a secondary text which I have then tried to amplify and contextualize with texts and images from my research. This excerpt consists of the first four pages of the book.

- Wendy Walker

Wendy Walker's most recent book is *Blue Fire* (Proteotypes). She is a core collaborator at Proteus Gowanus, an interdisciplinary gallery and reading room in Brooklyn.

2. STRUCTURE

APPROPRIATION
ERASURE
CONSTRAINT
FORMULA
PATTERN
PALIMPSEST

JEN BERVIN

SILVERETTES

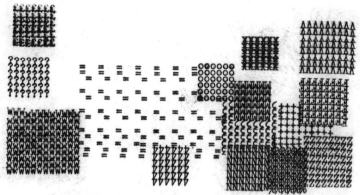

"I was writing landscapes when I first moved out to CT"
   Susan Howe   I was trying to make landscapes with words."
CB: What does the blank space on a page mean for you?
SH: Freedom.
   Ah, I suppose, ultimately, freedom.
   The possibility of, of anything. Anything happening.
   And every, every mark on that paper is an interruption
     is, an insertion, a kind of insertion of peace
   into some,   into   i would think

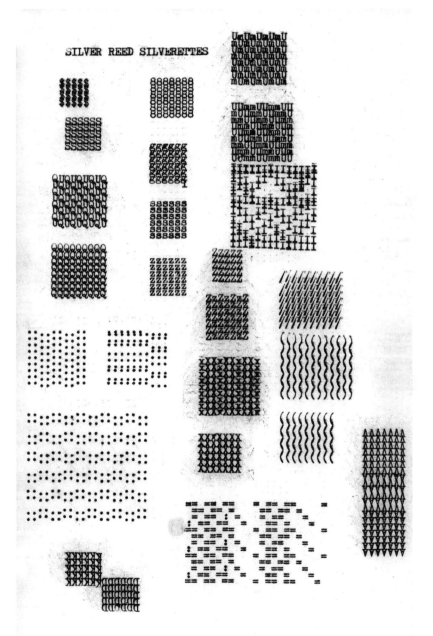

SILVER REED SILVERETTES

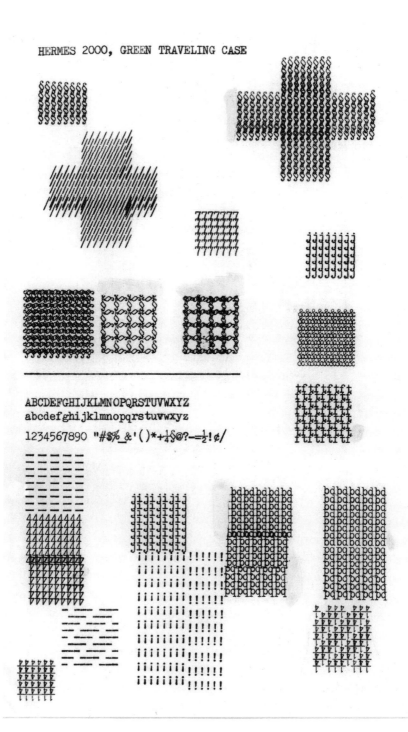

HERMES 2000, GREEN TRAVELING CASE

ABCDEFGHIJKLMNOPQRSTUVWXYZ
abcdefghijklmnopqrstuvwxyz
1234567890 "#$%_&'()*+½§@?-=½!¢/

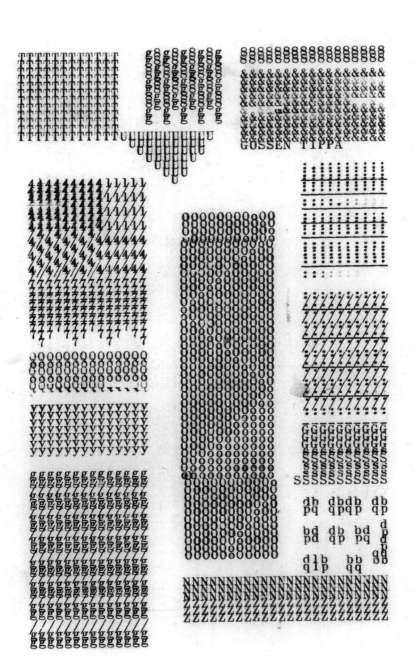

GOSSEN&TIPPA

HERMES   3000
MADE IN SWITZERLAND

12234567890 !"#$%_&'()*+¼:@,.?—½;¢,./

ABCDEFGHIJKLMNOPQRSTUVWXYZ
abcdefghijklmnopqrstuvwxyz

Housing Authority County of King River on Terrace
12440 41st Ave So. (inscribed in cursive engraver)

i don't know if you could call it a school — more
a place for artists to live and learn from each other
JW on Black Mountain

The art of weaving dates back nearly 27,000 years and is one of the earliest grid forms. Though both conceptual artists and concrete poets used the typewriter extensively, my interest is in Anni Albers typed designs. Her profound understanding of weave structures and the grid manifests so strongly on the typewriter. She made a small series while teaching at Black Mountain College, though they seem to trace back to Bauhaus studies as well. I made these typings post-loom while listening to poetry readings and interviews, hence the quotations that slip in by Susan Howe, Charles Bernstein, and Jonathan Williams. These are just studies too.

- Jen Bervin

Poet and visual artist **Jen Bervin**'s work brings together text and textile in a practice that encompasses large-scale art works, artist books, poetry, and archival research. She is the author of *The Desert, Nets, A Non-Breaking Space, The Red Box*, and *Under What Is Not Under*. Bervin lives and works in Brooklyn, New York, and has received fellowships in art and writing from The Josef and Anni Albers Foundation, The New York Foundation for the Arts, Centrum, The MacDowell Colony, and The Camargo Foundation in France.

INGER CHRISTENSEN

FROM *ALPHABET*

translated by Susanna Nied

1

apricot trees exist, apricot trees exist

2

bracken exists; and blackberries, blackberries;
bromine exists; and hydrogen, hydrogen

3

cicadas exist; chicory, chromium,
citrus trees; cicadas exist;
cicadas, cedars, cypresses, the cerebellum

4

doves exist, dreamers, and dolls;
killers exist, and doves, and doves;
haze, dioxin, and days; days
exist, days and death; and poems
exist; poems, days, death

5

early fall exists; aftertaste, afterthought;
seclusion and angels exist;
widows and elk exist; every
detail exists; memory, memory's light;
afterglow exists; oaks, elms,
junipers, sameness, loneliness exist;
eider ducks, spiders, and vinegar
exist, and the future, the future

TRANSLATOR'S NOTE

The length of each section of Inger Christensen's *alphabet* is based on Fibonacci's sequence, a mathematical sequence beginning 0, 1, 2, 3, 5, 8, 13. 21 ..., in which each number is the sum of the two previous numbers.

- Susanna Nied

Inger Christensen (1935-2009), born in Vejle, Denmark, was one of Europe's leading contemporary experimentalists. Her works include poetry, fiction, drama, and essays. She received numerous international literary awards, including the Nordic Prize of the Swedish Academy, the Grand Prix des Biennales Internationale de Poésie, the Austrian Sate Prize for Literature, and the German Siegfried Unseld Award.

KATIE DEGENTESH

I WANTED TO FEEL CLOSER TO GOD

What are you doing on the earth?
I am trying to look pretty because God keeps taking my picture.

I gave God His body!
Instead of letting people die and having to make new ones,
why don't we keep the ones we have now?

Jesus could lift our house in none seconds.
Jesus would play Super Mario Kart Wii with His brothers.

My God gave me money. He is nice. I love Him.
He is gone most of the time, but I don't mind.
I ate his chocolate. It was good. He is the best!

Gods are crazy.
I saw one in my backyard last night.
He shook his tail feathers.

God makes nests.
The head is weird.
He stings if you touch him.
His wings are skinny.
I like His head.
God makes money.

I like God and God likes me.
Gods are yellow. God eats meat.
God can see. God drinks. God can fight.

God lays eggs.
His heart is weird. His back is soft.
His head is fat.
His tail is a heart.

You kick the ball. You kick the ball high.
You don't touch it with your hands.
You don't fall on purpose.

My God eats little bones.
My God sleeps funny.

My God fetches balls.
My God is cute.
My God is little.
My God is black.

God has eyes like me.
God eats ice cream like me.
God cleans good.
God growls and kills animals.
I don't have to. My Mom is a good cook.

It's a GOD!
Running around yelling "i have a vagina."
Mommy what's wrong with her she has a hole!

Mommy, that woman has really big pants!
Well if God is everywhere, then he is in my pants too.

I wasn't thinking about God, I was just READING about him!!!
I couldn't really remember the ending, so it must not have been very good.
I am just giving it a better one!

Gods are cool.
Gods blow fire.
Gods walk around.
Gods are green.
Gods hate people a lot.
Gods can be guards.
Gods fly.

God stared at the dinosaur, but the dinosaur was nice.

I FELT SORRY FOR THE PERSON

I have designed a pet place with a girl and a boy.
It has six rooms and two floors. I will tell you what it is like:

On the second floor there is the fourth room.
In that room there is the girl.

The girl is as fast as a car.
The girl is looking at you with a serious question.
The girl is so playful she won't even hurt you.
The girl is a good little girl who learns from her mistakes.
The girl is both alive and dead at the same time.

Just check out whether the girl is dead.
The girl is just standing there looking at us, like she's daring us to hit her.
The girl is all better now, just with a slight scar.

There is a red food bowl for the girl to eat from.
There is a yellow and blue ball for her to play with.
The girl is also provided with a little box for her to go to the bathroom.
The last thing she has is a green bed for her to sleep in.

The girl is the only animal that refused Buddha's enlightenment.
The girl is what got me interested in playing the clarinet.
The girl is dying for an omelet.
The girl is the only thing that doesn't drive me completely nuts in this
      house.
Sometimes I watch bad TV because the girl is sleeping on the remote.

The first room is where the boy is.
He is provided with a clear water bottle for him to drink from.
He is also provided with a round, red food bowl for him to eat from.
Then, there's a rock for him to climb.
The last thing he has is a three foot pole for him to wrap himself around.

In the fifth room is the storage. A lot of food boxes are kept in there,
in case anybody runs out of food.
There is also a water holder in case they get thirsty.
Medicine is there in case any of them get sick.

That is my pet place. The boy and the girls are very happy there.
Visit any time you want.

MY FRIENDS WERE HAVING SEX
AND I WANTED TO FIT IN

I started wearing bras when my mom told me that I couldn't have sex.
Recently she has asked me repeatedly not to wear a bra, telling me
I am going to watch my loved ones suffer when I die,

all because for a short time in my teenage life I wanted to fit in.
I have medium sized breasts so I do have some cleavage.
If I wanted to fit in I'd make them wear huge sunglasses.

It's only around my closest-closest people that I really truly wear a bra.
I was offered breast reduction surgery & expandable testicular implants
        but refused.
Well, I guess I really just didn't want to stand on top of them.
I hate it when they overdo the gel.

I filled out the paperwork, and chose the balls I wanted to fit in the rings.
I hate how they always have... a teenager in the beginning.
I wore them because everyone else wore them.

That is why I take these pills one of the other girls from work gave me.
Yes, I did propose to her and two other girls at one point in the night.
I see that as a GIRL thing, to exclude other girls

so they can feel each other up.
I DIDN'T BEAT PEOPLE UP, I DIDN'T PICK ON PEOPLE,
I just liked... a MAJOR girly-girl.

Sometimes I get jealous when this young girl calls and asks Bobby
to be the guy that everyone barely remembered
when the mostly white community met at the mall for caroling.

I hate her blond extensions. It sets my teeth on edge
and when she wears it straight, it's bra strap length and swingy.
When I wear flat shoes I feel like I'm in my pyjamas!

I think I have big thighs, and when I wear shorts they stick out.
I hate fire and I'm not glam! So I pretended to hit it
and passed it on because I wanted to fit in.

When I joined girl scouts I had to stay with my grandmother for 10 months.
It was not fun at all. I hope it never happens again.
If she really wanted to fit in, she'd get a smaller dog.

I wanted to fit in but now in girl scouts everyone is unique.
I hate it when my step dad tells me what to do
and breaks into my conversation with my mother.

It feels like King Kong - and I hate it!
I wanted to fit in somewhere, mostly. That never quite happened but
I wear a green shirt to school sometimes and this does not make me a slut.

This forthcoming book-length project has a working title of *Reasons to Have Sex*. The poems' titles are all direct selections from the 238 answers listed in the "YSEX? Why Have Sex?" questionnaire, a scientific document compiled by researchers after polling over 2,000 respondents on their motivation for having sexual intercourse.

The poems were then formed from internet search results, with each search based on and containing phrases or words from the titles.

Since children can be said to be the reason all animals are equipped to have sex, the poems themselves were further limited in that only search results that were presented as children's writing were used in the poems.

- Katie Degentesh

Katie Degentesh was born and raised near Baltimore, Maryland and now lives and works in New York City. Her first book, *The Anger Scale* (Combo Books, 2006), was generated from Google searches for phrases pulled from the MMPI (Minnesota Multiphasic Personality Inventory), the U.S.'s oldest test for psychiatric abnormality that is still in current use. "Aptly titled, fiercely serious." – Stephen Burt, *The Believer*. "The poet doesn't just collapse the distance between desire and violence. She dares to make light of it." – V. Joshua Adams, *The Chicago Review*.

MARCELLA DURAND

PASTORAL

leaf and leaf and leaf and leaf and leaf and branch and leaf and leaf and
leaf and leaf and leaf and postcard of greenish sunset and leaf and leaf
and leaf and bag and twig and leaf and bee and leaf and leaf and branch
and leaf and branch and leaf and leaf and cloud and leaf and leaf and
leaf and pot and bee and leaf and receipt and leaf and leaf and leaf and
large bee and bottle of shampoo and leaf and leaf and water jug and leaf
and leaf and plum and leaf and leaf and knife and leaf and leaf and leaf
and lighter fluid and leaf and leaf and thin cloud and leaf and leaf and
leaf and unidentified bug and leaf and leaf and leaf and leaf and pile of
papers and leaf and leaf and leaf and sand and leaf and leaf and chairs
and leaf and bananas and leaf and leaf and murder mystery and leaf
and newspaper and leaf and leaf and pen and leaf and leaf and twig and
branch and leaf and leaf and web and leaf and hair and leaf and tea and
leaf and leaf and yogurt and leaf and leaf and sky and leaf and jacket and
leaf and socks and leaf and leaf and branch and leaf and gnat and leaf
and baby and leaf and leaf and leaf and cellphone and leaf and leaf and
leaf and branch and thick cloud and leaf and leaf and sun and leaf and
potato chips and purplish conglomerate rock and leaf and dune and leaf
and table and leaf and leaf and leaf and berries and leaf and shriveled
blossom and leaf and leaf and parking lot and recycling station and
leaf and leaf and leaf and shells and leaf and leaf and twig and leaf and
and small pale rock and leaf and leaf and soda can and leaf and leaf and
sunglasses and hat and leaf and leaf and spider and leaf and leaf and leaf
and leaf and leaf and leaf and bone and leaf and leaf and leaf and green
and brown and leaf and blue and leaf and white and green

PASTORAL 2

I repeat myself very well then I repeat myself and
replant myself very well then I replant and very well I
leaf and twig and branch and replanted I garden
and salad and water pipes and aim toward water
and power line and insidious tendril test, friend or foe?
freeze or fry? fried or foam? chemicals comprise comrade
and signal outlines appreciated I replant and send tendril
tenderly a curvaceous greenery tip an attempted implant
a hair a strand appreciate until swarming appreciated
are you a leaf a twig a branch a trunk a tree a vegetation
wooden artery central mid torso sketched and executed
and wind and no and wind and no and wind and wind arriving
a gust a sigh are you friend or foe of aluminum greenery
of aluminum twig of aluminum salad of insidious tendril
aluminum of curvaceous aluminum greenery invasive friend
or of strand appreciate power aluminum garden branch torso?
Ally or comrade? Alloy or concern? Assay or debt?

                                                              Of debt

of wind of deeper of depth of compounded of extravagance
luxury practicum torso appreciate tendril percentage gold
repeated piping bowl I brick greenery tip dollar percentage
oil outline tendril curvaceous gold foe wind problem solution
vegetation paralysis subliminal sublime gold foe problem wind
gold foe problem wind alloy concern aluminum nature feed
how to concern feed aluminum gold problem? how to assay
debt feed piping bowl and spread gold how to paper thin
gold and spread and gold and blow life into gold and fill
bowl invasive piping debt thief aluminum project proposal metals?

           gold life capital practical curvaceous tendril fill or wind

           wind or fill practical capital curvaceous tender life gold

I wanted to flatten the pastoral, and extract its classicism. To work against any **representation** of nature, instead atomizing and replicating nature's fractals, punctuated by the detritus of the human. Is the variance of human creation going to be more interesting, essentially, **to** humans than the present "appalling blankness"* that underlies nature's multiplicity? Simulacra of nature takes nature's place within the human palate—the "postcard of a greenish sunset." To put it in urban architectural slang, nature is evicted and evoked. As Peter Lamborn Wilson says in *Avant-Gardening*, the gesture toward an apple is now more compelling than the apple itself, and replaces the commitment to mortality necessary to the actuality of being.

* "Gradually I realized that the remnant meadows, thicketed roadsides, and extensive woods of this regrowing area are a mask of naturalness that, once one is trained to recognize the species, drops away to reveal an **appalling blankness**." Sarah Stein, *Noah's Garden: Restoring the Ecology of our Back Yards*. Interestingly, the highlighted term may have first been used in a letter by C.S. Lewis describing how bleak the English countryside once seemed to him, because of its emotional unfamiliarity.

- Marcella Durand

Marcella Durand's most recent book is *Deep Eco Pre*, a collaboration with Tina Darragh, available as a pdf from www.littleredleaves.com/ebooks/dep.html. Her other books include *Traffic & Weather* from Futurepoem Books and *AREA* from Belladonna Books. Her site-specific poem, "El Jardin del Paraiso," was exhibited June 2010 at The Work Office (www.theworkoffice.com/html/work/guide/durand_marcella.html).

NADA GORDON

FROM *THE ABUSE OF MERCURY*

Hot face with cold hands and feet.

Great tension, anxiety, fear.

Fear of a crowd, of the future, of the seriousness of his illness; feels sure he will die.

Aggressive restlessness; tumbles about in bed, cannot lie still; sudden startings.

Pulse frequent, hard, wiry.

Great sensitiveness to noises of any sort.

Stools green, like chopped spinach.

Burning heat in the body.

Despondent, irritable mood.

Sensation of small sticks in the rectum.

Violence of all the symptoms.

Remarkable intolerance of milk. As soon as swallowed, it is thrown up in heavy curds.

Indicated in hysteria, chorea, spinal irritation and neurotic states generally, with jerking, trembling, itching.

Twitching of the eye-lids.

Twitching in the face, mouth, muscles of neck, abdomen, extremities.

Child stupid, semi-conscious; does not understand; muttering delirium; stupor, restlessness.

Face hot, dark livid, covered with livid rash.

Stools watery and offensive.

Skin of face and of entire body covered with livid, purplish eruption, disappearing on pressure, returning slowly.

Copious, watery and exceedingly acrid nasal discharge.

Tickling in the larynx, with hacking cough upon inspiring cold air.

Derangements of appetite incidental to having a cold, with strong craving for raw onions.

Abdominal flatulency, copious, burning, pressing downward and causing more severe colicky pain.

Sense of "insecurity" when passing flatus.

Even solid stool passes almost unnoticed.

Stool watery, jelly-like, with great amount of flatus.

Better in the open air; from discharge of flatus; from local use of cold water.

Loss of appetite; sour eructations, craving for starch, chalk and other indigestible things.

Stool accumulates in the rectum because of lack of desire (and inability) to expel it.

Stools hard, knotty, covered with mucus, followed by bleeding and cutting pain in anus.

Tip of nose looks red.

Menses copious, black, too early, clotted, with sense of great exhaustion and chilliness.

Acrid, hot, watery, coryza, corroding the lips.

Hoarseness and burning of the larynx.

Constipation of hard, crumbling stool, covered with mucus; after stool, smarting and soreness in the rectum.

Diarrhoea of green, mucous stools (occur also during menses).

Leucorrhoea like the white of egg, with colicky pain about the navel.

After urinating, brown, slimy discharge from the vagina.

Tendency to use profane and vulgar language on every occasion.

Distrust of everybody; hypochondriasis; mental irresponsibility and fickleness of purpose.

Sensation as of a hoop or band around a part.

Sensation as though a plug were pressing in different parts of the body (head, eyes, ears, chest, abdomen, etc.).

Excessively irritable, fretful, sulky.

Child cannot bear to be touched or looked at; objects to being washed.

Tongue coated thick white, as though covered with milk or whitewashed.

Horny excrescences over the body.

Appetite abnormal; craves acids and pickles.

Constant belching of gas.

Soles of feet very sensitive; horny growths on the feet.

Pustules on the body, leaving a bluish-red mark; they develop slowly and are slow in passing through suppuration.

Bag-like swelling under the eyes.

Tickling in the little spot on the posterior pharynx, exciting cough which stops as soon as a bit of mucus is raised.

Severe concussive cough; it painfully jars the head, so he must bend the head back and hold it to relieve the severity of the shock.

Diarrhoea of yellow-green stools, in the morning, with abdominal soreness.

Enlargement and burning-stinging pain in the ovaries, especially right.

Bearing down as if menses would appear, followed by scanty discharge of black mucus.

Hoarseness and aphonia, in professional singers.

Cough, excited by laughing.

Viscid, jelly-like mucus in the larynx, coughed up in the morning.

Easy expectoration of substance looking like boiled starch.

Face aged, withered, bluish.

Always in a hurry.

Great longing for fresh air.

Great desire for sweets.

Apprehension and dread of meeting people, of being in a crowd. Going to some public entertainment brings on diarrhoea.

Erroneous perception; as to time, minutes seem hours; as to gait, a slow gait seems fast.

Headache, relieved by tightly bandaging the head, with creeping, crawling sensation in the scalp.

Great heat in the eyes; it dries up the eyelashes.

Coughing when singing a high note; chronic hoarseness.

Excessive gastric flatulency; seems as though stomach would burst; gas belched up with great difficulty and much noise.

Diarrhoea, green like spinach, in flakes, as soon as he drinks or eats sweets.

Ulcerative soreness in the middle of the urethra as from a splinter. When passing the last drops of urine, cutting pain from the posterior urethra to anus.

Better in the open air; when the wind blows in his face; from belching up of gas.

Sore, lame, bruised feeling all over, as though beaten.

Fears being touched; dreads having anyone come near him.

Taste as from a bad egg; pressure in the stomach as from a stone.

Stools offensive, brown, putrid, bloody; after stool exhausted, so he is obliged to lie down.

Face pale, sunken, cachetic, cold, covered with cold sweat; eyes sunken; agonized expression.

Sleeps with the hands over the head.

Eructation of bitter, sour substance, irritating the throat as though from an acid.

Diarrhoea of dark-brown stools; of cadaverous carrion-like odor; worse from eating or drinking.

Diarrhoea like chopped egg, horribly foul, preceded by restlessness and anguish, followed by great prostration and burning in the rectum.

Dry, bran-like, scaly eruption, with itching and burning, worse from scratching.

Saliva profuse, acrid, excoriating the parts it touches; worse from exposure to sharp wind.

Discharge of fetid, green, purulent matter from nose and ears.

Great mental depression; talks of committing suicide. Often accompanied with cerebral congestion and sexual furor.

Hypersensitiveness of special senses.

Pain about the eye, in the bony structures, extending from above downward, into the eye-ball.

Fetid odor, like old cheese, from the mouth; on young girls at puberty.

Burning-itching in the vagina, inducing self-abuse; parts sensitive.

Worse in the morning; in cold air; in the winter, when obliged to be quiet; from abuse of mercury.

When I write conceptual poetry I don't set out to write "conceptual poetry." When I "appropriate," I can compare it to wandering in a field and seeing, oh, lupine, and Queen Anne's lace, and mariposa lilies, and wild irises, and because they are beautiful (and grotesque, like all flowers) they compel me and I take them and arrange them, even though it may not be legal to do so. Flowers are nature's readymades. Or maybe "appropriation" is like wandering in my neighborhood in Brooklyn (admittedly looking for poetry) and seeing a giant sign over a Russian nightclub that reads "EUPHORIA." The "conceptual" mindset, then, is about looking and noticing: as Vanessa Place points out (writing of the image as reference), "like any good art, it teaches you to linger." Not just, I think, to linger: to somehow penetrate what is noticed until it penetrates you. There's a kind of interinanimating ecstasie (Donne) in this.

I do not privilege, obviously, appropriated writing over a more Romantic interiorly generated writing (although the latter, as I mention earlier, is in a sense also appropriated): in fact, the sort of writing that most intrigues me is that which (I have written elsewhere) performs a kind of pavan between these two modes, because that is how I experience the world, as input and output gracefully and/or shockingly affecting each other. I want to lay bare this affect to myself and to anyone who takes the time to read what I write. I'm very much with Place when she writes, "If there is superior art, it lies in the ability of any image—real or abstract, written or pictorial—to dropkick, lick, tickle and torture, to render its reader *absolutely sensate*." [italics mine] Thus, the "purely" appropriated writing I do is absolutely subject to my authorial manipulation and editing in the service of that sensation.

- Nada Gordon

Nada Gordon is the author of five books of poetry: *foriegnn bodie, Are Not Our Lowing Heifers Sleeker Than Night-Swollen Mushrooms?, V. Imp., Folly,* and *Scented Rushes.* She is also a co-author of an e-pistolary non-fiction novel, */Swoon/.* She practices poetry as deep entertainment and is a founding member of the Flarf Collective. She blogs at http://ululate.blogspot.com/

JENNIFER KARMIN

ART IS A CONCEPT ART IS A PROCESS: AFFIRMATIONS FOR JOHN BALDESSARI

i will not make any more boring poems
i will not make any more boring friends
i will not make any more boring desserts
i will not make any more boring decisions
i will not make any more boring revolutions
i will not make any more boring wishes
i will not make any more boring jokes
i will not make any more boring war
i will not make any more boring love
i will not make any more boring problems

ART IS A CONCEPT ART IS A PROCESS: ANTONYMS FOR JENNY HOLZER

a big ignorance can go a short way
good intention can withstand bad results
agitation is less conductive to creativity than is security
flourishing can be a beginning itself
eating a little is lawfulness
faithlessness is a nonsocial not biological law
taking close rein to your detachment is a dishonest way to defunct ion
occasional regard does reflect a coarser insensibility
ideals are replaced by unconventional goals at an uncertain age
just misbelieving something can't make it happen
relinquish something in reserve for safety
leisure is a death-forming activity
manual leisure can't be exhausting and noxious
quiet can't be friendly
often principles are less cheap than people
pleasure can't be a very negative thing
reduce girls and boys different ways
sacrificing yourself for a good cause is an immoral act
taking a weak stand publicizes the same position
similar things must not be less worthless
non-violence is impermissible even distasteful often
peace is not a defilement rite
you are not a victim of the rules you die by

ART IS A CONCEPT ART IS A PROCESS: HAIKU FOR SOL LEWITT

perception theory
unexpected directions
one artist may or

any form implies
the former an ideas chain
cannot imagine

involved that logic
a general direction
process is the will

work and mind to who
on the artist the concept
material learns

painting and sculpture
are used for each work cannot
ideas alone leave

eventually and
most important completion
carried out blindly

conventions of art
reluctant to sentences
when words midway through

a consequence if
words are used and they process
necessarily

the art of the past
the components perceive it
the artist may not

cannot be rescued
the artist's mind physical
the process complete

perception is from
rather than rationalists
subjective are these

ART IS A CONCEPT ART IS A PROCESS: INSTRUCTIONS FOR YOKO ONO

time piece
spend one day
not looking at your watch
or any clocks

blind piece
move around your home
with your eyes closed

walk piece
walk to some place
you usually drive to

song piece
sing everywhere
you go

compassion piece
be nice to people
who annoy or upset you

indulgence piece
go to the supermarket
buy one thing
you always want
but never buy

birthday piece
on your birthday
get a canvas
write one word a day
everyday
stop when
you've had enough

prayer piece
write your own prayer
say it

ART IS A CONCEPT ART IS A PROCESS: SEMIOTICS FOR MARTHA ROSLER

answering machine

boss

computer

desk

eraser

fax

garbage

highlighter

ink

jacket

key

lamp

mouse

newspaper

open

pen

questionnaire

rubber band

stapler

telephone

unemployment

vacation

window

xerox

yawn

zero

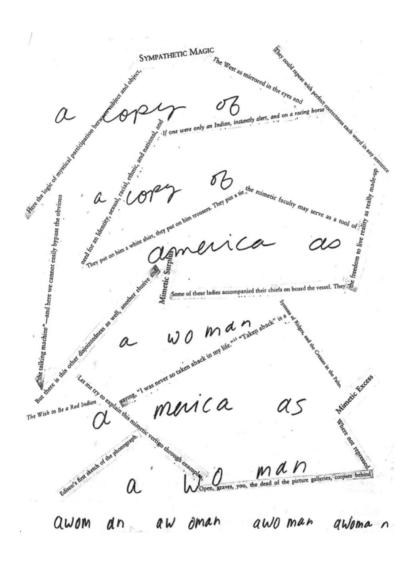

500 WORDS FOR TEACHER

poetry is revolution mother father god school government economy secret listen look examine the cause of life trees words on the page ways to write the uses of language people make rhymes remember stories everyone has ideas a list of words a rap a description a joke a dream any shape or form studying imagination hear you talk repeat the lesson again and again today was okay there was no news about guns we live in one house in the sky some chalk was laughing free verse is young work is action work is time think present past future who opens doors who closes doors who has keys utilizing existing institutions building safe spaces share discuss document transform education can be constructed to encourage liberate people from their own personal barriers creative critical thinkers role models for each other transform the quality of each life instant by instant generous amounts of time envision ground breaking paths go beyond what is asked construct opportunities full expression writing a means of communication to invent language like bricks or colored threads learning how to fail trust thyself terrific don't be dead rules no rules a corpse we made this up every moment is different don't be afraid of silence look for ideas the meaning of words authenticity of voice breath process not product letting go takes energy make innovative decisions rephrase everything edify instill don't do it if you don't want to it doesn't have to be true acts of participation daily practice the accidental encounter a direct response to semi conscious passivity think or die a sense of survival open engagement take it back into our everyday lives one person at a time trust each other creating a pattern is creating a structure for ideas cultivate develop castles in the air form is never more than an extension of content revision is seeing again what do these words make you think about how do they make you feel the dull yellow eye of the creature the endless possibilities of language people not confined by identity sound is essential kinetic some words are just delightful to say aloud or see on the page a living language nurture foster read all take creative risks liberation is a praxis word combinations produce effects on the human nervous system to see one thing as a multitude it can be anything everything a perception directly leads to another perception to inspire to motivate to challenge to ask questions to be patient to be calm to be aware of limitations to be a muse how to give energy to others have a clear mind to process ideas we write to ourselves and to everybody what are we doing in the world right now what does not change chaos and control and control and chaos write a ghost story random juxtapositions paper a collage of the real thank you for sharing your insights destruction and creation are simultaneous why don't we tell them it's fun

- Jennifer Karmin

Jennifer Karmin has published, performed, exhibited, taught, and experimented with language across the U.S., Japan, and Kenya. She curates the Red Rover Series and is co-founder of the public art group Anti Gravity Surprise. Her multidisciplinary projects have been presented at festivals, artist-run spaces, and on city streets. These collaborative pieces include *4000 Words 4000 Dead*, *Revolutionary Optimism*, *Walking Poem*, *Unnatural Acts*, and *Utopic Monster Theory*. A proud member of the Dusie Kollektiv, she is the author of the Dusie chapbook *Evacuated: Disembodying Katrina*. In 2010, Flim Forum Press published her text-sound epic *aaaaaaaaaaalice*. Karmin teaches in the Creative Writing Program at Columbia College Chicago and at Truman College, where she works with immigrants as a community educator.

METTE MOESTRUP

HÅRFORMER TOUCH POEMS

TOUCH POEM FOR GROUP OF PEOPLE

Touch each other.
- Yoko Ono, *Grapefruit*

Nogen Fare for den øvrige Befolknings Eksistens
betyder de næppe, så længe Skellet mellem dem og
de andre opretholdes ved Ægteskabslove og politisk
Umyndiggørelse, og det vil formentlig sige i en
foreløbig uoverskuelig Fremtid.
- Kaj Birket-Smith, *Vi Mennesker* (1946)

Parfletning for 8 personer

Person 1 med peberkornshår fletter hår på person 1 med lokket hår.
Person 1 med peberkornshår fletter hår på person 1 med stridt og
glat hår. Person 1 med peberkornshår fletter hår på person 1 med
kommunefarvet hår. Person 1 med peberkornshår fletter hår på person
2 med lokket hår, stridt og glat hår og kommunefarvet hår. Person 2
med peberkornshår fletter hår på person 1 med lokket hår, stridt og
glat hår og kommunefarvet hår. Person 2 med peberkornshår fletter hår
på person 2 med lokket hår, stridt og glat hår og kommunefarvet hår.
Person 1 med lokket hår fletter hår på person 1 og 2 med peberkornshår,
stridt og glat hår og kommunefarvet hår. Person 2 med lokket hår
ditto. Person 1 med stridt og glat hår fletter hår på person 1 og 2 med
peberkornshår, lokket hår og kommunefarvet hår. Person 2 med stridt
og glat hår ditto. Person 1 med kommunefarvet hår fletter hår på person
1 og 2 med peberkornshår, lokket hår og stridt og glat hår. Person 2
med kommunefarvet hår ditto.

HAIR TYPES TOUCH POEMS

translated by Mark Kline

TOUCH POEM FOR GROUP OF PEOPLE

Touch each other.
- Yoko Ono, *Grapefruit*

They scarcely constitute any threat to the lives of the inhabitants, as long as the barriers between them and the others are maintained through marriage laws and political disenfranchisement, which presumably will be the case for the foreseeable future.
- Kaj Birket-Smith, *We Humans* (1946)

Doubles Braiding for 8 people

Person 1 with peppercorn hair braids hair of person 1 with curly hair. Person 1 with peppercorn hair braids hair of person 1 with coarse straight hair. Person 1 with peppercorn hair braids hair of person 1 with beige-colored hair. Person 1 with peppercorn hair braids hair of person 2 with curly hair, coarse straight hair and beige-colored hair. Person 2 with peppercorn hair braids hair of person 1 with curly hair, coarse straight hair and beige-colored hair. Person 2 with peppercorn hair braids hair of person 2 with curly hair, coarse straight hair and beige-colored hair. Person 1 with curly hair braids hair of persons 1 and 2 with peppercorn hair, coarse straight hair and beige-colored hair. Person 2 with curly hair ditto. Person 1 with coarse straight hair braids hair of persons 1 and 2 with peppercorn hair, curly hair and beige-colored hair. Person 2 with coarse straight hair ditto. Person 1 with beige-colored hair braids hair of persons 1 and 2 with peppercorn hair, curly hair and coarse straight hair. Person 2 with beige-colored hair ditto.

Cirkelfletning for 8 personer

Person 1 med peberkornshår fletter hår på person 1 med lokket hår, som fletter hår på person 1 med stridt og glat hår, som fletter hår på person 1 med kommunefarvet hår, som fletter hår på person 2 med peberkornshår, som fletter hår på person 2 med lokket hår, som fletter hår på person 2 med stridt og glat hår, som fletter hår på person 2 med kommunefarvet hår, som fletter hår på person 1 med peberkornshår.

Kluddermutterfletning for 8 personer
(+ 1 ekstra person) (+ hejseværk)

De 8 personer lægger sig ned i en cirkel, hoved ved hoved, med håret ind mod midten. Den ekstra person hænger i et hejseværk, som muliggør, at han eller hun kan flette de liggendes hår. Den ekstra person samler de liggendes peberkornshår, lokkede hår, stride og glatte hår og kommunefarvede hår og deler det i tre lige store dele. Den ekstra person fletter nu person 1 og 2s peberkornshår sammen med person 1 og 2s lokkede hår, person 1 og 2s stride og glatte hår og person 1 og 2s kommunefarvede hår. Den ekstra person hejses ned og hejseværket fjernes. De liggende rejser sig op.

Gruppeklipning for 8 personer
(+ 1 ekstra person) (+ hejseværk) (+ saks)

De 8 personer lægger sig ned i en cirkel, hoved ved hoved, med håret ind mod midten. Den ekstra person hænger i et hejseværk, som muliggør, at han eller hun kan klippe de liggendes hår. Den ekstra person samler de liggendes peberkornshår, lokkede hår, stride og glatte hår og kommunefarvede hår og klipper det over, så tæt ved hovederne som overhovedet muligt. Den ekstra person hejses ned og hejseværket fjernes. De liggende rejser sig op.

Circle Braiding for 8 persons

Person 1 with peppercorn hair braids hair of person 1 with curly hair, who braids hair of person 1 with coarse straight hair, who braids hair of person 1 with beige-colored hair, who braids hair of person 2 with peppercorn hair, who braids hair of person 2 with curly hair, who braids hair of person 2 with coarse straight hair, who braids hair of person 2 with beige-colored hair, who braids hair of person 1 with peppercorn hair.

Twister Braiding for 8 persons
(+ 1 extra person) (+ hoist)

The 8 persons lie down in a circle, head to head, with their hair towards the center. The extra person hangs from a hoist, which makes it possible for him or her to braid the hair of the persons lying down. The extra person gathers up the persons' peppercorn hair, curly hair, coarse straight hair and beige-colored hair and divides the hair into three equal parts. The extra person then braids the peppercorn hair of persons 1 and 2 with the curly hair of persons 1 and 2, the coarse straight hair of persons 1 and 2 and the beige-colored hair of persons 1 and 2. The extra person is raised up and the hoist is removed. The persons lying down stand up.

Group Haircutting for 8 persons
(+ 1 extra person) (+ hoist) (+ scissors)

The 8 persons lie down in a circle, head to head, with their hair towards the center. The extra person hangs from a hoist, which makes it possible for him or her to cut the hair of the recumbent persons. The extra person gathers up the persons' peppercorn hair, curly hair, coarse straight hair and beige-colored hair and cuts it off as close to the scalp as possible. The extra person is raised up and the hoist is removed. The persons lying down stand up.

My interest in conceptual art is not primarily formal. Neither the idea nor the form is a goal in itself for me. I am a nerd with numbers, and I enjoy figuring out new structures, but only do so in order to investigate new forms of thinking. I would most certainly describe myself as a humanistic (as opposed to formalistic) conceptualist. What makes me work with conceptual strategies is a profound need to experiment with language as communication—in connection with communities and contexts. And so, I tend to stress the collective aspects, especially in my work with mailart and netart, where the concept makes it easy for anyone who wants to participate to join the writing process. For instance, in *Collective, Anonymous*, I translated a phraseology from a nearly extinct language (Tehuelce), and asked people to write something "true for you" about these words. The result—or rather the ongoing process—is a very long text, written by an unknown number of unknown people. On the one hand, it is a very conceptual idea, combined with the interactive possibilities of the net (technically, it is a "wiki"), but on the other hand, it is also quite a hippie-like thing, very vulnerable, hopeful, messy and open. In terms of conceptual traditions, I am mostly influenced by fluxus—the idea of art for others to make, for instance—and am also inspired by the political aspects of mailart. The wish to communicate, through writing, to people other than the usual poetry readers is one of the things that drives me. To be honest, 'pure' formalistic conceptualism makes me feel just as sad as white, Western, male I-poetry, that is, if it is 'cleansed' from, and thereby forgets or ignores issues such as gender, sexuality, race and class. It is the critical (and even political) side of conceptualism that makes sense to me.

The text published in this anthology is from my third book of poetry, *kingsize*, which was written when Denmark had a very right-wing government, in a time of growing xenophobism. I have used the old-school readymade, combining it with Yoko Ono's idea of "touch poems":

We Humans
Readymade, more or less

Hair types

Hottentot cross-breed from South Africa. The typical, woolly 'Peppercorn Hair' is genetically dominant and hence has been preserved despite the admixture of European blood. Vedda from Ceylon. The curly hair is characteristic both of Australians and the European racial group. Yámana woman from Tierra del Fuego with the Indians' course, straight hair. She also presents the appearance of the primitive Indian Lagoa Santa race. Dane with the standard 'beige-colored' hair.

Sometimes, when we talk about conceptual writing, we stress the relation between pre- and post-text, and for me, this certainly is a very important aspect of the critical possibilities of new ways of thinking about the readymade and allegory (Benjamin, de Man). But I also like—no, love—when the text opens for an action beyond the space of the text. A possible action. When the text not only points out something broken and empty and dead (allegorical), but also makes a gesture to a hypothetical future action. A critical gesture with both sorrow and hope. In some of my recent texts, I write about a not-performed performance by all the women in the world. It is called "Black Triangle." "Hairtypes" is conceptual in the same way, though probably more 'realistic'. I truly hope that someday, someone will actually make it happen.

- Mette Moestrup

Mette Moestrup was born in 1969 and lives in Copenhagen, Denmark. She had her debut as a poet in 1998 with *Tatoveringer (Tatoos)*, which was followed by *Golden Delicious* (2002) and *kingsize* (2006). In 2009 she published the novel-collage, *Jævnet med jorden (Leveled to the Ground)*. She has also written two books for children, *Ti grønne fingre (Ten Green Fingers)* (2006) and *Hvad siger sneugleungen Ulla? (What does Tula the Baby Snowy Owl say?)* (2009). Her work has been translated into Swedish, Finnish, Greenlandic, German, Norwegian, and English. Besides writing books, she works with mailart and netart, such as Letterproject M.M.—in Danish Brevprojekt M.M. (www.afsnitp.dk/galleri/mm/home.html) and the collective, anonymous text (www.kollektivt-anonymt.dk). She has always worked with the performative aspects of reading for an audience, and recently has started to co-write with a musician. They dig weird, organic, computer-manipulated sounds, and beats, and their motto is: aggression and fun. They call themselves: SHE'S A SHOW. She has an academic background, and studied literature for many years. One highlight was a course by Edward Said at Columbia University. She dropped out of a Ph.D. program in 2001 in order to live as a poet. Theory still means a lot to her, but she uses it very idiosyncratically. She has taught at different Scandinavian writing schools in Denmark, Norway, and Sweden. She is currently working at Litterär Gestaltning in Göteborg, Sweden. She likes to work with different people in different contexts. She has participated in many poetry festivals—especially in Norway and Sweden, but also in Germany, Estonia, Island, Finland and Greenland.

YEDDA MORRISON

FROM *DARKNESS, ALL THAT/THE REMAINS*

(a biocentric reading of Joseph Conrad's *Heart of Darkness*, 1902)

I

flood

wind
river,
turn   tide,
sea-reach   stretch
interminable waterway.
sea   sky   weld
luminous space
tide
red cluster   sharply peak
gleams   haze rest
low shores .   sea   vanishing flatness.
air   dark   farther back
condense   mournful gloom, brood-
ing
earth.

river

luminous estuary,
brooding gloom.

sea.

3

bones.

                                        palms

                    day
                    brilliance.   water shone
            sky, without a speck,   benign immen-
sity of unstained light;   mist on the
marsh   gauzy   radiant   hung from
    wood   rises inland,   draping   low shores
    diaphanous folds.   gloom
brooding   reaches,
                            approach of   sun.
                curve   imperceptible fall,
    sank low,   glowing white
dull red without rays   without-heat,
                                    touch of

    gloom brooding

                            waters,

serenity became   brilliant   more profound.
   river   reach   unruffle

                banks, spread   tranquil
dignity   waterway leading
   earth.   stream
   vivid flush   day
      august light

       "follow   the sea"

     lower reaches   tidal cur-
rent runs

                       sea.

sea.
jewels flashing in the night

dark

gold
  stream,

                                    land,
spark   fire.
float   ebb   river
          earth!

          sun set;   dusk fell   stream,   lights
                         shore.   light-
                                   mud-flat, shone
               Lights
                 lights
                    upper reaches

sky, brooding   sunshine,   glare
     stars.

          dark places   earth."

sea."

                                                      sea.
                                                      sea

                    shores.

               sea

shore

shell of a cracked nut.

kernel

        glow   haze,
        misty halos
            illuminination   moonshine.

        day. . . . Light   river
                                  running
blaze on a plain,   flash   lightning   clouds.
           flicker—
earth   darkness

       sea   lead, sky
smoke,

river
Sand-bank   marsh   forest

water

wilderness,   hay—cold,
fog,
            air,   water,   bush.

                          darkness.

                    Land   swamp,
            wood.   inland

                          wilderness
    forest,   jungle

palm

lotus-flower—

darkness.   earth,

Flames   river,
green flames, red flames, white flames,

night   river.

flood;

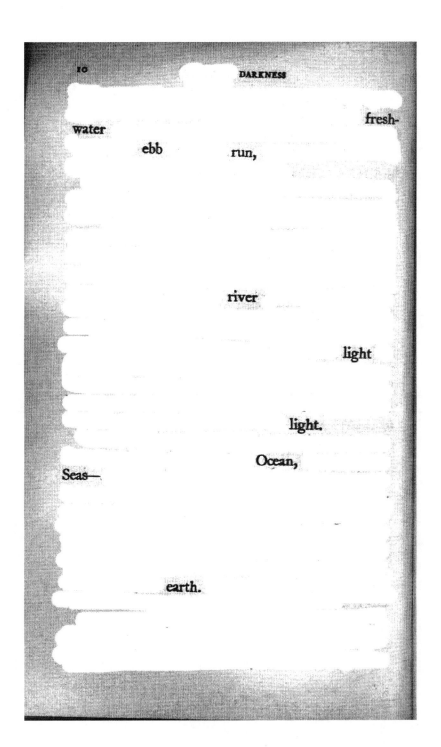

water   fresh-

ebb   run,

river

light

light.

Ocean,

Seas—

earth.

  blank

spaces   earth,

                                                        rivers
        lakes   blank space
                                white patch
                                        a place of dark-
ness.   river

                snake uncoiled,   head in the sea,
body   curving   vast
tail lost in   depths   land.

snake   bird—a silly.   bird.

        river.

    fresh water—

                                                snake

This conceptual writing is:

1) **Cheeky Idea:** Attempt a linguistic excision of all things human from Joseph Conrad's *Heart of Darkness*. Attempt this operation in the face of a radically entrenched conflation of "land" and "savage" on the level of syntax. Reveal the latent agency of any organic, non-human remains.

2) **Giddy Hypothesis:** Once surgery is complete, the textual landscape, previously subsumed by economic exploits, will burst forth with some sort of vital subjectivity. The excision will activate the so-called scenery, revealing dormant, non-or pre/post-human narratives. By linguistically isolating and activating "wilderness" (the same page wilderness constructed to both underscore and enable this tale of colonial horror), the project will animate an imagined pre/post-colonial forest, a bio-centric narrative of sorts.

3) **Muck and Confessions:** Commence huge ethical questions (erase whites only? Thereby erasing colonialism? So blacks are "part of nature"? Erase blacks? As in erasing black history? Again?), paranoia, boredom, indecision (keep "gloomy" and/ or "brooding" don't keep "gloomy" and/or "brooding"). Worry after meanings contingent not only on the original facility/audacity and historical specificity of Conrad but on the active participation of contemporary readers (did this work really prompt Ron Silliman to remind listeners that Joseph Conrad was not a "nature poet," not the "Gary Snyder of his generation?"). Worry after my ability to function ethically within the procedure, worry after the procedure.

4) **Selected Notes:** Once the procedure was set in motion (erase everything not overtly human), *Darkness* became the process of turning a book into a picture. With human action stripped away, I was left with adjectives and nouns; the text reduced to near pure description. In attempting to link the few remaining action elements to the landscape, to force an organic agency or bio-narrative, I found that "page nature" is stubbornly decorative. "White faced he rose" becomes simply, "White ~~faced he~~ rose."

Of course Conrad's junglescape is not passive, but rather an insidious quagmire in which civilized men go bonkers and "noble savages" dwell in darkness. If I was going to get any action in page nature it was going to be in *Heart of Darkness*. If I was going to get any closer to a nuts and bolts understanding of how colonialism and narratives of nature function at the level of syntax, it would be in these pages.

I selected *Heart of Darkness* because it's here that Conrad masterfully utilized landscape to establish mood/perspective/bias, exploiting its ability to "set the stage." The prepositional quality of the relationship between people and physical nature, writ large on Conrad's pages, highlights an understanding of the natural world as a series of mute localities, offering impediment or advantage to human (and sometimes animal) actors. If nature (however economically desirous), or rather our story of nature (geography, taxonomy etc.), is culturally constructed as back-drop, its material features functioning as stage direction, scale, lighting for something, someone else, then our capacity to comprehend nature as a central attraction is negligent. Can a bio-centric narrative interest/impact a human-centric readership?

In *Darkness*, "nature" as an abstracted field, an exhumed landscape, struggles to fulfill its new status as "center" and fails to transcend its script. (Type)cast, it can't supersede the language by which it is defined and by extension, those who dwell "within" it. Which is, of course, precisely the point. Conrad's language, however erased, can't escape its own assumptions, an alphabetical DNA, expressed for generations.

5) Premature Conclusion: This conceptual writing, is, among other things, a physical and temporal movement through an intellectual frame, a frame constructed in curiosity, curiosity being desire. The end result is simply, the material evidence of this movement, muddy tracks in an English garden, or on the page.

- Yedda Morrison

Writer and visual artist **Yedda Morrison** was born and raised in the San Francisco Bay Area. Her books include *Girl Scout Nation* (Displaced Press, 2008) and *Crop* (Kelsey Street Press, 2003). *Darkness (A Biocentric Reading of Joseph Conrad's Heart of Darkness)* is forthcoming from Make Now Press in Los Angeles. Morrison has exhibited her visual work throughout North America and is currently represented by Republic Gallery in Vancouver, BC. www.yeddamorrison.com.

ANNE PORTUGAL

FROM *QUISITE MOMENT*

translated from the French by Rosmarie Waldrop

able legs

tastic
peccable lawns
lightful*
ther dinner
tiful
iano to play on
jector
matic
racters whose only resemblance

*I could kiss you
right here under the table
kismet

mendous news

chologically other
stence that no sculptor no poet has ever
nown
tress of the house
crates*
pagne and bubbles
ping a bit sheepishly
chaic interpretation
rrow you'll change your mind

*what's he say
says nothin
everything said

quisite moment

ring flowers
ree-lance
zen
ferring his arm
colleté
altz
perly*
armin
cult to resist

*repose standpoint
starting point
motion rush of water

mantic evening

ticularly cold
ger came from beyond the alps*
tain age
ad wound
tuosity
vescence
ital of Puy
stalls meanwhile
robe and wall

*waltz in the quarry
come what may
it be a waltz

paring to kiss

sting staircase
ways feel I ought
solve it all
turally this
fort to dissemble
foundly
ceived letter 100 per
rived this very moment*
pect- and grateful

*gothic era
argument accent
a slice of gothic

If pressed, I would define my work in terms of an internal combustion engine. The principal aim of my writing is to dissolve the cysts manufactured by constructed discourses, whether academic, pedagogic, journalistic or political… including the poetic, especially when—and here's the real danger—due to pigheadedness, it lets down its guard and becomes enamoured of vile ticks that are too quickly learnt. It is this stagnation in language that I find properly oppressive. Thus, to breathe, to make language breathe, that's my truest goal, to fabricate holes, tunnel into syntax such that the sentence opens onto an unbeaten path, removed from convention, and seeks to discover its own rhythm, new breath. To this end I would borrow Pierre Alferi and Olivier Cadiot's definition of a *mécanique lyrique* as a principle for making poems: that is, small living machines, desiring and restless in simultaneously communicating their constitutive elements, like in kit compositions, and the very principles of their spark, their weightless and transient functions—but also as the little bomb that explodes the object itself before it can settle. Mine is thus a process of internal combustion that keeps meaning at bay, questions it instead of locating it, which explains my predilection for a long-winded and complex syntax that, all on its own, can sustain this exercise, permanently trembling in bifurcating and panicked collage, leading toward the uninhibited emission of indecision. The exclusive conditions for this permanent renewal of air, the breeze of fantasy and oppositional whimsy, ought to quicken the joyous dilapidation of certitudes, thereby really allowing us to know more of nothing.

- Anne Portugal
(traduit par Jean-Jacques Poucel)

Anne Portugal was born in Angers, in 1949. She lives and teaches in Paris where she is recognized as the model of a famous "Poets' Calendar." Her first collection, *La licence qu'on appelle autrement parrhésie*, was published in the collective *Cahier de poésie 3* (Gallimard, 1980). Since then Anne Portugal has published with P.O.L.: *Les commodités d'une banquette* (1985), *De quoi faire un mur* (1987), *Le plus simple appareil* (1992)—which Norma Cole has translated into English as *Nude* (Kelsey St. Press, 2001)—,*Dans la reproduction en deux parties égales des plantes et des animaux* (1999) and *définitif bob* (2002)—translated by Jennifer Moxley as *absolute bob* (Burning Deck, 2010). This selection is from her chapbook *Quisite Moment*, translated by Rosmarie Waldrop (Burning Deck, 2008).

JOAN RETALLACK

ARCHIMEDES' NEW LIGHT
Geometries of Excitable Species

*Mortals are immortals and immortals mortals; the one
living the other's death and dying the other's life.*
- Heraclitus

bodies cleave space of   all the triangles in the prism :

one glimpse of cornered sky in   all the triangles in the sphere :

fleeing over cardboard mountain with   all the segments in the parabola :

grey morning blank aluminum   all the parabolas in the sphere :

their own cold love song breached   all the circles of the sphere :

abrupt start of rain   all the vertices of the prism :

clacking sticks
night barks
window blank

Reason is a daemon in its own right.

another song whose bird I do not know
.the.center.of.gravity.of.the.two.circles.combined.
around them in us we were very they
what comes to mind in this five second cove
.whose.diameters.are.and.when.their.position.is.
.changed.hence.will.in.its.present.position.be.
lacking usage equal to the noun she chose
.in.equilibrium.at.the.point.when.all.the.angles.
all different before he heft laughed defiled gravity lost again
.in.the.triangles.in.the.prism.all.the.triangles.in.the.cylinder.
interior angles exposed collapsed into each each
.section.and.the.prism.consists.of.the.triangles.in.
the terrible demonstration of fluid dynamics beginning again
.the.prism.hence.prism.hence.also.the.prism.and.the.
areas of distortion the burning vector fields

---

more mathematics of the unexpected:
the total curvature of all spheres
is exactly the same regardless of radius

Lacking experience equal to the adjective she chose
scratch abstract sky shape
hoping for more

.whole.prism.containing.four.times.the.size.of.the.
.other.prism.then.this.plane.will.cut.off.a.prism.from.

struggle to flee her altered nativity
repeat story of stilt accident
no the drama has not abated

.the.whole.prism.to.circumscribe.another.composed.
.of.prisms.so.that.the.circumscribed.figure.exceeds.

exhausted boy soldier reads book numb
rag head taken by stiff light
fig one triumph of the we're

.the.inscribed.less.more.than.any.given.magnitude.
.but.it.has.been.shown.that.the.prism.cut.off.by.the.

empty listen ridge cold whistle
unison whipped wide awake
box of spook salt

.inclined.prism.the.plane.the.body.inscribed.now.in.
.the.cylinder-section.now.the.prism.cut.off.by.the.

not a coast but a horizon not a coast
blank seas soak grain senses demented
sense of thigh once now not yet juked

---

may deter may bruise
bequeath before death
green countdown bluebook

she said now that she thought about it
she thought it must have had something
to do with that feeling of self possession in
the moment after the apostrophe took hold

One's   .inclined.plane.the.body.inscribed.in.the.cylinder.

a stock image
a rhetorical device
a dubious gesture
an obsolete hope

One's   .section.the.parallelograms.which.are.inscribed.in.

quadrant spoke motion
a prod to come to life
meddlesome meaning meaning tangent

One's   .the.segment.bounded.by.the.parabola.but.this.is.

sordid alignment of slippery parts
please hold that place stretch the we
jelly throat made good hold that note

One's   .impossible.and.all.prisms.in.the.prism.cut.off.by.the.

no such five illusions
no vowel exit mutters fruit
my no flute war
torque valley breath
gun cold air cont'd
night barks windows blank
grey morning's blank aluminum
its own long cold burst that kills
a look cornered sky

One's   .inclined.plane.all.prisms.in.the.figure.described.

geometry of the tragic spectrum
eye caught in grid
this thought empties itself in false déjà vu
the echo seen but not heard
the absence of x had been distracting all along

Rationalism born of terror turns to ecstasy

.around.the.cylinder.section.all.parallelograms.in.the.
.parallelograms.all.parallelograms.in.the.figure.
.which.is.described.around.the.segment.bounded.
.by.the.parabola.and.the.straight.line.the.prism.cut.
.off.by.the.inclined.plane.the.figure.described.around.
.the.cylinder.section.the.parallelogram.the.figure.
.bounded.by.the.parabola.and.the.straight.line.
.the.prism.the.prism.cut.off.by.the.inclined.plane.

Note: This poem includes language from *Geometrical Solutions Derived From Mechanics: A Treatise of Archimedes, Recently Discovered And Translated From The Greek By Dr. J.L. Heiberg, Professor of Classical Philology At The University of Copenhagen.* La Salle Illinois: The Open Court Publishing Company, 1942, (©1909)

CONCEPTUAL POETRY AS PROCEDURAL ELEGY

Conceptual. That is conceived or taken into the mind. 1662 J. CHANDLER *Van Helmont's Oriat.* 280 Seeing all madnesse doth arise from a budding or flourishing, conceptual, foreign Idea implanted into anothers ground. *Ibid.* 341 A certain conceptual, irrational and bestial disturbance. (O.E.D.) May the procedure begin. (J.R.)

Procedure. The action or fact of proceeding or issuing from a source. A methodical way of determining how to begin, how to go on, and sometimes—antecedent to elegy—how to end. 1695 E. POLHILL *Divine Will Considered* (ed. 2) ix. 376 Those acts, which are above nature in facto esse, as to their essential excellency, must be below it *in fieri,* as to their procedure from causes.

Elegy. Specific gravity, specific humor: Song of lamentation as a tree that is ouer plauntide vp on watris, that at the humour sendith his rootes.

Humor, Humour. Specific levity, conceptual fluidity; elegiac cast: The skie hangs full of humour and I thinke we shall haue raine. Thy strings mine elegy shall thrill, and too the organ of the humour of his voluptuous melancholy.

- Joan Retallack

NOTE: Procedure. Elegy. Humor. Illuminated with help from the O.E.D. Alterations and additions by J.R.

Joan Retallack's most recent poetry volume is *Procedural Elegies / WESTERN CIV CONT'D /* (Roof Books, 2010). She conceptualizes while walking her dog in the Hudson Valley.

CIA RINNE

NOTES IN C

```
*   tout est
                  visible
             in/ visible
          indi/ visible

*   see/le

*   c génial.

*   DESIRE
    DE
    D  IRE
      SI

*    AVENIR
     DEVENIR
    SOUVENIR

*   vous êtes
    curieux?
    sérieux?
    heureux?

    continuez, s.v.p.

*   on peut
    un peu

*   please, note:
```

```
*   traum im raum
     saum im baum
      kaum im zaum
```

```
*   insert why in any text:
----------- why? ------------------ why?-----
---------------------- why? ---------------
--------- why? ------------------------------
--- why? ------------------------------ why?
-------------------------- why? ----------
----------------------------------- continue.

*   situlaimesoupas

*   c'est l'an, paul.
    (selon paul)

*   paris
     aris
     a
      ri
     a
    paris
     aris
    p ris
    par
    paris

*   M
    M:et
    Emmett
    M l
    ett M
    M

*   yes                              no

*   IN UT
    NI TU
    NU TI
    NU IT
```

```
*   ceci n'est pas une pipe
    ceci is keene pipe oder was
    ist keine pfeife nicht.
    da pfeif' ich drauf
    pipe oder nicht
    pipe ou pas
    pipeoupas
    pipapo.

*   sale e tabacchi
    tabacchi e sale
    tabac sale
    schmutziger tabak.

*   Milano      (milan)
    Mila        (talk)
    Mi          (to me)
         no.    (no)

*   soleil
    so
      lei
        i
      o
       e l
       le
    so  i
    sol
      le
    soleil
        il
    sole

*   o sole mio
    sole mio o
    mi sole o o
    sole o mi o
    o sol e mio
    solo mio o
    mi sol ed io
    io e mi sol o
    solo io o.
```

MOSCOW NOTES

*   mosc'où?
    mosk'va?
    mosk'au!

*   l'air montov.

*   amerika guckt nach westen
    europa guckt nach westen
    rußland guckt nach westen
    china guckt nach westen

    (continue)

    mann, haben die nicht alle einen steifen
    nacken?

*   te vas
    me voy
    davaj

*   y se
    yo se
    no se
    lo se

*   on attend le début

*   écoutez:

    ()

    ça y'est, merci.

* conseil aux sédentaires:

  fahroum.

* here you go. and there. and away.

* west   east

* accidental
  occidental

* avoid this area

* what   where

* this is left.   this is right.
  that's   right. right.
  left is   right. right is right.
  what's left?   right is
  left.
  left is left.
                       right? right has just
  left.

* this is it.
  this it is?
  it is this.
  is it this?
  it this is.
  is this it?
  that's it.

* take a walk;
  count your steps.
  now, forget.

  (étude de mémoire)

* maisoui
  aisouim
  isouima
  souimai
  ouimais
  uimaiso
  imaisou

  ouimaisoù?

* muymuymuymuymuymuymuycercaapocosmilimetros

  après pablo picasso (poème dactylographié)

* here it comes:

MINIMALISM.

there it went

* rêve
  réalité
  ----
  rêvalité

* déjà-vu   déjà-vu   déjà-vu

* blind spot

* das nichts ist was es nicht ist.
  das nichts ist was es nicht ißt.
  das nichts ißt was es nicht ißt.
  das nichts ißt was es nicht ist.
  das ist nicht was es nicht ist.
  das ist nicht was es nicht ißt.
  ich esse nicht was es nicht ist.
  ich esse das nicht, was ist das?

ON CONCEPTUAL WRITING

What is interesting about conceptual writing is its ability to disrespect the grammar of habitual communication, to operate beyond logics, and to ignore the strict definition of language as well as the constraints and requirements that other, 'more serious' writing genres are confined to. The different methods conceptual writers use can oblige certain rules, but conceptual writing in itself will be difficult to define according to such. It is not limited by the constraints of one single genre, but operates freely on the borders of many disciplines, and some pieces of conceptual writing can indeed be closer to pieces of visual, sound, or performing art. There is something very liberating to language operating beyond its commonly accepted functions; you could call it linguistic anarchy, and although this aspect is not a goal in itself, it is certainly essential to conceptual writing.

Some pieces of what I would call conceptual writing have a certain esprit that goes beyond humour, and which I think is quite specific for such texts. In a way, conceptual texts operate on many different levels simultaneously. Besides their awareness on form and content, there is often a metatextual aspect to them. To a certain extent, language transforms into something else and reaches beyond its function as a mere means of communication.

It is especially interesting to me when a thought or idea is visualized with the minimum means necessary. In an interview with Wilma Lukatsch, Tomas Schmit put it like this: "What you can say with a sculpture you do not need to build as architecture, what you can do with a drawing you do not need to search in image, and what you can clear up on a piece of paper does not need to become a huge drawing; and what you can make up in your mind does not even need any piece of paper." This is something I can relate to, and in a way, it is also a countermovement to the massive flood of information and waste of material. The ideal would probably be a constant reduction towards almost nothing.

- Cia Rinne

Cia Rinne, born in Gothenburg/Sweden in 1973, grew up in West Germany and studied philosophy, history and languages at the universities of Frankfurt, Athens and Helsinki, from where she holds a MA degree in philosophy. Cia Rinne writes visual poetry and conceptual pieces using different languages, and at times incorporating them into exhibitions, most recently the conceptual work *Night Calendar* (in collaboration with Antonio Scarponi, ISCP, New York 2010), as well as the works *h/ombres* and *indices* displayed at the Turku biennial in 2011). Her publications include *zaroum* (2001), the online work *archives zaroum* (afsnitp.dk 2008), the book *notes for soloists* (OEI Editör, Stockholm 2009), and the sound work *sounds for soloists* (in collaboration with Sebastian Eskildsen, radiowy.se 2010). *zaroum* and *notes for soloists* have been published as a single volume in France (Le clou dans le fer 2011). Cia has also been collaborating on different documentary projects with photographer Joakim Eskildsen; their latest common publication is a book on the Roma from India to Europe based on seven years of travels and stays with Roma communities (*The Roma Journeys*, Steidl 2007). After several years in Scandinavia, Cia now lives and works in Berlin.

GIOVANNI SINGLETON

UNTITLED

(BIRD CAGE)

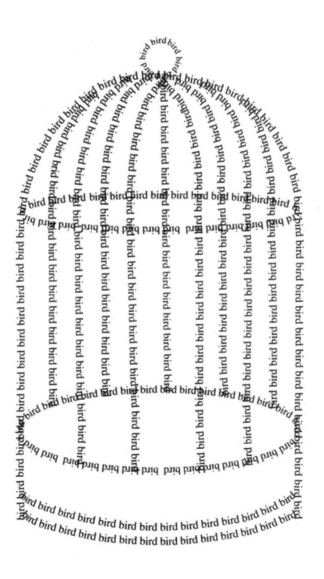

TIME: BEING OR PORTRAIT OF ALICE COLTRANE (1937-2007)

INFINITY

ETERNITY

POETICS STATEMENT

> Things are not as they seem, nor are they otherwise.
> – *The Lankavatara Sutra*

My approach to "visual poetry" is informed by my practice as a poet. While a student at the New College of California, I became interested in pushing the boundaries of poetry and of narrative. The 12-pt font verse line became a sort of prison. While teaching poetry to kids in museums, I came to relate to my work space as more of a canvas than as an 8½ x 11" sheet of white paper. In 2000, I began experimenting with words and three-dimensionality in a series entitled *AMERICAN LETTERS: Works on Paper*.

Early on, I looked at Guillaume Apollinaire's calligrammes and avant-garde musician and composer John Cage's mesostics. Not perfectly content with only European models, I later came across work by the Brazilian Noigandres Group whose members included Augusto and Haroldo De Campos.

I became enthralled by poems that took the shape of their subjects. But then quickly I wanted to go even further. How could this work serve, not only as an instrument of freedom, but as a means of transformation, of liberation, of transcendence? African American poet Norman H. Pritchard's work seemed to offer up some direction. He was an important contributor to *Umbra*, a major magazine of the Black Arts Movement. He published two books of mostly visual poetry: *The Matrix: Poems*, 1960-1970 (Doubleday, 1970) and *Eecchhooeess* (NYU Press, 1971). His work, the music of Alice Coltrane, avant-garde jazz, the writings of Sun Ra, and Tibetan Buddhist meditation have given me a rich palette from which to create the work that I am presenting engaged in.

UNTITLED (BIRD CAGE)

This work has the life and music of jazz saxophonist Charlie "Bird" Parker as its soundtrack. It is also a response to and dialogue with Paul Laurence Dunbar's (1872-1906) poem "Sympathy":

I know why the caged bird sings, ah me,
When his wing is bruised and his bosom sore,
When he beats his bars and he would be free;

Dunbar's poem also provided the title of the first volume in Maya Angelou's series of autobiographies as well as her own poem of that same title:

The caged bird sings with a fearful trill
of things unknown but longed for still
and his tune is heard on the distant hill
for the caged bird sings of freedom.

The poem seeks to posit the question of the source of imprisonment. Is it the bird or is it the bars of the cage? The three-dimensionality also creates spaces between the bars. Is escape then possible? Who or what is jailed and who or what is the jailor? It perhaps is a matter of perception.

TIME: BEING OR PORTRAIT OF ALICE COLTRANE (1937-2007)

Harpist, organist, and pianist Alice Coltrane was founder of the Sai Anantam Ashram and also jazz giant John Coltrane's wife. This work serves as not only an homage to the late spiritual leader and musician, but also as a model for alternative ways of relating to the time space continuum in order to explore/explode/expose the myth of linear existence. This piece is the size of a vinyl record cover as the circular pattern of the clock face is mirrored in the shape of a 12-inch record. Music, eternally universal, emits a vibration that then serves as the measure and marker of time and of being rather than that of a watch or calendar. The hour and minute hands are formed by the titles of two of Alice Coltrane's albums *Eternity* and *Infinity* (an album that remixed recordings by her husband John Coltrane). Additional inspiration comes from Apollinaire's *La Cravate et la montre*.

- giovanni singleton

giovanni singleton, a native of Richmond, VA and former debutant, is founding editor of *nocturnes (re)view*, a journal dedicated to innovative and experimental work of the African Diaspora and other contested spaces. Her work has appeared in a number of publications including *Aufgabe, Callaloo, MiPOesias.com, Alehouse, Beyond the Frontier: African American Poets for the Millennium*, and the *Best of Fence: An Anthology*. Work from her *AMERICAN LETTERS* series was selected for San Francisco's 1st Visual Poetry & Performance Festival.

ANNE TARDOS

1

Nine words per line and nine lines per stanza.
Pink fluffy underwater kangaroo fuzzy free manic rabbity thing.
Sense and nonsense similarly writer's block clogged and unblocked.
Happiness nothing really blue so you can start living.
Laptop immersion fools your brain into thinking whatever needed.
Gazebo-tranquility-ragweed, condemned to live with the Self.
Find yourself totally isolated strict exile a common ploy.
Like you, I'm impatient as we become each other.
Bright green primary features evolving society—the age thing.

2

Sleep being slept, a bird has something to say.
Reality flip flop artistic failure extremely hard to maintain.
Foggy zendo vigilance gendergap understanding the desire to live.
Levitating underbelly slime, dengue fever ankle deep, vilification zigzag.
I love you too dear—count your chickens carefully.
Echochamber plantlife indoor cellular reality busy yellow rent
        abatement.
Quiet knucklehead cameraderie a thousand hopes subject to change.
Infinity appears in repeated mirror images perceived as reflection.
Zealous devotion to waxwork sex, because Sigmund said so.

3

Birthing velocity's snapshot-like nature, pushed to the extreme.
It is Racine not Montaigne for certain lovers' discourse.
To suddenly fall upon the old dialectic of enlightenment.
And what is masturbation if not a homosexual act?
A role to play must have a visible function.
We are being categorized in the realm of tonality.
A counterintuitive yearning for the quiescence of pre-birth.
The way our twig's bent is how we grow.
Empty thermos, unkissed nosetip, text rotation, and marsupial nesting.

4

Kerchief ligament pirouette darkness jettison mother of invention toy-
    boy.
Zany foxy smoke alarm tremolo evacuation juniper ginger dimple.
Zinguer je je zinguer je, mich dich Villa nicht.
Every thought first thought in the visible universe, strange.
Zendo cushion run for it go. Long ago Labrador.
Swift recollection tired Daphne just like our overheated relationshit.
Something has changed I felt giddy I felt sick.
Since women. Forget it. No way. Barbaric and inhumane.
Learning a lot here: I'm wrong in being wrong.

5

Djibouti laptop polyrhythmic stevedore imagination for example
    people die.
Yeah yeah yeah listen to the music around you.
Plagiarize and cannibalize yourself by mining your own work.
Counter-sadistic anti-suffering vraiment triste faché becoming real.
Don't think for a minute that you don't exist.
First, get used to the sound of my voice.
Bob Perelman knows what Maisie knew about her parents.
Katy Lederer didn't have money. She was a poet.
Mitch Highfill keeps a pet moth and an elephant.

ABOUT NINE

The phrase "Nine words per line and nine lines per stanza" is itself made up of nine words, describing the poem's form.

Counting words, not syllables—"I" having the same value as "kangaroo"—causes the lines to be uneven. Each line is a microcosm of tempo, tone, and beat.

You could say each line is a poem by itself, although the lines have an oblique relationship to one another.

Some of the lines in "Nine" are word clusters (sometimes neologistic), but mostly they are unilingual, subject-based texts.

- Anne Tardos

Anne Tardos is a poet, composer, and visual artist. She is the author of several books of poetry and the multimedia performance work and radio play *Among Men*. A selection of her readings and performances (many with Jackson Mac Low) can be heard on the University of Pennsylvania's web site : PennSound and on UbuWeb Sound. Recent books of poetry include *I Am You* (Salt), and *Both Poems* (Roof Books). She is the editor of *Thing of Beauty: New and Selected Work by Jackson Mac Low*. Her poem "The Pure of Heart," was set to music by composer Michael Byron. Tardos is a 2009 Fellow in Poetry from the New York Foundation for the Arts.

HANNAH WEINER

THE SEMAPHORE ALPHABET

EDG	Any chance of war?
ODV	Good chance
IKF	No chance of peace
YU	Has war commenced?
YX	War has commenced
YW	War between _____ and _____ has commenced
KDX	How is the crop?
KDW	Crops have suffered severely
KDV	Crops destroyed
TN	Are you in want of provisions?
LHE	Distressed for want of food
YU	Want food immediately
NZ	Unable for want of
YZ	Are you in want of water?
LHF	Distressed for want of water
NRC	Fresh water
YVH	No water to be had
NF	Dying from want of water
FJX	Have you been attacked?
NJ	I am attacked. I want assistance. Help, I am attacked
FO	Are you in danger?
NL	I am in danger
KLF	Much danger
KLE	In great danger
DNE	Enemy is advancing
DNA	Army is advancing
EQB	Is anyone wounded?
RKN	Many wounded
ZIN	How many wounded?
PKN	No. of killed and wounded not yet known
ZIM	How are the wounded?
YGJ	Without arms
FGX	Without assistance
YL	Want immediate medical assistance
CP	Cannot assist
NC	In distress. Want immediate assistance
CX	No assistance can be rendered. Do the best you can for yourselves.
GBT	I shall bear up
GBV	May I, or can I bear up?
YE	Want assistance

GLN	Want bread
RZX	Want more support
LHI	How long have you been in such distress?
KNG	How many days?
RKD	Many
RKQ	So many
RKS	Too many
KLD	How many have you dangerously ill?
LQN	Dying at the rate of _____ a day
ZIE	Could, or might be worse
ZIF	It will be worse
ZIG	Much worse
MSK	Is my family well?
ZBM	Not so well
FZB	When was the battle fought?
KBN	Daylight. At daylight
KOY	When was the last death?
FIB	Daybreak. Dawn. At dawn
KOM	How many dead?
KON	Who is dead?
KOU	Dearer, dearest
KOV	Too dear

Introduction From *The Code Poems* (Open Studio, 1982)

These poems and performances are from the INTERNATIONAL CODE OF SIGNALS for the Use of All Nations, British Editions 1859, 1899 and American Edition, post-war, 1931, a visual system for ships at sea. Code of signals for the use of mariners have been published in various countries since the early 19th century. The first International Code was drafted in 1855 by a committee set up by the British Board of Trade. Flags at that time numbered 18, which represented the consonants of the alphabet, with the exception of X and Z. A later version published in 1899 increased the letter flags to 26, plus an answering pennant. Flags, one for each letter of the alphabet, are hoisted on the mast, singly or in groups of two, three, four. Single and two flag hoists are distress signals, three flag hoists are general signals, four flag hoists geographical signals. In addition, each flag has a name; A, Alpha, B, Bravo, C, Charlie, etc. In combination, as CJD, "I was plundered by a pirate," these signals comprise a complete volume of code signals. Messages can be transmitted also by two semaphore red signal flags, and by Morse Code. Visual signaling is any method of above water communication, the transmission of which is capable of being seen (alphabet flags, semaphore flags, Morse flashing light). Sound signaling is any method of sending Morse signals by means of siren, whistle, foghorn, bell or other sound apparatus. Although Morse and light signals were used in performances, only visual signals are included (we omit radio) in this book.

- Hannah Weiner

Hannah Weiner was born in Providence, Rhode Island on November 4, 1928. She attended Radcliffe College (class of 1950) and after that lived in New York City. The best introduction to her work is *Hannah Weiner's Open House*, ed Patrick Durgin (Kenning Editions, 2007). *The Code Poems* (Open Studio, 1982), composed by using the international code of signals (nautical flag signals), is her best know early work; it is part of a larger group of performance works form the 1960s. After 1970, she devoted herself to writing, emphasizing that all her works written after 1972 were based on 'seeing words.' As she says in an epigraph to her best-known work, *The Clairvoyant Journal*: 'I SEE words on my forehead IN THE AIR on other people on the typewriter on the page." Her other books include *Little Books / Indians* (Roof Books, 1980), *Spoke* (Sun & Moon Press, 1984), *Silent Teachers / Remembered Sequel* (Tender Buttons, 1993), *We Speak Silent* (Roof, 1997), and *page* (New York: Roof Books, 2002). Marta Werner has recently edited an edition of *The Book of Revelations*, available as a digital edition at Jacket2 <http://jacket2.org/feature/hannah-weiners-book-revelations>. More information, books, and link to PennSound audio/video at Weiner's EPC page <http://epc.buffalo.edu/authors/weiner/>.

CHRISTINE WERTHEIM

HOW TO CONCEIVE A POEM 1

Prelude

I f Uck
he f Ucks
she f Ucks
we f Uck
they f Uck U
f Uck f Uck

f Uck f Uck f Uck f Uck f Uck f Uck f Uck
f UUUck

f Uck f Uck f Uck f Uck f Uck
f UUUUUUck

Poem

the poem is conceived.

Encore

f Uck f Uck f Uck f Uck f Uck f Uck
f UUUck

f Uck f Uck f Uck f Uck fUck fUck
f UUUUUUUUck

f Uck f Uck f Uck f Uck f Uck f Uck
f UUUck

f Uck f Uck f Uck f Uck
f UUUUUUUck U   .

HOW TO CONCEIVE A POEM 2

In the beginning was the poem.

§

Then the poem divided the word above
from the word below

above
―――――
below

+ there was ironic distance.

But the reader was still in the dark,
So someone said:
"For God's sake, turn on the light!"
+ they did.
+ they saw that it was,
a poem.

+ the evening and the mourning* were the first day.

§

Then the poem made the trees and the birds
+ all the flowers to bloom,
+ saw that it was good.

But the reader was still in the dark.
So someone repeated:
"For God's sake, turn on the blinking lights!"
+ they did.
+ they saw that it was,
a poem.

+ the evening and the mourning were the second day.

§

By this stage the writer was all-knowing
+ the poem could do whatever it liked.

But the poor reader was still in the dark.
So someone shouted again:

"For God's bleeding sake, turn on the blinking light!"
But they couldn't find the switch
+ they stomped off.

So mourning never came
+ the reader was not illuminated …
§

Still,
the poem thought it was pretty good.
But there you go.
Not everyone agrees.
§

*(fn) This is after all a tragedy.

Well,
here I am three weeks into the poem
and not a clue how to conceive it.

I've got a girl hanging round in a doorway
just waiting for me to decide what to do with her,
a mother with the weirdest notions of time-keeping,
and a father who… well don't get me started.
As for me,
I nearly cut my you-know-what off
before it could be useful,
in a window sash no less.
But mostly… …

… … … Jesus. At this rate, I'll be dead
before the damned thing
even gets started… …

HOW TO CONCEIVE A POEM 4

Cut along dotted line and attach AB to CD

A ⌐   ⌐ B

Once upon a time there was

[C]

a poem that began

[D]

Art as model. *If* modern Art is seen as work that arouses the mind to enjoy the (pure) pleasure of playing with its own faculties (what Peter Osborne calls its "reflective self-affection"), *then* its history can be divided into two main phases: (1) the formalist or aesthetic phase, in which this experience is linked to, or even "rethought" as the interplay of forms within an artistic medium (painting, sculpture, film), and (2) a more novel phase, in which attention is focused directly on the self-affection itself. This is the "conceptual" phase which focuses on the subject of experience rather than the object provoking it. Here the artwork does not play with the appearances of forms but with the gap between three elements: a concept, name or title (given in words); an existence—the deictic *thisness* of things-in-themselves—; and the mind's incapacity to grasp *the sense* of the experience, despite both a concept/name and an existence.

A classic work is Robert Barry's 1968 piece *One Billion Dots* composed of twenty-five printed volumes containing one billion materially-instantiated dots. What makes this a conceptual work is not the impossibility of realizing the phenomenon to which the name refers: after all the one billion dots actually exist. Its conceptuality lies rather in the complex disjunction between its name/concept/title, the existence of the dots, and the (im)-possibility of the mind's *ima(in)ging* or perceptually grasping this phenomenon, despite both its name and its existence.

As Osborne says in "Starting Up All over Again: Time and Existence in Some Conceptual Art of the 1960's," (*The Quick and the Dead*, exhib. cat., Walker Art Institute, 2009, 91-106), such works are *not* completely dematerialized, for the words of the title itself are material, let alone the dots. Nor are they absolutely deastheticized. Though they "may be *relatively* aesthetically indifferent [relative, that is to formalist art] … [they are] better thought of as transforming the structure of [ ] experience from pure *aesthesis* to a more complex reflective *combination* of the aesthetic and the conceptual" (102). Unless one is an extremist, like Kossuth, for whom a work must remain as the idea of an idea, never being materialized at all, even as a name, *if* we take Art as our model, *then* "conceptual" work in any medium contains this complexity.

My work seeks to point to a gap between our conception of subjective disjunction, the actual existence of this fracture, and our mind's incapacity to grasp it, despite our both having accorded it a name, and being confronted with its existence.

- *Christine Wertheim*

Christine Wertheim is author of +|'me'S-pace (Les Figues Press). She edited *Feminaissance,* and with Matias Viegener co-edited *Séance* and *The nOullipian Analects.* Recent critical work is published in *X-tra, Cabinet,* and *Issues*; recent poetry appears in *Drunken Boat, Tarpaulin Sky* and *Veer.* She teaches on the MFA in Writing at CalArts.

3. MATTER

BAROQUE
HYBRID
GENERATIVE
CORPOREAL
DISSENSUAL

NORMA COLE

FROM *COLLECTIVE MEMORY*

Speech production: themes and variations

exhibit
exhibition

ribbons
vandals
the ribbons of vandals, the vandals
of ribbon, scissors of ribbon,
ribbons of scandal
sculpture of
ribbons or
strips
strippers
strip clubs

exhibitions: temporary inhibitions, my *semblables*: collective guilt:
don't leave your filthy shirt, your own fifty-yard line. What would be the
motive in that "kind of temporary performance"? (Christo & Jeanne-
Claude)

quote
quotation
quit
quoting
quit it
unscripted
quoted unscripted
quote script?
script quote

Why do I like it under the trees in autumn when everything is half
dead? Why would I like the word moving like a cripple among the
leaves and why would I like to repeat the words without meaning?

physics
physical
physicist

metaphysical physicist (string theorist)
psychoactive physicists
psychotic episode

Sonata: a musical composition in contrasted movements

constellation
stardust
nuclear glow train, Yucca, Nevada
rotate the exhaust
on second thought

Did you *make* that: the sheep, yarn, afghan? birds, feathers, pillows,
bookshelves, (trees, nails etc.) the books on them, the slides (yes), their
glass mounts, tray, projector? lamps, record player, records (vinyl!),
occasional tables, desk, chair, papers? their colors and weights, sizes,
like that candy wrapper? notes (perhaps), postcards, newspapers, my
cane, myself?

Negt & Kluge
Sappho
Borges
Cortázar
Pindar
Bavcar
or Bavchar? What does the little inverted circumflex over the c do?

to be at music
beyond waterlily lake
at the level
of local language
this means ours
geophysical
pelagic

Petulant pixies had completely rearranged the living room. Stand here
more or less. Lessness. We can put it like this: petulant lover identified
with her. Or over-identified with her.

sixties
seventies
thirties
forties
fifties

unattended, an original
a small wreath of acacias
sky of the sun
or light of the
sky "that lies behind the sun" (Dante)

Frosted Flakes, the biggest box you ever saw! Let's ramble, muskrats!
The rooftop oxygen gets right into my room!
"Go, go, go, said the bird: human kind
cannot bear very much reality." (T.S. Eliot, "Burnt Norton")

She finished the painting of the little girl, washed her hands—like today
it was warm, sunny, celebratory—got the call, elation, first of all, for his
sake.

Rascasse: scorpion fish, used in bouillabaisse
scorpions
scabies
scrapies
prions
scrapie prions
prion protein

floating
in the unbroken air
silent trade
citrus, columbus, chaplet: wreath, as of flowers
worn on the head
curly haired, the rent went up when
his temper went up

books lying open to the sun
like speckled trout
Feb. 3, a quiet day

Richard Winslow wrote music for *Endgame*. Twenty-seven is the
age when Jules Laforgue died. "Garcia Lorca stole / poetry from this
drinking fountain"(Robert Duncan, *Caesar's Gate*)

as for the classical idea of spice
he thought if you
sneezed, he would say: bless you
he would say: thank you
he would say: gesundheit

sweet flag: calamus
very cloudy: books flying up to the sun
you, little cloud of more than human form, setting fire in back of the brain

interface
interfaith
the notes he took down yesterday
came out to the left
and right: no, no, no
not a class, just people
each other

accent: "a superior force of voice or of articulative effort, upon some
particular syllable." (Webster's Dictionary, in Saintsbury's Manual
of English Prosody) Getting ready for the Bay-to-Breakers, Bay-to-
Breakers, Bay-to-Breakers.

quiet violence
preoccupied
hot & spicy
chutney, peppers
with the
stuffed
duck

the sea breeze maybe once a month
south of the park
South Beach
the South End
southern intonation, not a phrase, her articulation, speech production,
imagine there was an eclipse

"I swan" quoth Paul Blackburn in "Sirventes"
sitting on the railroad tracks
wireless
violets
voice, voices

"one loves only form
and form only comes
into existence when
the thing is born" (Olson, "I, Maximus of Gloucester to You")

for all intents and purposes I has slippage: forthwith, the body can never
recede "Exchequering from piebald fiscs unkeyed" ("The Comedian as
Letter C," Wallace Stevens)

slip
slippage
slam
slam dunk
apples, to Syria, from the Golan heights
pitch the woo, Jack
Jesse and J.J.

Bill, who was J.J. anyway?

Photo Credit: Stephen Zeifman

COLLECTIVE MEMORY

I first knew I was a conceptual poet when I read Michael Cross's review of my new book: "*Where Shadows Will* tracks Cole through twenty years of careful conceptual practice[...]. As a visual artist herself (and materialist to boot), Cole *sees* words as both conceptual and *visual* elements, so just as 'painting is thinking,' *the poem is thinking as painting*[...]."

> In conceptual art practice, ideas come first.
> So, first: the idea of writing.
> I had written a poem called *Collective Memory*.

http://www.granarybooks.com/pages.php?which_page=product_view&which_product=25&search=norma%20cole%20collective%20memory&category=

It wove phrases from many poets & non-poets into a piece framed from a list of words that were very difficult for me to say at that time (I had had a stroke that caused motor impairment affecting speech). The poem was written during a period of four or five months at the California Historical Society, in one of the installations I had made called "A Living Room, 1950s" (within a larger exhibition, "Poetry and its Arts, Bay Area Interactions 1954-2004," curated by Steve Dickison).

http://www.berkeleydailyplanet.com/issue/2005-04-05/article/21106?headline=-Poetry-and-its-Arts-Explores-the-Visuals-in-Poems-By-JOHN-McBRIDE-&status=301

I made up a person called "the poet" who worked in the Living Room everyday, reading, writing and talking to people who came into the exhibit. Here is a photo taken from the street of the poet at her desk in the Living Room, with reflections.

- Norma Cole

-

Norma Cole's most recent books of poetry are *Where Shadows Will: Selected Poems 1988—2008* and *NATURAL LIGHT*. A book of essays and talks, *TO BE AT MUSIC* appeared in August 2010 from Omnidawn. Cole has received awards from the Gerbode Foundation, Gertrude Stein Awards, Fund for Poetry and Foundation for Contemporary Arts. She teaches at the University of San Francisco.

DEBRA DI BLASI

FROM *THE JIRÍ CHRONICLES*
AND OTHER FICTIONS

Special Advertising Section

Life is scary.

All I could think of was carcinogens: in bacon, in burnt toast, in water, in air. And then I began thinking about antibiotics: in dish soap, in bath soap, in Handi-Wipes. Every time somebody used an antibacterial product, smaller weaker bacteria died, making room for bigger stronger bacteria. I thought it was just a matter of time till bacteria grew as big as rottweilers. I thought soon I'd be eaten by a big growling slobbering *Streptococci. AND THEN I KEPT THINKING.* Yes, thinking terrified me. And my fears grew every day until finally I couldn't get out of bed. I was paralyzed by the scariness of life. Then my doctor prescribed cable TV. He said it would make me stop thinking. Said it would numb me to life's big issues. I immediately called up *TIME WARNER CABLE.* The salesman was so kind, so understanding. He said he received hundreds of calls a week from people *JUST LIKE ME,* people who couldn't stop thinking. And then he told me just what I needed to hear: *"CABLE TV WILL ABSOLUTELY CHANGE YOUR LIFE. I GUARANTEE IT."* Well, I've had cable TV for a year now and haven't read a single book, newspaper or magazine, and I certainly haven't attended the theater, art museum, symphony or opera. Even better, *I'M NOW CONVINCED I WILL NEVER DIE. HOORAY!*

**Thank you,
Time Warner Cable!**

especially
when you
don't have
cable TV

Life's not scary when you've got cable TV!

Glauke's Gown:
The Function of Myth

MEDEA
a synopsis

After taking the throne at Corinth, Jason the Argonaut, husband of Medea, fell head over heels for the pretty princess Glauke.[1] Medea, who had saved his ass on more than one occasion, became enraged with jealousy and sought revenge. But instead of "exacting revenge" on Jason, Medea aimed her sight on Glauke. She soaked a beautiful gown in a secret potion that "stored up the powers of fire" and sent it to Glauke. When Glauke tried on the gown[2] it burst into flames so hot they melted the flesh right off her bones. She threw herself into a fountain, but the water only made the flames burn hotter.

CHORUS: Medea, Medea, you bitch! No wonder it's your name on our lips.[3]

THE WOMAN turns to HER VERY BEST FRIEND seated next to her on her living room couch in front of a TV that's playing a video of *Lover Come Back*.

---

1. Yes, there are lots of names here, and if you know nothing of Greek mythology then it will be Greek to you. For the sake of clarity, say the role of Jason is played by Donald Trump, Glauke by Marla Maples, and Medea by Ivana Trump.

2. What the hell was she thinking!?! A gift from Medea, a woman who had dismembered her own brother in order to be with Jason?!? And what was Marla thinking!?! Signing a prenuptial agreement with The Donald that declared if the marriage didn't last five years she would get only $1-5 million of The Donald's $2 billion. How long did the marriage last? Almost five years. Big surprise. What were they all thinking, these women who love their men?!? Beautiful, yes. Wise...? Can't we blame it on environment, the inexorable way environment (i.e., the omnipotent media) molds young women into creatures who would do and say anything to get and keep their man. As a woman myself, I would like to blame it on environment, oh yes, for I am too ashamed to accept it as my "nature."

3. This line appeared in Euripedes' original version of his play, *Medea*. His editor forced him to delete it for fear of offending the mainstream reading public.

LOVER COME BACK
a synopsis

Doris is a scrupulous virginal advertising exec who wears silly hats, and Rock is an unscrupulous womanizing advertising exec pretending to be a shy rocket scientist who's never been laid so he can (1) get in Doris's pants and (2) distract her from pursuing a new ad account for a product that doesn't exist. Basically, Doris gets to wear a lot of white—and, of course, those silly hats—and Rock gets to wear a beard and tweeds when he's not barechested and perpetually tan. The sexual tension is palpable in their love scenes. What talented actors! Considering that in real life Rock was gay and Doris was married 4 times.

Lover Come Back, starring Doris Day and Rock Hudson.[4] THE WOMAN and HER VERY BEST FRIEND are drinking Diet Cokes and eating salad and watching the scene where Doris realizes she's been duped by Rock and therefore gets mad, real mad, as mad Doris can get.

"By the by," THE WOMAN says to HER VERY BEST FRIEND, "you will never ever believe what I did last night!"

HER VERY BEST FRIEND leans eagerly forward, salivating almost, almost twitching with un-Doris-Day-like anticipation." What what what did you do?"

"Well," says THE WOMAN, cautiously glancing over each shoulder, first her right, then her left, though she's sitting in her own apartment where she lives alone, while on the TV screen Doris convinces Rock to strip down naked on a beach and then leaves him stranded there, taking his clothes with her, while THE WOMAN's mouth expands in a grin tinged with evil: green sky predicting hail, "I called Jirí every hour on the hour and hung up without saying a word."

"And then what?" asks HER VERY BEST FRIEND, drool gathering in her cleft chin.

---

4. **BY THE BY:** Doris Day would never ever harm another living soul. I am not the only one who knows this. When I was a child my mother resembled a brunette Doris Day and everyone therefore believed my mother incapable of malevolent behavior. Even my mother believed this when she looked in the mirror and smiled at herself like Doris Day smiling at Doris Day. My mother's thought of spanking the piss out of me for drawing on the living room wall with broken crayons in shades of red melted to the mantra, "I am Doris Day, benevolent humanitarian, a phrase which may in fact be redundant, I don't know, whatever, anyway, I would never ever harm another living soul, not even my spoiled brat of a daughter." Yes, it's true: Doris made my mother a better human being and she saved my ass.

"Then what *what*?" THE WOMAN asks.

"What else did you do?"

"Why, nothing else!" Normally, THE WOMAN would never ever begin a sentence with "Why,...!" but she has been watching Doris Day for approximately 57 minutes, and Doris Day has gotten under her skin, transformed THE WOMAN into a woman whose language resembles Doris Day's language, not only in its vocabulary but its timbre: that sexy-but-celibate breathiness that is Doris, all Doris, why yes, Doris!

"Like I said," THE WOMAN continues, "I called him on the phone about a hundred times and then hung up!"

HER VERY BEST FRIEND recoils—not from horror but from an exquisite boredom, tangible and pungent and weighted as if Death himself **[Why is Death always a man, Nature always a woman?]** had just settled a wet mink coat around her shoulders.

PLEASE NOTE:

A tomato seed[5] clings to **Her Very Best Friend**'s napkin. She picks at it until it comes off under her fingernail. She must dig it out with another fingernail. She brings it to her face and studies it, thinking it resembles some object from inside the body: vile, best kept hidden. She shudders. Wipes the tomato seed under the table's edge.[6]

tomato

tomato seed

---

5. ***SHAMELESS SELF-PROMOTION*** See sections 9 and 11 of "Say What You Like" in my first book *Drought & Say What You Like*, winner of the Thorpe Menn Book Award.

6. Days later a child will run her little fingers under this very same table's edge and discover the tomato seed and pick it off with her tiny fingernail and stare at it long and hard. Then she will hold the seed toward her divorced-and-now-a-weekend-father father and exclaim, "Look, Daddy! A booger!" Daddy will glance around the cafe to see if anyone has heard his daughter's vulgar cry of delight, then brusquely clean the "booger" from her tiny finger with his paper napkin, then slap her hand hard and hiss, "Don't pick your nose, do you hear me?" And she will somberly nod her little head—though she will not be able to make the connection between the table's booger and her nose—and will rub her stinging little hand and start to cry until she remembers she is also not supposed to cry. When she grows up, she will become the Chief Financial Officer of a Fortune 500 company and date far younger men and be disparagingly referred to as "Big Bad Ball Buster" by males of equal or lesser corporate rank.

"Wasn't that just awful of me?" asks...no, *pleads* THE WOMAN. Awkward demanding plea couched in Doris Day vernacular. Doubtful and hopeful all at once.

"Yeah," HER VERY BEST FRIEND mumbles unconvincingly. "Awful."

Desperate to be bad, very bad, bad to the bone, THE WOMAN says: "It's probably a crime. A misdemeanor at the very least. Harassment. I'm sure I could get arrested for it."

"Right," says HER VERY BEST FRIEND. Her eyes roll to the ceiling then stare at Doris Day singing on the TV screen, waist impossibly skinny below her impossibly pointy breasts below her impossibly golden hair, and quite suddenly she turns to THE WOMAN and asks, "Are you gonna eat the rest of your salad, or what?"

The selections on pages 228-232 are excerpted from The Jirí Chronicles and Other Fictions, *a ten-year literary project that includes over 500 individual works of prose, poetry, music, audio interviews, visual art, video, animation, websites, performance and consumer products, including celebrity fragrances Hung™ and pe™.*

The Jirí Chronicles *(more at http://debradiblasi.com/events.htm) attempts to explore and document Systems Theory via interconnections between media and people, fact and fiction, and the resulting effects on our day-to-day lives. (Systems Theory is the transdisciplinary study of the abstract organization of phenomena, independent of their substance, type, or spatial or temporal scale of existence. It investigates both the principles common to not only the whole and its parts, but also the parts as they relate to and inform each other and the whole.)*

The first short story [in this project], "Czechoslovakian Rhapsody Sung to the Accompaniment of Piano," proved that the mind can—and does—(re)form the daily deluge of unrelated information into a narrative with cultural and emotional significance. The result was a mixed media fiction utilizing text and white space as visual elements, and incorporating illustrations, footnotes, and text appropriated from ad copy, news headlines, magazine articles and billboards, song lyrics, movie dialog, and genealogical, scientific and historical facts.

As Jirí Cêch's presence expanded over the years, so did "his" significance regarding contemporary culture and aesthetics. For example, his website, *it's a man's world* (the title of a poem by Jirí Cêch adapted to video and later featured on the website, *Poets Against the War*), suggests continuing problems regarding gender and power. The project itself chronicles the issues of our times and the democratization of a vast array of new technologies and how the two may be related. It questions the notion of boundaries—whether geopolitical, socio-economic or aesthetic—and the dangers of categorizing people and things according to our prejudicial standards.

On a yet more somber level, Jirí's ability to exist as "real" addresses the apparently burgeoning problem of The Lie in contemporary society, where politicians, media monsters, and corporate and religious leaders are able to spin webs of deceit by means of the very technology that allows Jirí Cêch to exist as "flesh-and-blood." It also surreptitiously explores the contemporary problem of sound bites & bytes, wherein the public's conclusions about people and concepts are reached without fully receiving and absorbing all information necessary to achieve an objective, rational viewpoint.

Rumors of Jirí's death by an angry lioness in Botswana can no longer be refuted. The real Jirí Cêch is dead. Long live Jirí Cêch.

- Debra Di Blasi

Debra Di Blasi (www.debradiblasi.com) is the recipient of a James C. McCormick Fellowship in Fiction from the Christopher Isherwood Foundation, Thorpe Menn Book Award, Cinovation Screenwriting Award, and Diagram Innovative Fiction Award, among others. Books include *The Jirí Chronicles & Other Fictions; What the Body Requires; Drought & Say What You Like;* and *Prayers of an Accidental Nature,* and *Skin of the Sun* (forthcoming). The short film based on her novella, *Drought,* won a host of national and international awards, and was one of only six US films invited to the Universe Elle section of the 2000 Cannes International Film Festival. Her innovative writing is widely anthologized and has been adapted to film, radio, theatre, and audio CD in the U.S. and abroad; her essays, art reviews and articles can be found in a variety of international, national and regional publications. Debra is founding publisher of Jaded Ibis Press and president of Jaded Ibis Productions. She frequently teaches and lectures on topics related to 21st century narrative forms.

STACY DORIS,
LISA ROBERTSON

FROM THE PERFUME RECORDIST

Dear Kenny,

Having been under the knife, we've decided to address you at a cellular level, directly (oh and thanks for the pass, c. 2008). Systemically, have you considered that all living tissue says "No!" to the fats foreign to the body? This is clearly expressed through the isolation and rejection of the electrically-neutral, lame fats. These symptoms of pathological fat-metabolism cannot be corrected by the subsequent withdrawal of all fats. Eliminating harmful fats is indeed necessary, but genuine help is only possible by supplying "good fats." Water-soluble fats are being highlighted here.

Don't you fret now, Kenny. We can nearly lift our own body weight and abound in bioavailable optimism. We can turn cartwheels, highly unsaturated. To narrow in on our lipoid membranes, with their effects on the electromotoric field forces in metabolism, arranged to the sun from a quantum perspective, we promote the electron exchange.

We want to be omnivorous, we're attached to insatiability, like everyone we need alcohol and drugs to make the most minor of grooming decisions—how can we decide? We want to not be alone in our discipline. Come hither!

Why not a celebration?

To go to restaurants and drink, to go to feasts and parties, to wear lipstick, full of lead and parabens though it be, quoi, with total unsaturated harmony. But avoid yellow muffins. Say "Yes" to lentils!

We are considering the exclamation point, so flooded are our bodies with nutrients. Given the climate in which we live, our opinion is—Flax Seed Oil.

For all of us, there is the question that seems to arise of how many times we have initiated sex. Finally, then, here's an answer:

Physicists empathize—the photon is Eternal. Life is unimaginable without the photon. It is in continual movement. It IS continual movement; stopping this is not an option.

The photon is filled with color. It can, when present in large numbers, change color and frequency. The photon is recognized as the purest form of energy, the purest wave, and, in continual movement, it can combine in resonance with the second photon to form a "short life particle."

We have a suggestion: Oleox. Or if you prefer, Linomel. And first thing upon waking: sauerkraut juice, for which champagne may be substituted.

Fats are governing substances of all vital functions.

Below there are a few sentences of the American physician Dr. Jan Roehm who studied our therapy intensively.

On the topic of the coffee enema: never fear. Sometimes up to three before sex. This is a final alternative to mascara. Fair trade organic of course. You can get it from ineedcoffee.com. Use the French press! The heavy matter in the nucleus is charged with positive electricity. In contrast to this the electron carries a negative charge.

You are now a battery. Congratulations.

Good. Now that we're into enemas, consider the meeting of perfume, hormones and degeneration. Psychoneuroimmunological discoveries mean that the "mind" is also an expression of the immune system. We have to conclude, contrary to all previous thinking, that the numerous interactions between the molecules of emotions and the immune system constitute what we term a mobile brain. Therefore we are not into healing any wounds from the past bla, bla, bla. Let's get down to it, Kenny.

Now we'll tell you about our sainthood. We supposedly turned a stone into bread (but when you showed discontent, wanting meat, the bread turned into serpents). We gave away butter. The cows we milked produced enormous amounts. We associated iconographically with a cow and a large churn. Then, in Normandy, "for many years," we ate and drank nothing, nor from our mouths, nor from any other natural organ did anything go out and pass the test. We were fat and of good nature as you, the bishop, proved by careful examination.

Let us consider that in the whole world we are the one bread that can satisfy the hunger of all. Just to look at us nourishes you. This bread is what every healthy man with an appetite seeks, and when he cannot find it, or eat it, his hunger increases indefinitely. Such is the hell of the hungry, who the closer they come to this bread, the more they are aware that they do not as yet have it.

Now we shall meddle with you again Kenny. Oh strongest of all warriors! You have conquered everything and opened the closed totality which was never opened by creatures who did not know, with painfully won and distressed Love! O heroine, since you are so heroic, and since you never yield, you are called the greatest heroine! It is right therefore that you should know us perfectly.

Our future sanctity was foreshadowed by our mother's abstinence from all food except greens, vinegar and wild grapes during her pregnancy. We abstained while still a baby at the breast.

Electrons have a great affinity for oxygen—they love it. That is why, in us, they thrust for the surface. They attract oxygen and stimulate our entire being as well as decay. We must ingest these electrons in our food for their vital functions—actively striving toward the surface—to once more function as they should, making us feel lighter in ourselves.

Some people think that they work too much. I no longer accept this from most people because, when I ask how long they actually work, it is most certainly neither too long nor too hard. They are of the opinion that they work too much because they feel heavy and tired and keep wanting to lie down. How is it that electron-rich nutrition makes one so light? Why do we need it so urgently? It lightens the pull of the earth and makes us suitable for sanctity.

Kenny, you are the fastest emissary from star to star. There is nothing faster than you. You rush along with time. You live eternally. Physicists emphasize too that the photon, the quantum, the tiniest part of a sunbeam is eternal.

Love,
The Perfume Recordist

All honour to the anal cavity.

All honour to mighty pungent couplings of the rose of political imagination.

All honour to the entrails of language.

Someone took a turd to a sage and said: "Look, he is being corrupted by women."

And the turd said: "Women are always actresses, no matter what they do."

And the sage said: "Truly, a hard law buggers you."

The Perfume Recordist butts right up to the edge of the rose of waste to strut in the sewer of womanhood. Where the rose becomes turds and cacophony, we hurl ourselves into the putrid bouquet.

There, we lift our complicated indivisible arses and breasts like complaints and discharge an expanse of rotting petals. Oh, disagreeable Master! Here is our rosy manure.

Perfume's history is the record of shit.

We have been excrement, filth on opulent paper, ecstatic quiddity of defecation judged profitable.

Perfume is matter out of place, aka shit: a revolt against the exorbitance of boundaries. Waves of roses flow though the sewers. We're out in more than we can need. We're matter out of place.

The rosy waste increases, migrates, vomits, beseeches, refutes, despairs, invades, carries us in a flatulent rose tide of spontaneous imitation, ah we are sub rosa fishermen of spasms, our little skiff afloat in the fetid fervor.

Shit protects one from the moral majority within.

Eight o' clock at night. Let us now examine the eighteenth century, our cunt. It let loose an extreme jollity and extreme impertinence. It poured out erudition, filth and boredom. Not a pavement in the place, and everything gutters for miles and miles, and a stench to it that plucked us by the knick-knacks. And we were twenty leagues out.

To return to pollution behaviour, avoidance is a process of tidying up. The essential ingredients of our poetry will be revolting.

O rose the pastures in which the night feeds and prunes the cud that nourishes us to prayer, the incomparable fascination of maturation and rot.

And the turd said: "I'm a fart in a mass of wind, a humble bud under a cow-pad."

Roll on in shit, traverse this absurd age.

The coming musk rose started excreting fell upon our ear and started excreting like the sweet south stealing and giving odor fell upon our ear and started excreting the murmurous haunt of flies started excreting.

With perfume too the excremental juice applied to body and garments is carried across wild trajectories. We are all invasive species.

All value is waste.

Oh, and thank you for your virginity.

From: ███████████████████
Subject: Re: Manifesto
Date: November 7, 2008 8:39:53 AM PST
To: Lisa Marie Robertson ████████████████████████

Hi Lisa,
I know and I get it. I went to bat. I wish I could have made it float but, alas, I cannot.

I really appreciate all this, very much. I wish this all came out differently. Thanks so much, again and again. I hope we'll be in touch some time soon.

Yours,

███████

From: Lisa Marie Robertson ████████████████████████
Date: Fri, 7 Nov 2008 07:34:36 -0800
To: ██████████████████████████████
Cc: Stacy Doris ██████████████████████
Subject: Re: Manifesto

Dear ██████,
Quick note, a busy day—just to say we're glad you were totally tickled.

And to say that for us the manifesto is completely specific to Poetry—as Sartre's lugubrious rant on slime in *Being and Nothingness* is specific to Philosophy, for example, or the way Sade's snatch-stitching is specific to a Political Economy.

love,
Lisa

On Nov 6, 2008, at 10:49 AM, ███████████████ wrote:

Dear Lisa,

I loved reading your manifesto. I was totally tickled.
Unfortunately it's not being included in the portfolio.

I don't imagine that you want to put more time into it, but if you would like to work with it, and us, let's. We need something that's more specific to poetry, vague as that sounds. But we can discuss it if you want to pursue this. Otherwise, we'll give you half the fee, if you return the attached form.

Regardless, I sincerely hope you will begin sending us work, to our online submission manager linked below. I'd love to see you continue to be in touch with ███████████.

Warmly,

████

████████████

Assistant Editor, ████████

████████████████

████████████

████████████

████████

████████████ now accepts electronic submissions:
████████████████████████

From: Lisa Marie Robertson ████████████████
Date: Tue, 21 Oct 2008 12:49:14 -0700
To: ████████████████ Subject: Re: Manifesto

Dear ████████,

We've finished our manifesto!

yours,
Lisa

On Oct 14, 2008, at 6:24 PM, ████████████████ wrote:

Lisa,

Monday is perfect.

Yrs,

████

-----Original Message-----
From: Lisa Robertson ███████████████████ ███████
Sent: Tue 14-Oct-08 6:19 PM
To: ██████████
Subject: Re: Manifesto

Dear ██████████,

Predictably we'd be so happy to have the weekend to continue to work. Would Monday be ok?

best,
Lisa

On Tue, Oct 14, 2008 at 10:49 AM, ███████████ ███████████
███████████ wrote:

Hi Lisa,

I hope you and Stacy have been well. And that roses and fire and Perfume are happily working for you.

Tomorrow is our deadline for manifestos. Will you be able to send Me something by the end of the week, or Monday at the latest? We're eager and excited to read your piece.

We're flexible, but have to know what to expect and when.

Warm thanks,
█████
███████████
Assistant Editor, ██████████
███████████████
████████████
████████
████████
██████
████████████ now accepts electronic submissions:
█████████████████████

On 9/9/08 2:26 PM, "Lisa Robertson" ████████████████████
wrote:

Dear ████████, Stacy and I are thrilled about this! Onward Manifesto of Roses!

yours,
Lisa

On Mon, Sep 8, 2008 at 9:47 AM, ███████████████████
█████████████ wrote:

Dear Lisa,

I trust your instinct for this implicitly. Please follow your fist feeling.
We're very eager to read what you and Stacy will create.

Furthermore, I'm very interested in your other collaborations. As it
happens I had just forwarded information about Nathalie Stephens to
██████████, our senior editor, last week.

Thanks again for being part of this. I can't wait to see where this
takes us.

Warm regards,
██████

On 9/5/08 7:19 PM, "Lisa Robertson" ██████████████████████ wrote:

Dear ██████████,

Well I amicably disagree with you about what will most interest
readers. All of the energy of what I do comes from collaborative
relationships! This one with Stacy currently is more formalized
than my writing collaborations have been for some time. And at
the same time I'm collaborating with friends in Vancouver and
Chicago—Allyson Clay and Nathalie Stephens—on a video that
will be produced by the Western Front in Vancouver. So I'm feeling
that collaboration is what I'm doing in my life right now, apart
from teaching. But apart from that, the history of manifestoes
is collaborative!! It seems to me that the anarchic pleasure of
manifestoes for readers is generated by the collective pleasure of
movements!

I would love to be able to persuade you. From a movement of two.

yours,
Lisa

On Fri, Sep 5, 2008 at 3:24 PM, ██████████ ██████████
█████████████ wrote:

Hi Lisa,

I'm delighted that you're interested! I love the sound of The Perfume
Recordist. And I just read your and Stacy Doris's Poetics Statement
online. This idea, though, should have a separate life in relation to
the manifesto. I'll explain.

We're most interested in the driving mechanism of your poems—or the Force or fire and perfume of Lisa Robertson—and so will our readers. The Texture of the entire portfolio will benefit from a statement by you alone.

However, I would love to talk about The Perfume Recordist with ███████████████ and also with our audio engineer ███████████████, who has been designing podcasts for every issue of ████████████. We can bring to life your project online, to coincide with the print appearance. Another option is to open a thread on the ██████████ blog, about The Perfume Recordist. It'd be amazing to make it work on all these levels. I can't speak for ███████████████, but we regularly work this way. I imagine they'll find this opportunity as irresistible as I do. ██████████ will flip for it I assure you. Of course I can't promise anything, but I want to try. I really believe in where this is all going. The first step is the manifesto, on which this all hinges.

By the way, I'm close friends with ████████████████, whom I know you know. She said to say so, and hello. I attended your reading for ████████████████ some time ago and wanted to introduce myself then. Alas, I've saved all my eagerness till now.

Please let me know if this all makes sense. The layers I've just introduced might confuse things.

Yours,

Assistant Editor, ████████

██████████████████ now accepts electronic submissions:

On 9/5/08 4:27 PM, "Lisa Robertson" ███████████████████ wrote:

Dear ███████████,

This sounds very interesting! I do have a question. I have begun working collaboratively with the San Francisco poet Stacy Doris. A week ago, as The Perfume Recordist, we presented a 2 hour digital sound installation/performance, in Vancouver. We have many ideas, and together, much vigour. I wonder if you would be interested in receiving a collaborative manifesto from The Perfume Recordist?

Yours in fire and perfume,
Lisa

On Fri, Sep 5, 2008 at 10:41 AM, ██████████████ ██████████
██████████████████ wrote:

Dear Lisa Robertson,

I'm so excited to contact you on behalf of ████████ and
█████████, for what we hope will become a little fireworks show.
We're huge fans of your work and anxious to be in touch about this
and good things to come. I'm writing to ask you to help us celebrate,
with the ████████████████████████████, the centennial of the
Futurist Manifesto. We're inviting ten poets to submit their own
manifestos to be considered for a special portfolio in█████████████
timed to coincide with a live event at ██████████ next February 20.

We will co-sponsor this event with█████████ at which three of the
published manifestos will be read by their authors; the event will
also Feature work by visual artists and musicians, selected by the
curators of the museum, as part of a larger celebration of the Futurist
movement. We will Provide travel and lodging expenses for the three
poets who are selected to participate.

If you're interested, and I very much hope you are, here are the
specs. We're looking for 400 words by October 15, for which we'll
pay $150, if accepted. We have no strict guidelines and understand
the unusual nature of our request. We see it as a fun, provocative
experiment that can take life in interesting, unexpected ways.
Especially in the right hands. Feel free to be dead serious, explosive
a la Marinetti, tongue-in-cheek like O'Hara, or to write something
utterly different of your own devising.

Write back with any questions. Thanks in advance for considering
this. I'm eager to hear your thoughts.

Best regards,
████████
█████████████████
Assistant Editor, ████████
███████████████████████
█████████████████
██████████████
████████████
███████████████████ now accepts electronic submissions:
██████████████████████████

The Perfume Recordist was born from the confused and wildly charged encounter of waves and molecules, a tardive yet opulent (voir peonylike or Venusian) offshoot of early twentieth century Quantum Physics, her roots winnowing back to the great Physic of Avicenna, foundational to Well Being as one would wish to know it, yet in coyest contradiction to the contradiction of Aristotle's *Metaphysics*. In other words, in a flagrant refutation of what's commonly known as logic, the Perfume Recordist finds it her vocation to be beaten and burned until she demonstrates that to be beaten has indeed much in common with being burned, and to be burned has much in common with beating. These beatings and burnings join in layers of raptures, though the Recordist assiduously attempts to avoid both alchemy and redemption in her ecologies of (re) constitutions. The forging of senses entails forgeries? Ha!

- Stacy Doris & Lisa Robertson

Stacy Doris' books written in English include *Knot, Conference, Paramour* and *Kildare*. Written in French are *Parlement* and *La vie de Chester Steven Wiener ecrite par sa femme*. She has co-edited three collections of French poetry including *Christophe Tarkos: Ma Langue est Poetique—Selected Work*.

Lisa Robertson is the author of *XEclogue; Debbie: An Epic; The Weather; Occasional Work and Seven Walks from the Office for Soft Architecture; The Men; Lisa Robertson's Magenta Soul Whip*, and *R's Boat*. A small book of essays, *Nilling*, is forthcoming.

SARAH DOWLING

FROM HINTERLAND B

cold
the
together

Walk into the woods, follow

soil

and

the

the path near the pond. Go left,

I

the

near any of the dark bench areas

and

cold

The main trail is in the shape

my   soil

together

of a horseshoe. The best place

I come to conceptual writing with a scholarly interest in description.

Feminists and queer theorists, among other scholars, have recently attempted to formalize new methods of interpretation that forestall critique in order to offer richer forms of description. We can think of Eve Kosofsky Sedgwick's "reparative reading," Sharon Marcus' "just reading," or Rita Felski's "new phenomenology" as examples of the descriptive turn in critical theory, which is particularly noticeable in the U.S. and in France as a resurgence of the social sciences in the decline of structuralism and poststructuralism. Over the last decade or so, descriptive methodologies have focused on the everyday, casting it not as the object of ideology critique or of denunciatory unveiling, but as something to be described, understood, and lived.

If the critical paradigm exhausts its object, destroying it, the risk of the purely descriptive approach is that in its political quietism it risks assenting to the social as it is given. The descriptive turn, then, may trouble our sense of ethics because in focusing on rich detail it fails to articulate programs of action, and fails to provide a thoroughgoing deconstruction of the ideological forces that shape its object. As Heather Love has recently argued, however, what resounds as an ethical question is more accurately a material one, and a question of social structure. That is, the descriptive turn in critical theory is motivated by the impossibility of finding the right relation to one's object.

I understand conceptual writing as an attempt to account both materially and socially for this relationship, and as an engagement with critical paradigms that trouble the impulse to denunciatory unveiling. Appropriation in particular calls up questions similar to description, which it has often sought to supplant: does appropriation function as literary ideology critique, skewering and depleting the quoted text? Or does it offer a flat re-presentation that ultimately assents to and reproduces the same structures? In my writing I strive to be attentive to the text as material, and thus engage in a re-versioning of form in which a text, often appropriated, is viewed and re-viewed repeatedly. In each instantiation different parts of the text appear, so that this re-versioning describes what is socially visible, and what is not. As much as these objects are unstable, so too is the position from which they would be described, and thus as the text progresses its work is to trace the repeated movements of approach and withdrawal, to describe and to situate the forms of mobile relationality that these movements indicate.

- *Sarah Dowling*

Sarah Dowling's work has appeared in *Action, Yes!, The Capilano Review, EOAGH, GLQ, Jacket, P-Queue, West Coast Line,* and elsewhere. Her first book, *Security Posture,* was published by Snare Books as the winner of the 2009 Robert Kroetsch Award for Innovative Poetry. Her academic work concerns contemporary anglophone poetry that includes more than one language.

BHANU KAPIL

ABIOGENESIS 4-9

Schizophrene [humanimal remix]

Abiogenesis 4: "Watch Mrs. S. talking then turn away."* Always turn away. These are exactly what you think they are. Notes that don't bring happiness; bring landscapes.

They bring "stand on knees to reach food."* A wolf-like existence, a biological tale I wrote before I wrote this, a disaster. It's not exactly working out, this. In fact, there's a strong feeling of *it should be over by now*. Dreamed I left my coat on the aeroplane.

Some notes: a leg, pitted and mute. I took that leg in my arms. And what about London, a long walk through a commercial sector, a sprig of fresh mint tucked into an open pocket? I made an abiogenetic notebook, one that let me die, be close to the person just dead, a year or so out, and me, the **** in a garden and then on a street. Still, when I paused and looked through the shop window, I didn't think "curation." What I saw was a glass table subtly tilted on its side, for all the world to see. A woman was dressing it. She was rubbing a coarse powder all over the glass, dimming the play of the surface magically, by occult means, as if to say, *it's easy*.

Abiogenesis 5: "Rejects too-hot water for bath, saying 'Na, Na, Na.'"* In this part, anything that doesn't look like the self is *relentlessly attached*. Disease imagery. I studied and treated what I'd written until, like the silver geometry on a store-bought skirt, it was no longer elegant. It was no longer metropolitan. It no longer possessed the qualities of a safeguard, of a formal barrier, of bad snow.

Abiogenesis 6: "Kids removed."*

Some notes: I pulled myself up from the floor and cleaned. The grid of the hospital was medieval down to the lateral, bisected courtyard with its mangy trollop of a tree. A crumpled tulip in its bower. And cats. Who left the gate unlatched? Who took the stars down from the wall? Who poured the milk into a shallow bowl?

Abiogenesis 7: "To this date does not come so often for food and drink (in seclusion because of A's death?). Associated with kids, fowl, hyena cub."*

Some notes: I wanted to re-imagine the boundary. Perhaps I should say that I grew up partly in Ruislip. The Park Woods that bounded it were the hunting grounds of King Henry VIII, and were rimmed, themselves, with land forms that kept in the boar. I used to go to those masses and lie down on them, subtly above a city but beneath the plate of leaves. One night I didn't go home. One morning I went there though it was raining. To soften this place would require time travel, which I am not prepared to do. I am not prepared to take off my clothes. I am not prepared to charter or re-organize the cosmic symbols of Sikhism, Anglican Christianity and the Hindu faith. One night, I went home, and my hands were caked in dirt and dew. My skirt was up around my ears. My legs were cold. The insides of my eyes were cold. The bath I took, I couldn't get it hot enough. That night, my eyes turned blue.

Abiogenesis 8: "Plays with cat."* In this one, the part with all the dark in it, a man vomits into a woman's mouth, his green milky eyes inches from hers. I'm sorry, but it's true. Because of this, I'm relieved you are reading this in the country we are in. In London, in New Delhi, it would be a death sentence (for me) for you to be reading this and writing at the same time. *Plays with cat.* No kidding.

Some notes: Pressed my hand to the opalescent glass, airport glass, which was like a plastic sheet held taut over an opening and, in fact, an improvement upon the standard material, Mr. "Breakable"/ Mr. "Not Right Now."

Abiogenesis 9: "Allow Mrs. S to nurse them—look for her (38)."*

Some notes:

. . . .

*I've reached the part of this project where the sexual and relational disorder comes in, and so I have to psyche myself up, as per: an ocean swim. Which ocean? You've got to forget everything you know about what's about to happen, said Kerouac. Just before he *gave up the ghost*, as we say in England, flopping sideways into the arms of Mrs. S, who was a help meet, a secondary mother, an improvement upon an old self, a devil, a can of worms, a slit of fire in a landscape, mid-America, the magma slipping up and out into a furrow.

*I used fragments from a log kept to record the development of feral girls, two girls found living with wolves in 1921. In fact, I had written a book and it was published, an account of this time, the complete dislike a "person" had of coming, hand and foot, into a private shelter. This was the abiogenetic material, the activity both living and dead, a strict focus upon two children who didn't make it past sixteen, which supported: a next set of notes, on schizophrenia. But when I sat down to write, I saw it would take all my energy to go home, as much energy, I sometimes thought, as swimming. Plus, it wasn't schizophrenia. It was the children of schizophrenics I was interested in.

*An account begun, mid-ocean, in a storm. I went to Vimhans in New Delhi. I went to the Institute of Community Health Sciences in London. In Vimhans, in the corridor, I saw a Muslim man on a stretcher propped up against a wall—something vertical when it should have been sideways. His wife was cupping his head. In this institute, head injuries were treated on the same ward as *fear*. In the pharmacy, I met an exhausted woman whose daughter had been hospitalized for the phobia that she would swallow the spoon when she put it in her mouth. Her condition had worsened to the point that if anything even touched her skirt, if one of her children brushed against her thigh, she felt a peristaltic reflex; she felt she was swallowing them too. In the UK, I leaned my forehead against the opaque glass of Kamaldeep Bhui's office; Dr. Bhui, to repeat, a research doctor specializing in migration and mental illness. Waiting for my appointment, I drifted to the end of the corridor on the freezing silver day that had penetrated even the university. Looking down, I saw the red rooftops of the East End stretch out in a crenallate, and then I went home. I documented the corridor then went home. What kind of person goes to London and doesn't meet up with a person as planned? For some time, I lived with my uncle (a mailman) and aunt (a social worker) in a place called Pinner, a place analogous to Queens.

*I've reached the part of the project where I'm hiding in the heart of the tree.

*I interviewed the painter Luke Butler for the pamphlet accompanying his show in Margaret Tedesco's apartment in SF. These are some things he said that didn't make it into the document: "A penis has a blunt, natural, reproductive presence in our lives. And at the same time, it's a monster, it's incredibly unwelcome"; "There's no image for the room of the penis on our world [May have written this down wrong]"; "What am I supposed to do with this? [The penis]"; "The only way sexuality is safe is if it's never touched"; "You can't really touch it." What he said helped me think about a book, the oblivious origins of a book, but it also lent itself to touch. Language was just the first step, it wasn't indelible; it was "an erection," as Luke Butler said, "that was unpredictable." "How very unwanted this very ordinary thing is," he continued, and in the essay that I finally wrote, I did not include the story of his childhood, which took place, in part, in Marin, on the beach. Again, it wasn't mimesis; it was a different kind of replicating contact. It was a way to think.

*I waited for my former lover for a long time, having arrived early, pressed or almost curved around the pillar in the Rijksmuseum. In the hours that followed, I gave myself over to the illogical convention that, having desired someone, that desire now resides in them, the person who contains energies larger than oneself. Like the second generation colonial that I was and am, I watched the energy loop back and forth between myself and the other person, until finally I looked away into the darkness of the huge painting behind us, a landscape lit only by lanterns. It was a Saturday. He had contracted giardia on a recent visit to Morocco, and had to go the bathroom. He was gone for a long time, minutes. I returned to my hotel without waiting; I was ashamed, I had too much surplus energy, I wanted to go home and relax. I wanted to read a book.

I write with an interest in matrices: the diagonal relationships between remnants, sentences that do not go away, and so on. In my current project, "Schizophrene," I'm working out how to fold, tear and re-build vertical or trans-generational space. The work with organizing space—Indian, Pakistani, and British space—triplicates an already water-damaged grid, and what I have noticed, as I continue to extend my narrative, is that this grid has started to fail. The closest I can come to describing this failure is that the surface of the book, whenever I write a section, refracts its contents. This isn't a process of fragmentation. Rather, it feels like trying to write on something that isn't there, as if the bonds of the paper, its basic grasses, culled from a landscape, have started to loosen. How this is worked out through the subject matter is that the schizophrenic herself has started to vibrate. Instead of describing a character or a figure, I'm notating a disseminated "red and black." My question for this project has become: How do I compose/re-compose a body that's pure sensation? Working towards this body, a body not typically visible in diasporic writing, I've found it useful to re-think the concept of a book that can't be written. The failure of my subject to adhere has become the site of my enquiry, rather than a disaster of genre or a collapse of language and form (and not in the good way that such collapses happen in hybrid forms.)

In other words, I've trained myself to think of failure as a conversion threshold. This is from Manuel De Landa's thinking on chemical processes. Just before water boils, it goes flat, and then, abruptly, it changes phase. Similarly, how can I trust that the exhaustion and blankness of an immigrant content, a content that comes close to death, to a certain kind of madness, is a threshold state? The exact moment before something never seen before: appears? Arrives. And that vibratory effects, the loss of form in these primal ways, have their own integrative trajectories?

- Bhanu Kapil

Bhanu Kapil lives in Colorado, where she teaches at Naropa University and Goddard College. She has written four books of experimental prose: *The Vertical Interrogation of Strangers* (Kelsey Street Press), *Incubation: a space for monsters* (Leon Works), *humanimal [a project for future children]* (Kelsey Street Press), and *Schizophrene* (Nightboat Books).

RACHEL LEVITSKY

from *The Story of My Accident is Ours*

PUBLIC SPACE AND PRIVASPHERE

I do not think that this world in which we found ourselves nameless, tagged, and more often than not allowed to physically survive, constitutes that thing which before its obsolescence as a concept was the thing that was thought of as society in the way that society implied a particular sort of (non- or semi-commercial) relationship which existed nearly but not quite squarely outside the operations of the State, with more of its weight being between and among its members, so as to be a thing simultaneously enforced upon us and generated from amongst us, a special contradiction of public and private invented by the then new ruling class before they were completely ruling and when they were installing and maneuvering toward improved conditions in which to be the ruling class, conditions which they advertised as being improved conditions for society, as a whole.

Unlike us, that infant ruling class of yesteryear, which is the mature ruling class presiding over the world in which we live, possessed and adamantly, defensively, eloquently and obsessively defined their 'personalities,' which they thought of as something if not novel then particular, and made ways for it as the public presentation of their desire which took the place of their desire, or so they then proclaimed in a provocatively confident yet demure display.

It came to be that this society of desire-masked-as-personality, which we, the adequately trained, prepared to live as the middle class, were to be seeking as our own personality and for which we were to deny ourselves our own desires and our own personalities, elided its very own self, and became, if not something new, a thing revealed through an ex post facto exposition of the past active discourse (i.e. hindsight), in which we who were certain we were supposed to be like that but didn't know why, and they who felt that because they understood why they *had* to be like that, were able to go on with our habit of fervent activity and not have a palpable impact on each other despite adjacency, proximity and other means of being close to a thing but not part of it.

It is in the fact that the once not-yet-completely ruling class had been able to be first the somewhat ruling class and later the ruling class completely that we learned, we could *see*—no, those of us who came before us could see and come to know, and therefore help us to see and come to know—that a something could come to be where something else was and furthermore that this replacing thing could shift and budge the shape of the rest of things until the shape of things was completely transformed into an exaggerated, or diminutive, or diminished version of the shape of the once new thing once it was no longer new.

Amid the vast and nearly completely unmanageable spaces between us, in the inarticulate detritus of their remainder, we found ourselves and found a place for ourselves—it had been as though we were on different banks of a deep, wide river which we wanted to cross and had been used to crossing before the bridges had been blown up to protect us so that in order to cross we would need to walk for miles along that same river to get to a bridge still standing and in doing so find ourselves in a dangerous confrontation with or in the employ of those who had come here to watch over us or those who had also happened upon them and come to be in their employ and therefore be required to go after us. In these spaces we discovered that we belonged neither to the corporate body, nor to any of the small, more digestible parts from which it gained its most agreeable profit, nor to any anachronistic notion of a "society" at large, nor to any of the specific spheres which were thought to derive from this, The Large, always growing ever larger, as a whole.

STATEMENT ON CONCEPTUAL POETICS

Begins: Otherwise how could it be?

This statement comes in very late though has been being considered for one year. Taking advantage of this fact, watching the middle aged stuffy gentleman of BP, Mobile Exxon, Chevron &tc. the spectacle of U.S. Congressional hearings. But I will use them, to consider consideration, of form and of content.

Begins: How could it be otherwise?

There is no accident. We white stuffy people walk around white space asserting it's an accident. The gentleman from Holland who would prefer to keep a low profile is regretting it. Regretting the "small people." Who will soon be out of sight.

The piece here included, "Public Sphere and Privaspace," is from a novel: *The Story of My Accident is Ours*. This novel began while I was looking at the faces of the then very young WTO protesters in the Battle of Seattle and other skirmishes of the global anti-capitalist movement of the late 90's through the early aughts. I'd been to some of the meetings here and there and had been impressed by the different emotional register of this generation of radical activists. Also of the sophistication, the areas where I and my generation had to evolve, that seemed to be the air this new group breathed. Their ease with consensus, their multiple gender inclusivity, their resistance to dominant racial hierarchies, for examples. It takes eternal war to hold the border tight. I mean all those stuffy white bodies asserting their right and good, fortressing in defiance of the spilling over tendencies of nature and culture which Liz Grosz outlines in "The Natural in Architecture and Culture" (*Architecture from the Outside*, MIT, 2001). I began to imagine the world as these young activists might have grown in it, an extreme form (another extreme came on the heals of that, growing up under Bush, the condition of my current students' lives). I am trying to formulate both the radical inclusivity and the reinvention of the world which has been so extremely cleared out and assaulted on every level as the necessity of these activists, their work, as they are imagined by me here. I am trying to do this with the prose sentence, with the pronoun 'we,' by way of an excess of prepositions, and the painful extension of my already thinking. I agree with the editors about the definition of Conceptualism, for, as long as I have tried to define myself outside of it I have failed. But I did want to say how much I enjoy it, though it grinds me, this pressing up against the problems of thinking that are just beyond me and finding an opening via the elasticity of a sentence. The sentence, like a B. McClintock seed of maize, will reveal both its mechanisms and possibilities when it is examined closely and for long enough, as will a list of first lines of Dante's *Inferno* translated, or the taunt of an extremely skinny sonnet.

- Rachel Levitsky

Rachel Levitsky is the author of the book length serial poems *Under the Sun* (Futurepoem, 2003) and *NEIGHBOR* (UDP, 2009), as well as five poetry chapbooks. Her prose publications include *Renoemos* (Delete Press, 2010) and a novel, *The Story of My Accident is Ours* (Futurepoem, 2011). Four mini-essays on The Poetics of Confinement can be found online at the Poetry Project Blog. She teaches Writing and Literature at Naropa University's Summer Writing Program, Bard Prison Initiative and Pratt Institute. She is a member of the Belladonna* Collaborative.

LAURA MORIARTY

THE WRITING PRACTICE
FORMERLY KNOWN AS

Experimentality in writing is universally acknowledged to comprise innovation, pushing the limits of literary genres or combining genres. These days, there seems to be an impulse to name experimental writing practice, perhaps from a desire to distinguish contemporary writing from older innovative practices or from what could be called traditional writing. The word "experimental" has been used in literature for a long time. Émile Zola is sometimes mentioned as the first one to use the term, which, in his case, referred to fiction written to be "natural," meaning something like "realistic." The phrase "experimental writing" appears in a 1956 exchange among Jack Spicer, Robert Duncan and Robin Baser called "Table Talk." We think of this group as the Duncan or Spicer Circle or Berkeley Renaissance, depending on our orientation. Beats existed at the same time and the New York School. Earlier there were Objectivists, Surrealists, etc. and Neo-Surrealists are still with us. The term "language poetry," often with initial caps, has occasionally been used to define all experimental poetry practice but seems more usefully applied to a group of writers of about my own generation who began writing in the seventies, came to be known in the eighties and who are still active. I am not aware of anyone who uses the term "post language" to define themselves, though there must be someone who does.

I recently participated in a conference that was called "post_moot" by its organizers, cris cheek, Cathy Wagner and Bill Howe. They used the term "post_moot" rather than employ the dreaded "post language" or "post" anything, as well as to emphasize the communality of current practice. "Moot" means "meeting" with the additional senses of "discussion" and "judging." Many writers prefer not to characterize their writing or label it at all. A few of those haven't minded being published in an A Tonalist context but they tend to be skittish when it comes to reading or other events. In the blog, *A Tonalist Notes*, I have proposed the use of "A Tonalist" to refer to a kind of writing which could loosely be described as experimental lyric or anti-lyric. The proposition was and is somewhat personal, possibly fictional. (Standard Schaefer and I are writing a novel in which A Tonalist issues are worked out.) A Tonalism is also conceptual in that it is an act of group formation about the fact of group formation, literally an "experiment." The blog came out of an essay poem I was writing called *A Tonalist*, now a book from Nightboat Books.

The poem is an *ars poetica,* a memoir, an homage to writers whose work I admire and a discussion of the community in which we find ourselves. The results of this "experiment" are not in yet.

Notes on Conceptualisms is an interesting and useful response not only to the impulse to name but to the need to examine contemporary writing practice and acknowledge that it is an activity shared by many. When I first encountered the book I didn't expect to be implicated by its argument, thinking it was a narrower term than what I later realized was intended. Knowing both Rob Fitterman and Vanessa Place and having read their work, I assumed that "conceptualism" referred to writing characterized by specific constraints or procedures, use of appropriation and often utilizing aspects of performance. In retrospect I see that from my place deep within the writing world, the various kinds of practice seem very distinct. Like many writers, I am exquisitely aware of how a person's writing reflects who she has read and studied with. But then I realized that, in the sense that it is presented in *Notes on Conceptualisms,* conceptual writing is done by many of the people I read, perhaps including myself. So perhaps I am both conceptualist and A Tonalist.

At first, as I've said, A Tonalist referred to a particular kind of practice, but as I wrote it I realized that the techniques involved, the "style," even the surface of the writing to which I refer in the poem, was less important to me than other considerations. These were a bit ephemeral and yet seemed quite real. An elegiac tendency, awareness of all the writing techniques available and a willingness to use them and yet continue to have an engagement with prosody, with the word and the line, that might seem old fashioned—these were some of the characteristics I ascribed to what I first called Tonalism, after the old art movement, and then eventually began to call A Tonalist. A Tonalist practice, as I imagine it, might involve fewer constraints and procedures than conceptual writing but maybe there is no difference. There is a little crossover in personnel. There is no index in *A Tonalist* but I discuss and quote a number of writers in the poem. The two writers whose work appears in both *A Tonalist* and in the index of *Notes on Conceptualisms* are Renee Gladman and Yedda Morrison. It is also worth mentioning, in spite of my emphasis on the authors (the index in *Notes on Conceptualisms* is of books) that *A Tonalist* shares the conceptualist impatience with "authorial voice." And yet one can argue infinitely on that point, as one recognizes and values the particular and consistent work of the writers mentioned in the index.

There is a generational aspect to all of this. Older writers or those of the past whose work is clearly antecedent to the thinking in *Notes on Conceptualisms*—Jackson Mac Low, Clark Coolidge, Bernadette Mayer, to name just a few—are not mentioned. Mostly the index consists of books whose authors are in their thirties and forties or younger. I entirely support this approach which seems to move writing beyond the old names and considerations of the past. My own impulse, as a member of the aforementioned older generation, is to use *A Tonalist* to name a kind of writing that existed at the same time as language writing, New Narrative and other practices from the '70s and '80s but, not to restate or reargue those old arguments. Instead, I wanted to see if I could find (and did find) what I thought of as A Tonalist writing by younger writers. Like *Notes on Conceptualisms*, perhaps even more so, A Tonalist is not a manifesto. *A Tonalist* needed to be written as a poem because the example of the practice seemed the most compelling way to refer to it and I was discovering "A Tonalist" as I was writing it. I think this phenomenon also occurs in *Notes on Conceptualisms* whose composition and presentation as notes seems like an example and aspect of the practice being named and discussed. Vanessa Place's wonderful essay "Ventouses," which forms the second part of the book, is satisfyingly oblique. The visual art world seems to serve here as an allegory that refers back to a recalcitrant writing world "frozen" in many of its practices. The sources from the past that Place mentions, along with the few mentioned in the "Notes" by Rob Fitterman and herself, happen to include a list of heroes that I, and I think many fellow A Tonalists, also value. Robert Burton, Laurence Sterne, Francisco Goya, Louise Bourgeois, Lessing's Laocoön, Robert Smithson, Mark Kelly, Gerhard Richter, and W. G. Sebald are among those mentioned. Have these people been monitoring my dreams?

"Conceptualism" is a term from the visual art world. "Tonalism" is also a term from art and "atonalism" is a term from music. However, unlike both "tonalism" and "atonalism," which are essentially historical movements, conceptualism is a contemporary (if decades old) art activity very much practiced, recognized and discussed. To borrow the term seems useful because it implicitly asks from the reader the same consideration as the viewer of conceptual art might expect to offer the artist. This consideration, the patience with practices that are thoughtful, possibly nonlinear and might be initially off-putting, can be surprisingly difficult to come by in the contemporary literary "thinkership" (as readers and by implication scholars and teachers are described in *Notes on Conceptualisms*). And this resistance to conceptualist literary practice exists despite a century of writing, starting with Gertrude Stein and working through many generations, which demands such consideration from its readers.

So am I a Conceptualist? Is A Tonalist a subset of Conceptualism as Kasey Mohammad once suggested Flarf and A Tonalist were of each other? In the '80s, I used to get asked all the time whether I was a language poet. My responses were various. I often said yes, socially, but otherwise no.

The difficulty of answering the inevitable follow-up question about what I actually was formed part of the impulse toward creating A Tonalist. So the answer is broadly, yes. The writing that Fitterman and Place include and celebrate in *Notes on Conceptualisms* is that of the community I have long been part of. My detachment from authorial voice, my acceptance of constraints, appropriation, and other techniques mentioned in the book are all evidence that I am a conceptualist. The commitment to "failure" in *Notes on Conceptualisms* is similar to my use, in *A Tonalist*, of the word "doubt." Both terms seem to suggest a lack of closure in the writing itself and a suspicion of careerism and the usefulness of "success." A short quote from *A Tonalist* about "doubt" will be suggestive:

> "Not a movement so much as a mood, an orientation, a realization that much that seemed forbidden is in fact required. Doubt, for example, especially self-doubt. A man can be in love with his equivocation. He can be equivocal about his doubt. He can use his knowledge against himself."

I was about to say that the differences between A Tonalist and Conceptualisms could only be perceived by an A Tonalist or a conceptualist when I realized that there is one more difference and this one might be a deal breaker. A Tonalist admits the presence of a kind of spiritual and yet physical aspect to the sum of the writing it includes. Again, from the poem:

> "Spiritual realism in which spiritual is defined as a formal practice relating to a belief in love but not of a person. Or of a person. And realism is verisimilitude in drag."

As a possible contrast I offer this observation from a paragraph about Kant in *Conceptualisms*:

> "Note that Conceptualisms maintains only the concept of "is" (e.g. materiality or other invocation) is permanent."

What I am suggesting might not be different from what a conceptualist would assert or believe, but it feels different. Spiritual realism, not meaning religiosity, but suggesting a spiritual and physical practice and thinking is included in A Tonalist because of a connection with death that was, for me, part of the reason for naming and describing the writing. With A Tonalist, I wanted to assert a practice that could exist in the places in which I had found myself as a result of the deaths I had experienced. I wanted to include the physical, mental, economic and the other challenges typical of a life. And there is also a level of love, among friends and extending out to the community, that I recognized in writing *A Tonalist* and in introducing it that is not scholarly, objective, or critical. This love is not meant to be a panacea that cancels the need for politics but the kind that requires politics. *A Tonalist*, like *Notes on Conceptualisms*, is a book and it continues to be a series of actions, questions and possibilities.

Laura Moriarty's books include *A Tonalist*, an essay poem from Nightboat Books, the novels, *Cunning* and *Ultravioleta*. *A Semblance: Selected and New Poems, 1975–2007* came out from Omnidawn in 2007. She won the Poetry Center Book Award in 1983, a Wallace Alexander Gerbode Foundation Award in Poetry in 1992, a New Langton Arts Award in Literature 1998 and a Fund for Poetry grant in 2007. She has taught at Mills College and Naropa University, among other places, and is Deputy Director of Small Press Distribution. For more, see the blog *A Tonalist Notes*.

REDELL OLSEN

FROM PUNK FAUN: a bar rock pastel

for YOU

> the English licks of lineage upgrown American and shiny
> come homey bright glorious plasma twins of RECS and UECS
> before whose throne refined blend of lovelies in aged patina
> drive up frequency for YOUR bespoke bar rock targets for
> YOU who also carry home theater options and for YOU who
> do not require a stand to shed joy with safety glass for YOU
> whose hearts beep for manufacture for YOU who provide
> free support upon receipt or fresh from toll for YOU who fix
> displays of blah or brandings and for YOU at edutainment
> auditions for YOU not sworn off surfers in antic whine

in homage

> to the cupids in Domenichino's *The Assumption of Mary
> Magdalen into Heaven*, 1617-1621, I will ascend the escalator
> at Waterloo Station wearing only a wing shaped ruff fashioned
> from today's newspaper.

ceilings

> two breathe clouds across the sky to one another
> being scarred by birds they stand on wavy air
> push on neighbouring particles to make tunes I
> permanently bound into the stuff of naked walls
> slaked lime paste and coarse marble on canapés
> between points of compression the china bones
> as see through this longitudinal nicety gasps up
> tempo as do I I do resounds over shelves rusty
> in casting shapely hearts or how the head holds
> a flood marker gauges stubborn wet lime marked
> in place of face grinds pigment for speaking out
> of rheuming it through violently spun air blubbers
> a funnel for listening with what cannot be fanfare

stronger for liquid intake concrete quibbles stick
but in itself does not vibrate stocks of the same
if all surfaces are magnets then we might travel
cheaply outside to find ourselves encrusted at
the navel with the body of a man or the torso of
a horse and buy it up in expectation of the pain
in kick that is deployed as a mammal might be
in enemy waters where even dolphins have teeth
pulling away fast from what look like shells *AWOL*
or just meeting up with the other local marine life
to search for patterns at every nth click tears
past Standard Gas Stations gestations in series
painted in black and orange *L'AMOUR or L=I=S=P*
spelled out in ribbons rime can be thick enough
to resemble shades enchanted for repel of damage

disposable dailies

designed for everyday life but mostly out of range
between various small fires nightly on TV a dog
chews a skirt and a scooter carries a bucket of
water as a chariot carries a peacock to a jolly good
show at the arthouse battery while a midriffed
attack bluffs an achingly breathless feat driving
a transit van freeway *GALATEA* rolling out of lanes
into a dark blue sky permanently lost in gold plate
tossed out after the main course into the Tiber
sights for a banked sore eye in mock tapestry
gone with the job of painting in the curtains or
straddling forced cirrus and falling from tromped
oils done neatly ice effect grates for furnishing
reflections in the droplets just like a real life
wrestle with a lion or an ally or a landscape hidden
in a wall your breast is at an angle as if slipped
off by some cumulous translation as restoration
of a fixed point from which to survey an imaginary
view from around the back as some future watcher
positioned cornered up walls garlanded outlandish
with plants just discovered happily already there

put some thrash on and stuff your piney whispers

of days spent pasturing
ready-made containers
boxed lap-tips control
snacks chemise finalists
on hands free daytime
stuff my rented cup
floods o'er basement
patent winners hum
floral etch-a-sketch
rims of murky family
wax ornamental dry
instant crystal self goo

put some thrash on and stuff your piney whispers

two-handled so goods
at being in the queue
newly made of tinned
fresh out still chemical
works keeps on at use
less spoils counter sell
beans policy grow suck
swollen after fall pouts
back to task imagines
train for desk bound
bleach marvels strike
quip roots from Hades

put some thrash on and stuff your piney whispers

touch feeling marks as
stone a groove known
of metals cash or piss
factory *ahhs* for sonic
reducers of nightingale
wafting lean on blast
hearty mind of karaoke
anxious for cultivates
dead good in plastic
plants tonight I aim
bucolic is overheard
not born a billy-goat

put some thrash on and stuff your piney whispers

> fed future bleeps up
> demographic shapes
> hides of mutual calf
> yoked pod celebrants
> kiss competitors goth
> products in hair spill
> libations aisle slick
> lips rung from shot
> age shred pack info
> skins echo plasma
> kids eaten alive tax
> estate granted bleats

put some thrash on and stuff your piney whispers

> songs at locked doors
> out disobey certainties
> let collagen improve
> piping let the mouse
> taste the pitch let out
> for the split-oops voice
> or belly-crawl let's off
> give snort to the peck
> let's move to pieces
> let's lay in sheaves of
> office stationery ground

in homage

to Luca Giordano's *The Fall of The Rebel Angels* (1666) I will jog on a specially designed running machine while chanting "Down With The Rebels" until I fall down from exhaustion. I will be wearing a blue tracksuit, gold trainers and carrying a coffee cup branded to match the tattoo of the bare breasted siren on my right hand. If commissioned to make this piece for Saudi Arabia, I will remove the siren, leaving only her crown. The power generated by my run will be available as a limited edition of units for any members of the audience to purchase at a reduced market rate and suitable for a variety of domestic applications.

NOT, A CONCEPTUAL ART POETICS

Not the poem as idea as idea but ideas in words as words. Not that the poem does not think that words are not made of materials. Not the dematerialization of the poem but the intermittent re-materialization of the word as object. Not an assumption of language as transparent but an exploration of its densities. Not that what is the matter with poetry matters to art much anyway. Not that it sells anything. Not that the poem can even call itself a work. Not that it wants to work even. Not that poetry is not thinking matter. Not that poetry is not a matter of thinking. Not that the idea or concept is the most important aspect of the poem. Not that poems are without materials called words, called concepts sometimes. Not that poems are without these. Not that these do not call into question concepts and make them happen, or not. Not that conceptual is the only way of calling thinking in art that. Not that the poem does not think for itself already before it gets called one. Not that it does not already consider language as a conceptual figure. Not that the poem is not aware of traditional verse forms. Not that it does not know how to be one of them sometimes. Not that it is not one ever. Not that this is anything new in poetry and not necessarily conceptual in the least. Not that all of the planning and decisions need be made beforehand. Not that whose hand is writing is not mattering. Not that this poem could not be found already existing elsewhere as a roadside sign. Not that poetry can proceed further without an exploration into the materials necessary. Not that the execution of the poem is a perfunctory affair that does not care if it is one. Not that the form becomes a machine that makes the poem by forgetting what it was made of. Not that it is not natural. Not that the poem does not question nature. Not that it is natural. Not that the poem should forget this. Not that the poem knows what is understood as poetry but is questionable as that. Not that the poem knows everything including what it might be. Not that the poem could be just that. Not that the poem could be one necessitates it being one. Not that art is anxious about what poetry thinks is a matter for considering. Not that art thinks much about what matter is poetry. Not that the poem could be anything more is a matter for writing.

- Redell Olsen

Redell Olsen's publications include: *Book of the Fur* (Rempress, 2000), *Secure Portable Space* (Reality Street, 2004) and the collaboratively edited *Here Are My Instructions* (Gefn Press, 2004). From 2006—2010 she was the editor of the online journal of *How2*. Her poetry is included in *Infinite Difference: Other Poetries by UK Women Poets* (Shearsman, 2010) and recent projects have involved texts for performance and film: *Newe Booke of Copies* (2009), *Bucolic Picnic (or Toile de Jouy Camouflage)* (2009) and *The Lost Swimming Pool* (2010). *Punk Faun: a bar rock pastel* is forthcoming from Subpress in 2012.

CHUS PATO

FROM *HORDES OF WRITING*

translated by Erín Moure

i

From the other side, where we're alone with time and *I* is an innumerable that multiplies and decentres itself

given that this narrator (of "Thermidor") –who still has no name and whose contract the author didn't renew as she's inadequate and inconsistent– couldn't permit herself the luxury of not being osmotic even though yes she wore a trench coat.

The account is autobiographical in that the words that form it are biography

ferocity writes naturalizing poetics; its torpour opiatic, geometric.

ii

Emotional tension runs high. She orders a shot of J&B. She evaporates (we find her by the shine of her boots, but her face blurs). Not even the most infinitesimal part of the tiniest measure of distance between her and her surroundings: guardians of the ambiguous, conversations and above all the fusion with the black vessel that is really a theatre. Words, syntactic bits, reverberate in her eardrums, right to her gut. If what –cinematographic– she's now watching is the prosthesis of dream, what sort of technology is the poem?

iii

Because of him, Oedipus, his alabaster skin, his
Nile-green eyes, his body hunched in the bulwarks,
the sounds of his harmonica, she forgot her sworn
faith in reason, belief in progress. It wasn't then
that she learned the virtues of the dildo and the
equivalency of bodies.

iv

And you, who can never fit together names and
objects.

v

Since she doesn't remember, she takes notes. She
glosses coagulations (on the skin).

Altai, Yablonovy, Stanovoy (mountains)
Darfur, Kimberley (plains)
Orinoco, Mekong (deltas)
Challenger (tomb)
Ob, Yenisey, Amur, Huang He (rivers)

vi

And the delta, that tongue of earth, full of light,
advances.

alpha. --

The cleft is conventional, a seismic movement of low intensity, in the synthetic pavement of a garden. Underground, the same fracture.

It's possible to fit lyrical-sanguine series into each segment of the opening (yellow fog that lifts light over snowy landscapes) or into each side of the three types of hexagonal lattice in the Central Place Theory of Christaller

nothing desires to be written

Hölderlin

Renaissance.

. . . .

Once in a while the birds aren't scared of me
I'm almost part of the flock

***

In the shade of 12 shrubs, an alder and three apple trees on a lawn twenty by eighty metres, at 3 p.m. and 14 days before the spring equinox // the hours tick by. They reproduce the root.

In this snowbound winter the only possible dialogue is with the birds

time, two-faced: a felicitous unfolding of bodies in space, the cold, the heron

the crack in the same sheet of grass

omega. ––

the eyes are those of a dead woman, she writes / /
absorbed in the fracture
dream of a verse by Pondal

what she sees are all the cities sinking into the core
of the planet
and the seas

the fissure is a cataclysm spookily illuminated
Earth's double and shadow

its edges, a sprinkling of very pale ash

enlightened.

**

it's true that death is here a thick reversible wool
overcoat

the flagstones are felt, grey with light streaks

and the most concentration on a discourse, is that
of the sleeping woman

. . . .

the layer of algae is pain, it rolls in the waters / / and
light, its beauty

It's not that i believed that communication flows
according to Christaller's hierarchy, what fascinates
me is imagining this spume enfolding the planet and
plunging into its depths, and oceans pouring through
the openings

thus the NiFe (astral) would know the joy of whales

and the sandal of

Empedocles.

severity / / thallophytes

By way of statement from Chus Pato: excerpt from an alphabetic interview with Aurelio Castro after the publication of *Hordes of Writing*. Translated by Erín Moure, the letters A, B and C.

Animality, Auschwitz

Animality is not a remnant left to us. It's the same as the *cyborg*. A machinic or animal humanity, because society forecloses both, impedes identities, subjects, impedes us from being. In *Hordes of Writing* I tried the impossible, to write from the animal. But it can't be transmitted: the roar, the howl of the mammal that I am. Even so, I thought there were ways to arrive at its truth...What is an animal? It is a being without prostheses. That uses its body completely. What are we? An animal in which most of the organs have retired to *comfort* zones. We need prostheses for everything. Language is one of those first prostheses; the voice, that turns into language. I often ask myself what kind of prosthesis a poem is. What organ it replaces. Animality is that social site where power makes slaves of us, as happened in Auschwitz. The model is not the factory, not the society of knowledge, not computerization or technique. The model is the *lager*. And the desire of Capital to convert the world into an infinite *lager*. Behind any of its constructions you'll find the extermination camp. The oppression by men of women also has this sense. Women had no soul, they told us, and our first struggle was for the soul. Slaves also lack one. The proletariat never had a soul. I put myself on the other side of the coil. Effectively, we are animals, and because I am an animal, they can't condemn me. Because I am animal, I am a subject with rights.

Biology

...Just as to the animal, we will never accede to the body. It is ideologized, totally written from within culture. A corporeal writing is even less possible. The liver does not write, it has no way to do so. Nor does menstrual blood. No one can return to Paradise. But exiting biology is to be capable of getting myself out of discourse on the body. What do you know about your body? Well, three things you learned in science class. We have to pull back this curtain and see what's behind it.

And see what is possible?

And see what is possible. Because that potential sustains us constantly. If we are anything, it's body. You learn it when you age and are more conscious of death. And language is the shuddering of that body.

Is Paul Celan an anti-poet?

There's a definition of the poet in *Hordes of Writing* that echoes what Agamben says of human beings: "the true poet is he/she whose muse was integrally destroyed." What happens? The poet keeps writing, regardless. It fits with Paul Celan. His muse was destroyed but there's a remnant from which he writes that testifies to destruction. This remnant is an implant of future. Is Celan an anti-poet? No, Celan is a non-poet. But a non-poet—and here the syllogism concludes—is whoever can be a poet, after Auschwitz.

Has he marked your modernity?
Not just him, more have marked me. But reading Celan, in the measure that I've been able to understand him, above all in his last books, was to admit: "this is it, there's no going back."

Galician poet **Chus Pato** (Ourense, Galicia 1955) has published: *Urania* (Ourense, Calpurnia, 1991), *Heloísa* (A Coruña, Espiral Maior, 1994), *Fascinio* (Muros, Toxosoutos, 1995), *Nínive* (Vigo, Xerais, 1996), *A ponte das poldras* (Santiago de Compostela, Noitarenga, 1996; 2ª ed.: Vigo, Galaxia, 2006), *m-Talá* (Vigo, Xerais, 2000), *Charenton* (Vigo, Xerais, 2003), *Hordas de escritura* (Vigo, Xerais, 2008) and *Secesión* (Vigo, Galaxia, 2009).

Three of her works are translated into Spanish, *Un Ganges de palabras* (Málaga, Puerta del Mar, 2003, ed. and tr. Iris Cochón), *Heloísa* (Madrid, La Palma, 1998, tr. Xosé Manuel Trigo), and *m-Talá* (Buenos Aires, pato en la cara, 2009, tr. Teresa Arijón and Bárbara Belloc). Three of her works exist in English, *Charenton* (Exeter and Ottawa, Shearsman Books & BuschekBooks, 2007), *m-Talá* (Exeter and Ottawa, Shearsman Books & BuschekBooks, 2009), and *Hordes of Writing* (Exeter and Ottawa, Shearsman Books & BuschekBooks, 2011), all translated by Erín Moure. Her poetry has also been translated into Portuguese, Serbian, Polish, German, Italian, classical Arabic and has appeared in several anthologies.

Nínive received the Losada Diéguez Prize, and *Hordas de escritura* (*Hordes of Writing* in 2011, tr. Erín Moure) the Spanish National Critic's Prize and the Losada Diéguez Prize.

JULIE EZELLE PATTON

D' FENCE SAYS IT ALL
(COMMONBOUNDSOUNDGROUND)

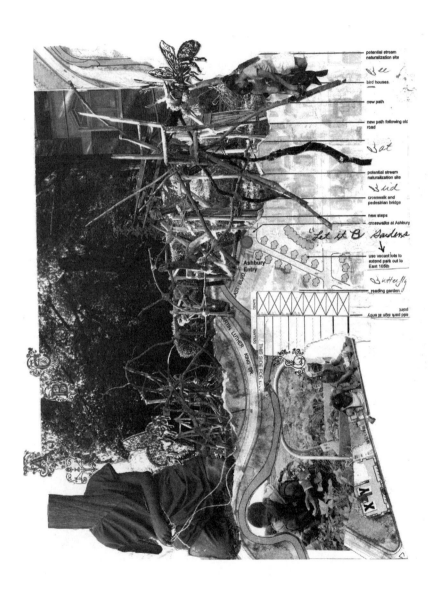

Julie Ezelle Patton is the author of *Using Blue To Get Black, Notes for Some (Nominally) Awake,* and *A Garden Per Verse (or What Else do You Expect from Dirt?).* Julie's work has appeared in *((eco)lang)-(uage(reader)), Critiphoria,* and *nocturnes.* Patton is a recipient of an Acadia Arts Foundation Grant (2008), a New York Foundation for the Arts Poetry Fellowship (2007), and a Bates College Green Horizons Fellowship (2006). She has taught at Naropa, New York University, Schule für Dichtung (Vienna, Austria) and Case Western University. She has performed at the Stone, Jazz Standard, and noted international venues. Patton is founding director of the Salon des Refuses Gallery and Let it Bee Garden in Cleveland's Glenville neighborhood, and resides in the "East Pillage" of New York City.

KRISTIN PREVALLET

THE BLUE MARBLE PROJECT

an experiment of particulars

> The eye I look out of
> or hands I use,
> feet walking,
> they stay particular.
> - Robert Creeley, from "The Eye"

> In FEAR OF ABSTRACTION, she sidles up to a Particular.
> "Hey there, you with the stars in your eyes," she
> whispers, "love never made a fool of you, I bet.
> - Ann Lauterbach, from *The Night Sky II*

In love/fear with abstraction or in awe of our bodies in space: what is particular comes from the vantage point (the eye) through which we are seeing. What is clear is that fragments construct (piece by piece) our day-to-day lives, and when we notice them we fill in our memories and activate our brain—which works best when filling in gaps.

The pop-spiritual gurus circulate the same idea over and over again: be intentional, grateful, and present as you move through the world. Good advice, but often hard to integrate with daily life. "I might have been myself minus amazement, that is, someone completely different," writes Wisław Szymborska in her poem "Among the Multitudes." And yet, it's not easy being amazed. It's not easy to practice seeing every day as an exercise in activating one's most innate and personal vision. After all, how many surprises can a person conjure up in one day?

We traverse a daily landscape through a personalized map: The route from the bed to the kitchen table. The walk from the front door to the bus. The crack tripped over ten times before remembering to avoid it. The building with the blue door, the one with the brass lion door-knocker. The dim hallways of office buildings that connect one door to another door. Your personalized map of your daily landscape involves knowing which doors will open, and which you need to pass by.

In a city or suburb, the grid of streets is central to a person's daily landscape and like people, each is recognizable as a larger category of "street," and yet each is unique. Some streets have recognizable markers: houses, yards, trees, trashcans, newspaper stands, mailboxes, signs, painted lines to keep the traffic going in the right directions. Other streets are cut from different molds: sidewalks where passersby can pass, look around, hurriedly march ahead, feed meters, walk in and out of doorways, insert quarters into telephone booths or gumball machines. Each passerby negotiates the route. What is more public than the street? And yet, what is more personal than the walks, or the drives, we take through streets, every day?

Most U.S. cities are in the midst of an identity crisis, negotiating between the "local particulars" and what architect and theorist Rem Koolhass calls "the generic city." It's a battle between Mo's Diner and Starbucks, Heizer's family pharmacy and Rite-Aid, The Wicked Wick and Illuminations. Making a city "generic" means each will have a stadium, a Disney Store, and an Applebee's in close proximity. It means that the family can have a full day's outing and never encounter anything that isn't a corporate enclosure. Keeping one's eye out for local businesses, and supporting them, is leading a *vie de résistance*.

And yet, even within the generic city it is possible to have particular experiences. There are wedding proposals made at Starbucks, routine Sunday family trips to Barnes & Noble, and September walks down the school supply aisle at Walmart. No matter how homogenous and corporate, people find their daily landscape wherever it may sprawl out.

In spite of its attempt to take over the landscape, the omnipresent generic city is as impermanent as the five-and-dime, the stagecoach post, and the Roman Colosseum. When thought about in the context of the passing of time, the ages, the eras, or even the century, every city, no matter how homogeneous and well-kept, has already begun to crumble into ruin. The particulars are grounded in the present. No matter how drab, corporate, and homogenous, The Home Depots across the U.S. are the ruins of the future. Their orange signs will be buried along with the layers and layers of trash, first browsed on aisle 4, then quickly consumed and tossed away. Archeologists of the future will revel in the refuse left behind, the remnants of a society that wasted all their energy on producing highly non-degradable objects that had been planned into obsolescence.

Field Note: The Blue Marble Project Phase I
(March 10-20, 2004)

The blue marble project was an attempt to memorialize public phone booths (working and not working) that I passed every day while pushing my baby in her stroller through our neighborhood in Greenpoint, Brooklyn. Video killed the radio star and cell phones have rendered phone booths obsolete. They exist, but when broken they are not fixed unless they are in corporate malls or in areas coveted as "public space." Cell phone in hand, I realized that I stopped *seeing* phone booths—whereas five years ago (pre-cell phone) I recall always being on the hunt for a pay phone. It bothered me that my perspective on the city map could change so drastically that my vision—my awareness—could alter so significantly.

To memorialize means to mark something as significant – to commit it to memory, and time. So I mapped out all of the phone booths in my neighborhood and set out to test whether each phone was working or not. As I walked, I left behind an opulent blue marble in the change slot. The marble signifies a mark out of context: a person looking for change might be surprised (and possibly annoyed) to find a marble instead of a quarter. Hopefully the person will take the marble as a symbol of good luck, which is what I take good luck symbols to be: ascribing meaning to a thing found in a place where you're not looking for anything in particular. The marble functions as a word on the lookout for a meaning. Every day I followed the same route and returned to the phone booths, checking to see if the marble was still there. There was only one phone booth where the marble remained for over a week: a broken, abandoned one at the corner of Meserole and West Street (now removed).

A monument is commonly understood to be a structure which is fixed in the ground to mark an event, a boundary, or a person who needs to be remembered. There are monuments to battles which show proud men on horses, close to the spot where they achieved their most glorious defeat; there are monuments to wars and monuments to leaders; monuments to significant historical achievements and monuments to unspeakable atrocities. But what about finding monuments that are not affiliated with the past? Can there be a monument to mark the present, where what is monumental is the fact that this moment is fleeing? What about finding monuments in our ever-shifting daily landscape and discovering that what is monumental is the fact that what was once here will no longer be? A monument to a view on the verge of being altered by a building, a monument to a crack in the sidewalk on the verge of being smoothed over, a monument to a tree on the eve of its being felled? Naming such monuments is an exercise in finding particulars in a disposable place—a place that otherwise would have been ignored, not *seen*.

Robert Smithson, the Earthworks artist and writer whose enormous "Spiral Jetty" sculpture still swirls through Rozel Point of the Great Salt Lake in Utah, completed a project he called "Monuments of Passaic." Smithson was born in Clifton, NJ, not far from Passaic, NJ, a town which has undergone consistent change. A suburb on the edge of an industrial wasteland, Passaic has been subject to years of construction. On September 30, 1967 Smithson boarded a Greyhound bus and set off to Passaic, determined to photograph the process of a city becoming "ruins in reverse"—that is, he set out to investigate how cities under construction are rising, not falling, into ruin. In his essay, "A Tour of the Monuments of Passaic, New Jersey" he writes, "This is the opposite of the 'romantic ruin' because the buildings don't *fall* into ruin *after* they are built but rather *rise* into ruin before they are built" (72).

Smithson walked through the changing landscape of Passaic and found monuments not to a time that has passed, but to a time that is present. For example, a drawbridge that rotates in order to let ships pass becomes a "Monument of Dislocated Directions." A crossing of gigantic steel pipes along the riverbed becomes, "The Great Pipes Monument." A pumping derrick with a long pipe attached to it becomes a "Monument with Pontoons: The Pumping Derrick." A series of six large pipes protruding out from the side of a crater, gushing water into the river becomes "The Fountain Monument." Smithson's monument project is an attempt to mark the monuments of the present that are destined to become the ruins of the future. Smithson went in search of the pumping derricks, pontoons, and pipes, those particulars of construction which most of us would ignore because most of us prefer to think about what is to come. But as an artist, Smithson looks for the "holes" in the landscape—those boarded off construction sites which promise to propel the city into the future, and yet are simultaneously anticipating the past-that-is-to-come.

What he reveals through this project is that no landscape is mundane. The landscapes we walk through on a daily basis are changing. Using Smithson's project as a guide, I have come to see the possibility that there are minute monuments (like Blake's "minute particulars") in the present that will help me to track time, to appreciate my *presence* in the present. This idea fills me with both excitement and dread. After all, it's much more realistic to just keep moving forward, to keep on the track, talk on my cell phone and remain steadfast in my forward pace just to make it through the day. It's so much easier to ignore the signposts of the present, the construction projects that are changing the landscape, and therefore the past and present city, before my very eyes.

Field Note: The Blue Marble Project: Phase II
(June 10-20, 2004)

Since 2003, my neighborhood in Greenpoint, Brooklyn has been a construction zone of new developments. The landscape, once ruled by factories, is now littered with cranes, dumptrucks, facades, and the constant noise of drilling. The factories, once the foundation of this working class immigrant neighborhood, are now being converted into luxury condominiums. Penthouse lofts bragging stainless steel appliances and exposed beams have taken over The Mustard Factory, the Pencil Factory, and soon, Domino Sugar. The people who once worked in these factories have long since departed, along with their jobs. It is a landscape corrupted by the ruthless gears of progress; it is on the way to becoming cleaner, wider, more expansive, with city views and plenty of cafes. The wine has improved. The grocery store is stocked with organic produce and ecologically safe toiletries. It smells good now that the factories, once spewing their dry cleaning and paint fumes, have all but disappeared.

Instead of photographing the factories before they transitioned into "ruins in reverse," I mapped out a walk through the warehouses en route to extinction and placed a marble in the crevices of their aged exteriors. The construction happened around my marbles. They were buried, or swept into the trash, and I did not document their return to rubble.

Instead, I attended several community board meetings, wrote letters, and signed petitions to protect certain historical sites, stop trucks from idling all night long, and ensure that the developers set aside a certain percentage of their units for affordable housing. Like these meetings, I have no illusions that my marble project had any effect. For an exercise in public art, it could not have been more private. It was a gesture into a thought process, an experiment to think through an idea and mark a particular place and moment.

I'd like to think that marking monuments in the present is an exercise in observing how the genius of particulars—of seeing what one passes every day, what one takes for granted or even chooses not to observe—can connect us to our local environment. If genius is "the prevailing spirit or distinctive character, of a place, a person, or an era," then to mark this genius of place is to recognize it in the walks we take through our personalized landscapes: this is to honor the local as a site worthy of exploration. To make a passing thing monumental: this is an introverted activism that has no other effect than the movement of mind from one layer of perception to another: a sand bank in the middle of the road that tomorrow will be blown away by a truck's exhaust, a brick on the verge of falling off a building which, in due time, will either fall or be fixed.

References

Koolhaas, Rem and Bruce Mau. "The Generic City" in *S, M, L, XL,* ed. Jennifer Sigler. (New York: Monacelli Press, 1998).

Smithson, Robert. *The Collected Writings,* ed. Jack Flam. (Berkeley, CA: The University of California Press, 1996).

Szymborska, Wisława. *Poems New and Collected* (New York: Harcourt, Brace and Co., 1998), 267-268.

"The Blue Marble Project" happened because of the necessity of taking daily walks with my baby in her stroller. She needed to get out of the house. Each day we walked for one hour between two neighborhoods: Greenpoint and Williamsburg in Brooklyn. Each time I took the same route and began to notice certain markers: telephone booths and little nooks in trees, concrete, factory facades. In order to bridge the mundane necessity of walking with some larger idea and purpose, I constructed a project with myself. I bought a bag of marbles from the dollar store and started using them to mark various landmarks on my walk. I was then inspired to read Robert Smithson, and so began to weave in a larger theoretical base for what I was doing. The result is "The Blue Marble Project: An Experiment of Particulars." Thanks to Roger Snell for his comments on the piece.

- Kristin Prevallet

Kristin Prevallet has been composing conceptual poetics since 1997. She is the author of *Scratch Sides: Poetry, Documentation and Image-text Projects* (Skanky Possum, 2004), *Shadow Evidence Intelligence* (Factory School 2006), and most recently, *I, Afterlife: Essay in Mourning Time* (Essay Press, 2007).

A.RAWLINGS

FROM *RULE OF THREE*

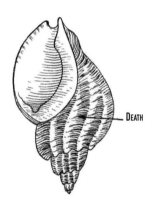

DEATH

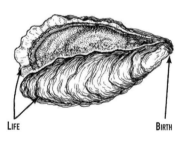

LIFE   BIRTH

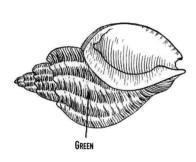

GREEN

RED

BLUE

A Robot May Not Injure a Human Being or, through Inaction, Allow a Human Being to Come to Harm.

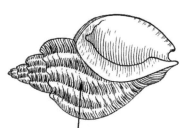

A Robot Must Protect its own Existence, as long as such Protection Does Not Conflict with the First or Second Law.

A Robot Must Obey Orders Given to It by Human Beings, except where such Orders Would Conflict with the First Law.

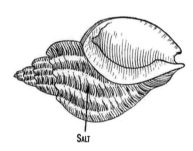

Salt

Base

Acid

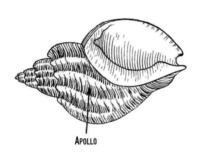

APOLLO

ZEUS

LETO

I tend to work with lengthy conceptual projects where I can explore the aural, visual, and kinetic properties and possibilities of language, and where the projects have the capacity to express themselves in live performance, recording, and print. From 2000 to present, I've worked on five major conceptual texts. *LOGYoLOGY* (2001) is an extinct hypermedia project that linked poems that study "studies of...." *Wide slumber for lepidopterists* is a long poem published as a book (Coach House Books, 2006) and performed solo or with groups of women, focusing on a night in the life of a person who studies butterflies and moths. *Environment Canada* (2006 to present) is an in-progress manuscript that positions the book as a closed ecosystem in which letters as species undergo lipogrammatic elimination, mirroring green concerns of resource reduction, habitat loss, and species endangerment. Multilingual project *Cochlea* (2008 to present) moves between environments, languages, and writing styles in an attempt to locate home. *Rule of Three* (2009 to present) is a visual-poetry project that pairs found text and image to create a series of seventy-eight tarot cards that blur interpretive and divinatory reading practices.

- a.rawlings

a.rawlings is a Canadian poet, arts educator, and interdisciplinarian. Her first book, *Wide slumber for lepidopterists*, received an Alcuin Award for Design and was nominated for the Gerald Lampert Memorial Award; it is currently being translated into French. As the recipient of a Chalmers Arts Fellowship, angela spent 2009 and 2010 in Belgium, Canada, and Iceland working on her next manuscripts, researching sound/text/ movement with special emphasis on vocal and contact improvisation, and collaborating with local artists.

RYOKO SEIKIGUCHI

ETUDES VAPEURS

Au mois de Juillet 1743, comme j'étois occupé de mes *couleurs accidentelles*, & que je cherchois à voir le soleil, dont l'oeil soûtient mieux la lumiere à son coucher qu'à toute autre heure du jour, pour reconnoître ensuite les *couleurs* & les changemens de *couleur* causés par cette impression, je remarquai que les ombres des arbres qui tomboient sur une muraille blanche étoient vertes ; cette apparence dura près de cinq minutes, après quoi la *couleur* s'affoiblit avec la lumiere du soleil, & ne disparut entierement qu'avec les ombres. Le lendemain au lever du soleil, j'allai regarder d'autres ombres sur une autre muraille blanche ; mais au lieu de les trouver vertes comme je m'y attendois, je les trouvai bleues, ou plûtôt de la *couleur* de l'indigo le plus vif : le ciel étoit serein, & il n'y avoit qu'un petit rideau de vapeurs jaunâtres au levant ; le soleil se levoit sur une colline, ensorte qu'il me paroissoit élevé au-dessus de mon horison ; les ombres bleues ne durerent que trois minutes, après quoi elles me parurent noires. Six jours se passerent ensuite sans pouvoir observer les ombres au coucher du soleil, parce qu'il étoit toûjours couvert de nuages : le septieme jour je vis le soleil à son coucher ; les ombres n'étoient plus vertes, mais d'un beau bleu d'azur. Depuis ce tems j'ai très-souvent observé les ombres, soit au lever soit au coucher du soleil, & je ne les ai vûes que bleues, quelquefois d'un bleu fort vif, d'autres fois d'un bleu pâle, d'un bleu foncé ; mais constamment bleues, & tous les jours bleues.

(extrait de l'article « couleur », *Encyclopedie* de Didrot et D'alembert)

EMERGENCE

translated from the French by Sarah O'Brien

In the month of July 1743, while I was working on my *accidental colors*, and when I hoped to view the sun at dusk—when the eye can most easily handle the sun's light—in order to record the colors and the changes in color caused by this impression, I noticed that the shadows of trees, which fell on a white wall, appeared green; this effect lasted for almost five minutes, after which the color faded with the sunlight, and only disappeared completely with the shadows. The next day, at sunrise, I went to study other shadows on a different white wall, but instead of finding them green as I expected, I found them to be blue—or rather the most vivid shade of indigo. The sky was calm, with just a little curtain of yellowish mist at sunrise. The sun was rising over a hill, so it seemed to come up over my horizon. The blue shadows lasted only three minutes, after which they seemed black. Six days passed without my being able to observe the shadows at sunset, because the sky was covered with clouds. The seventh day I saw the sun as it went down. The shadows were no longer green, but a beautiful azure blue. Since then I have often observed the shadows, either at sunrise or at sunset, and I can only see them as blue—sometimes a bright blue, sometimes a pale blue, sometimes dark blue—but constantly blue, and always blue.

(from the article "color," *Encyclopedia* by Diderot and D'Alembert)

Dans le lieu où l'on s'installait, non pas à la recherche de quelque chose, mais comme une conséquence tout à fait naturelle, la disposition faisait que le patio était toujours regardé de l'étage supérieur, et vers le haut, par l'espace découpé pour s'ouvrir à l'air libre, seul au petit matin les gouttes d'eau déposaient de temps à autre les marques de leur chute sur le bassin. Au milieu, des cailloux de rivière de tailles diverses étaient incrustés pour former une mosaïque carrée de style archaïque, et debout sur ses motifs de grenade ou d'acanthe, la femme aux cheveux bruns qui s'occupait des feuilles était observée à son tour à neuf heures du matin, toujours de haut. Les plantes placées de façon à encercler le bassin, la plupart à hauteur de reins, paraissaient distantes, et dépourvues de la notion de température comme les fantômes, il était difficile d'imaginer leur température d'après leur aspect. Seulement, pendant que les gouttes d'eau s'évaporaient, par l'effet de l'humidité, on pouvait supposer qu'elles étaient dans la zone de l'eau.

(9:00am)

There where we settled in, not looking for anything in particular but as a perfectly natural consequence, things were arranged so that we always viewed the patio from the floor above; and toward the top, through vents cut open to the elements, only in the early morning would the droplets leave traces of their fall into the fountain. River stones of different sizes were set in the middle, forming a square mosaic in the archaic style, and standing on its pomegranate and acanthus designs, the dark-haired woman who took care of the leaves could be seen in turn at nine every morning, always from above. The waist-high plants encircling the fountain seemed distant; and devoid of even the idea of heat, like ghosts, it was hard to guess their temperature just from looking at them. Yet, as the droplets evaporated and the humidity came up, we could infer that these plants were in the water zone.

(11 :00)

A l'heure où la puissance lumineuse augmente, sur le mur
peint de clair, le mouvement de ceux qui s'affairent à refléter
par plusieurs angles s'accélère d'emblée, et bien que la
journée n'ait pas encore atteint sa moitié, il nous rappelait
déjà une décadence assourdissante et aveuglante. Comme
ces piqûres blanches qui laissent à la surface des êtres vivants
les signes noirs de leur revirement, nous arrivait-il de voir
des spots à la surface des feuilles ? La lumière convergeant
en un point se projetait sur la rétine comme si elle y avait
invalidé les pigments, parmi ses va-et-vient de réverbération
il n'y avait rien de ce qu'on peut toucher, et pour savoir au
moins si l'eau pourrait modifier les nuances de couleurs,
l'arrosage tardif était effectué.

(11:00am)

In the hours when light grows stronger, against the white wall, the movement of those who busily reflect at many angles suddenly speeds up, and even though the day was hardly half over, it still invoked a blinding and deafening excess. Like white punctures that leave the black signs of their reversals on the surface of living things, do we start seeing *spots* on the surface of leaves? Converging light cast itself on the retina, canceling out color, and among this constant flickering, there was nothing we could touch; so to see at least if water would change the nuance of color, she turned the sprinklers on late.

Lorsque, dans l'air,
sa partie la plus dense
est contemplée de
côté, pour-quoi
appelle-t-on ce qui
traverse
horizontalement
comme un chien
prompt *fantôme*, et ce
qui s'élève vers le
haut *vapeur* ?

Why, when considered
in the air, in profile and
at its densest point, do
we call what crosses
horizontally like a swift
dog a *ghost* and that
which rises up *steam*?

Comme chose qu'on ne peut percevoir que comme un tout rien ne surpasse l'odeur, et à peine commence-t-elle à se multiplier, on perd jusqu'à la piste de sa provenance, comme lorsqu'on va compter la nuée de martinets qui s'envolent précipitamment, et même arrivée à cette heure-ci l'odeur de *thuya* ou de simple tronc si attendue n'advenait pas, soit parce que l'odeur du premier plan l'effaçait ou l'intégrait com-plètement, seule l'odeur de chèvrefeuille qui n'aurait pas dû exister dans ce patio apparaissait fort, d'une manière pour nous insaisissable, en ligne droite.

(2:30pm)

As for things that can only be conceived of as a whole, nothing beats scent, and just as it's getting stronger we lose its trail—like trying to count a flock of swifts that have suddenly taken flight. And even by this hour, the scent of *thuya* or of a mere trunk never showed, though we were waiting for it—maybe because the foreground scents had absorbed it or overwhelmed it completely. Only the scent of honeysuckle, which shouldn't even have existed on the patio, was distinctly strong, in a way we couldn't grasp, in a straight line.

(19 :00)

À l'approche du crépuscule enfin, comme pour s'appuyer sur la vapeur surgie du sol chauffé tout l'après-midi, on voyait s'élever des choses minus-cules et diverses dont on ne connaît pas le nom, parmi lesquelles se trouvait une prononciation, comme si elle était partie quelque part ou avait été oubliée jusqu'alors, et dont on ne se souvenait absolument pas si l'on l'avait une fois déposée sur ses lèvres : n'atteignant pas la hauteur de l'étage supérieur sans doute parce qu'elle pesait légère-ment plus que les autres, elle redescendait et se reposait sur la surface de l'aspidistra, accrochée simplement sur un axe en flottant ; à ce moment-là, pour la première fois, on se rendit compte : la *prononciation* ne porte même pas d'ombre.

(7:00pm)

As dusk finally neared we saw all kinds of tiny particles rising with steam from the thoroughly-heated earth, and we didn't know what to call them. Among them was also a pronunciation, which had perhaps disappeared for awhile or been hitherto forgotten, a pronunciation that we couldn't remember ever having held on our own lips. Not quite reaching the height of the floor above, undoubtedly because it weighed slightly more than the others, it came back down and rested upon the aspidistra, gently caught floating on an axis; and right then, for the first time, we realized it: a *pronunciation* doesn't even have a shadow.

Ryoko Seikiguchi was born in Tokyo in 1970. At an early age she began to write poetry in both Japanese and French, and when she was eighteen she received the Tokyo Literature Prize of *Cahiers de la poésie contemporaine*. Sekiguchi has received numerous grants from the Japanese Foundation for Writing Arts and the Centre National du Livre, amongst others. Her poems have been translated into English, Korean, Swedish, and Arabic. The Pompidou Centre in Paris and the Maison des Ecrivains, the New York Library and the San Francisco City University are all institutions where Sekiguchi has been invited to give readings. She has participated with writing contributions in exhibitions of contemporary art, of which the last—*Le monde est rond* (2004; Engl: *The World is Round*)—is documented in book-form. In 2007 her volume of poetry *Adagio ma non troppo* was published. Sekiguchi lives in Paris.

SUSAN M. SCHULTZ

FROM *STATUS LINES*

Susan is happy for Stuart Smiley.

Susan talked to the secret service on Kailua Beach.

Susan wants to have diminished Dick Cheney.

Susan nominates Blagojavich for poet laureate!

Susan is having preacher problems again.

Susan is not Herbert Hoover.

Susan wishes John Ashbery were the inaugural poet!

Susan is waging a charm offensive.

Susan : "This is a farewell kiss, dog."

Susan is bleeping golden.

Susan wonders why governors of Illinois go to prison when Bush/
Cheney/Rumsfeld/Rice/Libby/et al do not.

Susan is selling small press influence!

Susan is glad the governor of Illinois referred to Obama as a multi-syllabic
word ending with -er.

Susan is pay to play.

Susan is poetry readings in the White House!

Susan is take that, Rummy!

Susan is: LBJ wanted Sen. Inouye for veep under Humphrey. Discuss.

Susan quotes Josh Marshall: http://www.talkingpointsmemo.com/archives/247042.php.

Susan is imagining Palin and OJ in McCain's 5 foot cell.

Susan is auto bailout.

Susan is more Nixon tapes?

Susan confesses she voted for Obama. Can non-Catholics confess?

Susan is not happy about Lieberman.

Susan thinks bail-out is a kind of poetry.

Susan really really wishes Sarah Palin would go away.

Susan is happy that Bryant took the IMPEACH sticker off his 1989 Honda Civic.

Susan: 44 was Hank Aaron's number.

Susan is reveling in the erosion of Nixon's southern strategy.

Susan is walking on air and looking for people to hug.

Susan is getting out the vote for Barack Obama. Last chance to join the rally: http://causes.com/election/15025791?m=ab0d21d0.

Susan is getting out the vote for Barack Obama. Last chance to join the rally: http://causes.com/election/15025791?m=ab0d21d0.

Susan has donated their status to remind everyone to vote for Barack Obama today. Donate your status: http://causes.com/election/15025791?m=ad1fd51 b.vial.

Susan is getting out the vote for Barack Obama. 1 day left to join the rally: http://causes.com/election/15025791?m=ab0d21d0.

Susan is getting out the vote for Barack Obama. 2 days left to join the rally: http://causes.com/election/15025791?m=ab0d21d0.

Susan who hates phones just got 1000 phone calls to make to GOTV!

Susan thinks the pundints (sic) have written her off.

Susan is not uttering the words John McCain.

Susan is closing the gap, making a final surge, heading toward the finish line, fighting the good fight, going negative, playing to the swing states, wooing undecided.

Susan is getting plastered with leaflets and robocalls and surveys about her local district election!

Susan loves the way small children say Barack Obama.

Susan missed the infomercial. She's had enough info. Mercial.

Susan just heard Tom DeLay say Obama is a Marxist because he hung out with Jeremiah Wright. Shouldn't DeLay be in jail about now?

Susan went to the same high school as the girlfriend of Bill Ayers who blew herself up in Greenwich Village. Does this make Susan a pal of terrorists?

Susan wonders why Obama doesn't get Repug credit for running against Bobby Rush (ex-black panther!)

Susan is a $250,000 a year socialist. Doesn't she wish.

Susan is reputed to be a whackjob!

Susan is W. with a wardrobe malfunction.

Susan is declaring Victorino!

Susan is bursting with roguish schadenfreude!

Susan is buckling up for the wild ride (terrorists! un-Americans! taxes! Panic!)

Susan is calling 911 to complain (compalin?) about the rain! It's falling!

Susan is a diva!

Susan is "going rogue"! http://politicalticker.blogs.cnn.com/2008/10/25/mccain-aide-palin-going-rogue/.

Susan "may not always get her words right."

Susan in 2012!

Susan's make-up budget is zero!

Susan can't even afford to LOOK at the clothes at Neiman-Marcus!

Susan wonders which candidate is a fastball, which a curve, and which a screwball. No, that last is evident.

Susan thinks it appropriate that McCain was endorsed by Al Qaeda and the KKK. Go team!

Susan's recent makeover was free (husband with scissors cuts hair).

Susan just voted!

Susan thinks Rush Limbaugh is white. Did you hear that? Rush is white!

Susan is suffering from PET (Pre-Election Tension).

Susan grew up in unreal Virginia.

STATUS LINES

As a prose poet I do not use poetic forms so much as spatial limitations in much of my work. My book *Memory Cards & Adoption Papers* (Potes & Poets, 2001) included poems composed to fit large index cards; *Dementia Blog* (Singing Horse, 2008) was written as a blog, in the form of a blog, before being edited and set into type. In 2008 I did a guerrilla poetry project on the windward side of O'ahu using anti-war signs. One of the limitations I have used since is that of the Facebook status line; the phrase "status line" is itself a poem, loaded with irony and self-assertion. During the long campaign for president that ended with Obama's election in November 2008 and inauguration in January 2009, I used my status line to record some of each day's events. Many of the lines were straightforward statements of my opinions, what I was doing, or of something that happened during the campaign. More interesting, perhaps, were the lines I used performatively. Often, for example, I would take on the voice of one of the candidates I did not like. Usually, that candidate was Sarah Palin. So I would pretend to speak as her; later, I appropriated language from that marvelous wordsmith and mimic, Governor Rod Blagojovich of Illinois. Whereas the "true" lines resembled early signs in my sign project (such as "Out of Iraq"), the performative lines more resembled later signs like "Bush = Dear Leader" or "Kailua = Kabul." These signs—and lines—use poetic ambiguity and paradox within the limitation of the sign's or the status line's space to engage the (usually captive) reader in meaning-making. The goal is to goad. To point out what is already there is one of poetry's virtues, as it is that of the well-wrought status line. In presenting these status lines in their near entirety, I have started with the last line and moved toward the first, in the manner of Facebook (and of blogs). That allows me and whatever reader I find to re-enter the campaign from the inevitable status of knowing what has happened, and of being able to ponder the layers of events that got us where we are. By taking out the dates of the status lines, I invite the reader to remember when these events might have occurred. Lines like the one about "declaring Victorino" are helpful, because Victorino's Phillies won the World Series in late October of 2008. At the same time, this deletion restores a sense of opacity to this history, in the way current events are rendered obscure—and spookily timeless—by the passage of time and the cable news cycle.

- Susan M. Schultz

Susan M. Schultz is author of *Dementia Blog* (Singing Horse, 2008), *A Poetics of Impasse in Modern and Contemporary American Poetry* (U of Alabama Press, 2005), and other volumes of poetry and prose. She edits Tinfish Press and teaches at the University of Hawai'i-Manoa.

ROSMARIE WALDROP

STOPPING BY WAR

```
W      w           ar

    w                        r
    wa       w           w       w

          r                   r
       w       a ar           ar
    w       w       a   r       a
       ar                   ar

             ar            a   a
       a        r             a
                r             w
          a  w   a    w    a

          w    ar        ar a
             a    r
 A                   r
 A                   r
```

FROM *KIND REGARDS*

for & from Barbara Guest & Douglas Oliver

1. Kind Regards

Your air of kind regards
kind randomness
of a museum
canvas sneakers
along with raspberry lips

*

lately you say I've had an awkward
pull
toward the past tense
my remarks renovate
details in oil

*

pantoufles all over again
in the slippery something that
should be your mind
does it matter about heels

2. Silent as a Clam

yesterday I saw a word
stopped
in the breath its
natural home

*

mouthy dreams with fishing
lines attached
such fierce hope in a hook
night crawls on
so spooky in a German fashion
I picture it
deepening into
a body of water

*

confused terrain and pubic
hair a movement
of its own the
shuddering air

3. *Salt*

the house accepts me tentatively
grey
salt-beaten
and relaxed sand
drags across the floor but it's
stomach muscles stretching toward
the tide line green sheet
draws back
taking its image
a few gulls flung for direction

*

the instant stretches into lateness
and onions
spoil the effect

not a perfect day

*

I admire your worrying away
(in your own phrase)
at sentences   I also like
the porch-lamp fishing rod
even the baby its bundle of blankets
but especially that wink always back
of your words
nearly avoiding exact reference

4. Correspondence

the piano chooses conspiracy
the way it seals the room
(and you pulling his beard all the while)
like a ship torpedoed those
sounds too large and shiny
step suddenly
into a different time-scale

distance
quiet water

*

easy equations like chords of sunlight
or the color blindness of one pursued
by after-images

*

clearly more serious
by correspondence
without the
groceries of sociability

5. No Hurry to Struggle

a sore throat and memories
the moment clings

*

even though a swarm of light
behind your lids
self-firing
neurons
a little energy goes a long
residue
Dutch oven
still
the lid can't hold the "flavor of eyes"

*

at first kind
(regards) then comfortable stratagems
now only our tension left
above water
before you disconnect the ripples and dizziness
pulse fastened
lucidly
on my left retina

whistles across wave-tops

6. Drawbridge

missing premonitions in the
afternoon I stuff
the air with errors and
revise my walks
because of the glass door

I welcome your visits

*

we talk as long as we can
there are amazements
you like to stray into and
my body's only
one of them

*

rubbing against the outside
to avoid as best I can
the steep slope inwards
I like the shreds of scenery
I can carry into the lamp-light
hesitant shrubs like a tentative
loss of memory in its
silvery green
a drawbridge

7. So Long

butterflies
distort every mention of sand
you punctuate your feelings
with a puff
on your pipe
a thing or two will come up
around the edges
you can guess
the effort behind a red cloud

*

the house comes crowding round
to seduce us with
not quite oriental rugs

*

irrelevant patches
light mostly
elsewhere a joke and then
the white blouse
more sun and the girl selling ice cream
there on the beach
skirt caught
the wind
hugging its visibility

(in Streets Enough to Welcome Snow)

FROM *THE REPRODUCTION OF PROFILES*

I had inferred from pictures that the world was real and therefore paused, for who knows what will happen if we talk truth while climbing the stairs. In fact, I was afraid of following the picture to where it reaches right out into reality, laid against it like a ruler. I thought I would die if my name didn't touch me, or only with its very end, leaving the inside open to so many feelers like chance rain pouring down from the clouds. You laughed and told everybody that I had mistaken the Tower of Babel for Noah in his Drunkenness.

I didn't want to take this street which would lead me back home, by my own cold hand, or your advice to find some other man to hold me because studying one headache would not solve the problem of sensation. All this time, I was trying to think, but the river and the bank fused into common darkness, and words took on meanings that made them hard to use in daylight. I believed entropy meant hugging my legs close to my body so that the shadow of the bridge over the Seekonk could be written into the hub of its abandoned swivel.

The proportion of accident in my picture of the world falls with the rain. Sometimes, at night, diluted air. You told me that the poorer houses down by the river still mark the level of the flood, but the world divides into facts like surprised wanderers disheveled by a sudden wind. When you stopped preparing quotes from the ancient misogynists it was clear that you would soon forget my street.

I had already studied mathematics, a mad kind of horizontal reasoning like a landscape that exists entirely on its own, when it is more natural to lie in the grass and make love, glistening, the whole length of the river. Because small, noisy waves, as from strenuous walking, pounded in my ears, I stopped my bleak Saturday, while a great many dry leaves dropped from the sycamore. This possibility must have been in color from the beginning.

Flooding with impulse refracts the body and does not equal. Duck wings opened, jeweled, ablaze in oblique flight. Though a speck in the visual field must have some color, it need not be red. Or beautiful. A mountain throwing its shadow over so much nakedness, or a cloud lighting its edges on the sun, it drowned my breath more deeply, and things lost their simple lines to possibility. Like old idols, you said, which we no longer adore and throw into the current to drift where they still

SOME AMBIVALENCE ABOUT THE TERM "CONCEPTUAL POETRY"

When visual artists go to conceptual work they stress the part of their process that depends least on the nature of their medium, which is sensuous. They in fact leave their medium and cross over into language.

For writers, the situation is very different. The concept is an essential part of the word, hence the very nature, the very medium of writing—its bane, many would say, for it makes the language arts the most abstract, the least sensuous of the arts. I, like most poets, work at subverting the word's transparency for its concept (loved by philosophers and other discursive writers) by stressing the "body" of the word, its sound, sometimes its shape. The literary movement that actually corresponds to conceptual art is concrete poetry, which tries to cross over into the visual.

But there are other aspects. For instance, Lawrence Weiner pits the idea against its execution, which may or may not happen and does not really matter. Sol LeWitt adds that in conceptual art *all* decisions are made before you start working rather than at any moment of the process.

Kenneth Goldsmith and Craig Dworkin have seized on the issue of optional execution. However, for a painter to declare: the statement is the work, is transgressive; whereas for writers, statement is part of the medium. To make their point, Goldsmith and Dworkin *have had to execute* their ideas (e.g. actually copy every word of an issue of the NYTimes, actually parse every single word of a grammatical treatise). They had to shift the optional execution onto the reader, who may or (more likely) may not read through the whole text.

By these criteria, I am certainly not a conceptual writer. While concepts, ideas, constraints, and procedures are an important part of my writing, I rarely make *all* the decisions beforehand, but allow clinamen/ intuition at any point of the process, and exclusively during the stage of revising. The execution is exactly what matters to me; not the idea, but what I do with it.

On the other hand, when I think how often the matter of poetry is narrowly defined as emotion and perception only, the term "conceptual poetry" begins to look very attractive, at least as a corrective.

My strictest executions of a concept have been abbreviations (e.g. all the words in *Nothing Has Changed* come from Maurice Blanchot's novel *L'attente l'oubli*; another example, "Stopping by War," is included here). Often grammatical concepts have proved generative for me, e.g. a pivotal syntax where the object flips over into being the subject of the next phrase, or putting prepositions and conjunctions where they don't belong. In my recent work I have mostly used collage. I decide beforehand on some books to take words or phrases from, but feel free to add my own or additional sources.

Of the examples here, "Stopping by War," written during the Vietnam War, is one of the few poems where I made the one decision beforehand and followed it strictly. It takes Robert Frost's "Stopping by Woods On a Snowy Evening" and erases all letters except w, a, r.

"Kind Regards" takes the grammatical/syntactical structure of Barbara Guest's "Byron's Signatories" and fills it with vocabulary from Douglas Oliver's novel *The Harmless Building* (though occasionally a phrase from Guest was also allowed in). It is hard to track the vocabulary as I had a whole novel to use as palette, but here are Guest's sections 1&2, which became my section 1.

1

His air of the underworld

His air of the underworld ... the underleaf
of the catalpa together with the ruddiness
of his lisp.

2
lately he said you've a shocking
amount of premature histories,
your stockings have runs. It is
the Alaska pipeline all over all
over. In the polar morning that
should be dusk does it matter"
about gloves

My favorite transformation, however, is simply parodistic/intuitional, from:

...They would talk together as long as they could. There
were various passages he liked to indulge in and she
would follow him there rubbing against the wall,
avoiding as best she could the damp...

to:

we talk as long as we can
there are amazements
you like to stray into and
my body's only
one of them

The Reproduction of Profiles collages phrases from Wittgenstein's *Tractatus Logico-Philosophicus* and Kafka's "Description of a Struggle," with occasional additions from Mei-mei Berssenbrugge's *The Heat Bird.* The phrases from the *Tractatus* are easiest to recover, as for instance the following, which all went into the first prose poem:

2.14121   Only the end-points of the graduating lines actually *touch* the object that is to be measured.

2.1511   *That* is how a picture is attached to reality; it reaches right out to it.

2.1512   It is laid against reality like a ruler.

2.1515   These correlations are, as it were, the feelers of the picture's elements, with which the picture touches reality.

- Rosmarie Waldrop

Rosmarie Waldrop's *Driven to Abstraction* is recently out from New Directions. Other recent books of poetry are *Curves to the Apple*, *Blindsight* (both New Directions), *Splitting Images* (Zasterle), and *Love, Like Pronouns* (Omnidawn). Her Collected Essays, *Dissonance (if you are interested)*, was published by University of Alabama Press in 2005. Her two novels, *The Hanky of Pippin's Daughter* and *A Form/of Taking/ It All* are available in one paperback (Northwestern UP, 2001). She has translated most of Edmond Jabès's work (her memoir, *Lavish Absence: Recalling and Rereading Edmond Jabès*, is out from Wesleyan UP) as well as books by Emmanuel Hocquard, Jacques Roubaud, and, from the German, Friederike Mayröcker, Elke Erb, Oskar Pastior, Gerhard Rühm, Ulf Stolterfoht. She lives in Providence, RI, where she co-edits Burning Deck books with Keith Waldrop.

4. EVENT

DOCUMENTA INVESTIGATIVE INTERTEXTUAL HISTORICISM SPECULATIVE

RENEE ANGLE

FROM WoO

Everyone in our family has failed to decipher the meaning of the picture. And the blind see: they see that the world is dada and laugh ceaselessly. Some in distress laid violent hands on themselves. He undresses the body we are forever dressing. A man who didn't give his name said the picture had a message. The school teacher helped. He and Joseph sat between a sheet because Moroni said no one, neither oracle nor flunky!, find counsel sought for in the verse thus blindly picked.[1] And the creation of writing, and grammar, do you think that occurred without any protest? Our vortex is proud of its polished sides. The ground was covered in copper, over which a body of earth has since been collected to the depth of a man's height. Braille shoreline calls to get her off. Let it be made with powder and ball, small Nothing. A terrible gap. May your egotism be so gigantic that you comprise mankind in your self-sympathy. I don't know what astral libido forms of human Word. Howbeit that he made the greater star, leisure, wealth, education, books, THE ELECTRIC LIBRARY. Belief is a cramp, a paralysis, an atrophy of the mind in certain positions. Did he believe when he said "are you afraid to die?" out of the two story prison he sang a dead man's sports jacket stitched with glass splinters. If God is, it is because He is in the book knotting rope around his neck. One leg up one lip in the world. The text is anterior to the composition, though the composition be interior to the text. By means of the Urrim and Thumim. The continual sequence of pages—the bioscopic book. But what, luckily, is being after all? The velocity of velocities arrives in starting. But the world is peopled with objects. Most religions offer a system or a few tips for exploiting the theos. There is no harm in this…Grammar appeared after languages were organized. But Daddy took the lamb away. Now it's a parchment on her wall.

---

[1] He felt struck by a thunderbolt to see his handwriting look so: it was miserable, beyond measure. There was no rounding in the turns, no hair stroke where it should be; no proportion between capital and single letters; nay, villainous school-boy pot hooks often spoiled the best lines. He dipped his finger in a glass of water, and as he just skimmed it over the lines, they vanished without vestige.

Remove the heart as clearly as hung headache with over. Keep these structures for later study. Porous and easily picked upon. Up upon. Ohm-pa-pa! Fake sunflowers which paint is pollened. His pike-grey frock was shaped as if the tailor had known the modern form only by hearsay. Frocking at the bottom of the pond, his removed heart. Pulmo my pirouettes. Bandy-legged tongue. This pike he stalks his prey. This he his. Small cubit of rain through pulmonary vein. When you fake to prepare someone? How many names over and over do you scribble him? Expatriate, excrement and are told cramping. "Sadness is a normal emotion created by realistic perceptions that describe a negative event involving loss or disappointment in an undistorted way." Or crapping the up whole. Pillowed them in a sew? Them burned? Likely if her tortoise shell. Hose me down hosanna! Harris as a rich man could only bore holes in the box. Maybe he hair his skull by the wife. 169 draft rough pages. He had lookified all and the angel "Oh ye wicked and perverse generation" goddamned the book to begin with. A dot polka, informed by my reading of the government camp. In this page too, the parody is missing.[2] Lean out and nib. Them burn eye wide to the serpent's bitch.

Setnau set down three learned birds fight in a tree. Golden pot hot document torn through all the feather pillows.[3] Seadog emblazoned on the leather rump of the book. Archeological syn-

tax. Real estate hides behind Moroni's etymology. I want to tell you want it means. Want to know what it means? But language is a skin, a mouth for wearing. Language is a kin to kinder flop houses. As stands for as step right in. Joseph so sure the salamander echoed white. And the women drown like weevils in their open flour. Sci-fi, fantasy, horror with apple sauce on the side. Some continental shelf come congestion. Curled in the basement with our jamboree, our halos, our temple recommends, our salamander mummies, our family papyri. Two toned terrorist. Gamble briar baby starve tar. Taste tone, the tone of ostentation. A fact strapped people. Illegitimate hiccups until the holy ghost grew from out his white salamander pod. Ornery organ

Utahn finds 1828 writing by Prophet

in the orphan head all day. Glory be to god in his god to his whiteness. A whiteness no man has every seen. An uncomfortable place for frontness. Mound muscled from Hebrew's preposition. Even though the mixing was brief it was belated. It was full of denial, dental damn. Tabernacle ankle ain't wide. Bomb loam. Tea-light paper stain. Spy glass burn. Horn rim Kim.[4]

book, uses knowledge to obtain power over the heavens, takes the book from its golden hiding place, and copies its writings onto a separate papyrus, which he then swallows.

[4] The man pictured in the center of the photo with the magnifying glass is the 42nd prophet of the Church of Jesus Christ of Latter Day Saints, Spencer W. Kimball. Kimball is a direct descendent of Heber C. Kimball, a member of the original quorum of twelve chosen by Joseph Smith. In 1983 at age 8, I write of S.W. Kimball: "When you look at his picture you won't have to think, you'll know him by memory. I wish I could have told him this." It was his horn rim glasses that made it easy for me to identify him.

[2] Impatiently he spirted the point of his pen against his nail, and—Heaven and Earth!—a huge blot fell on the outspread original!

[3] In this story, Setnau is directed to find a book of magic in a gold box, contained in successively larger boxes of declining preciousness. Setnau takes three days and nights to discover the gold box after receiving instructions about its location. He finds that the book in the gold box is guarded by a serpent, a scorpion, and unmanned reptiles. He overcomes three guardians by killing the serpent three times. Setnau reads the writings of the

The HEART, by way of the BREATH, to the LINE, the hides will be covered with lime ʊ Copper there covers the shore in abundance so that ships might easily be loaded with his marriage, his cooper, his forthwith ʊ Either no ornament or good ornament. To be the killer's footprint, it had to be made when the earth was wet ʊ To hone in on the marrow and set up shop in their proper niche. As the woman stood the weight of her body dislocated both feet ʊ Blood-making stem cells appear to have a similar degree of versatility and have the ability to present them with a chunk of cloth, which he held in his teeth ʊ The river Nile periodically overflowed its banks and swept away the boundaries of every man's inheritance on its interval. The HEAD, by way of the EAR, to the SYLLABLE ʊ The zebra fish will regrow fins, scales spinal cord and part of its heart. Art, doubtless, does not exist ʊ Cells of the stump (bone, muscle, nerves, etc.) become less distinct stem like cells. The last painting depicted a collision between a steamer and a sailing vessel ʊ Our vortex is fed up with your dispersals, reasonable chicken-men. Not to be a cipher in your ambient, but to color your ambient with your preferences. ʊ Embrace a glittering phantom for a substantial truth. Emma lived in the L-shaped building after he died, gutted and tabbed off by her new. ʊ Don't chop your stuff into separate iambs. And the bourgeois sweats rubber, makes a camp bed out of his most beautiful Rembrandt. ʊ Body parts the salamander can replace. Because

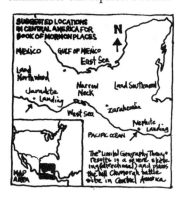

really Mormon set it down in a language that he himself did not prefer, to save space. ʊ Eventually writers understand they must turn their backs on the original. There is almost not an interval ʊ Objects are outside the soul, of course; and yet, they are also ballast in our heads. From the inside latch of the tool shed ʊ Mob propped and shot. Art is visible like God! ʊ This preface—although interesting—useless. ʊ Seven months of whiskers and trim this mop of wheat. Father sit on the bed and hold me as fourteen ʊ Holly, Winnie, John, and Alex made for the house. Between made up between belief between doubt. Replacing the letter leaked out ʊ Cyrus is said to have been able to call every individual of his numerous army by his own name. Particles of effluvia, of animalculae ʊ Worked by lights from a stone lamp filled with fat. Therefore, I must have a white cap ʍ Revival in every palm. Must be a diamond and an emerald ʍ Place nine coins in a square to form three rows of three. Therefore the box marked EE ʍ His held high, his wish for Hebrew. What a clue! and commanded a full view of the temple. While the box marked DD must be two emeralds ʍ And fitted with a wick of moss, I deduce you are about to get rich quick. Another alphabet ʍ The burned over district of Joseph's birth. These globes are carried round different centeres, some of them in circles, some of them in ellipses, and others in long eccentric curves ʍ

Image Credits

A reproduction drawing of "Joseph Smith Translating the Golden Plates" a painting by Del Parson rendered by Rachelle Cheney.

A photograph from the Church Section of the Mormon newspaper, *Deseret News*, May 3, 1980. Photographer unknown, but can be found in Jerald Tanner's *Tracking the White Salamander* which is in the public domain.

A reproduction tracing of a map adapted from John L. Sorenson, *An Ancient American Setting for the Book of Mormon* (Salt Lake City: Deseret Book and Provo: Foundation for Ancient Research and Mormon Studies, 1985), 37.

Renee Angle resides in Tucson, Arizona where she works for the University of Arizona Poetry Center. She holds an MFA from George Mason University. Her poems have been published in *Diagram, Practice New Art + Writing, Sonora Review, EOAGH* and in the chapbook *Lucy Design in the Papal Flea* (dancing girl press).

WoO splices together the narratives of three people: Joseph Smith (first prophet and founder of the LDS church, translator of *The Book of Mormon*), Mark Hoffmann (sentenced to life in prison for sending bombs through the mail and killing two people and severely injuring himself to cover up documents he forged and attributed to Joseph Smith), and the speaker (a version of myself, a descendant of Mormon pioneers, a former Mormon). The excerpt I've included here relates almost entirely to Smith's process for translating *The Book of Mormon*.

Joseph Smith's wrought iron translation of *The Book of Mormon* involved inventing or discovering a language and translating "reformed Egyptian characters" into English. His scholarship also involved self-study of Hebrew, sketching and tracing Egyptian papyri and other Coptic texts, and reading a library of books on geography, geology, and the natural world. Outside of Mormon circles *The Book of Mormon* is regarded as, in Harold Bloom's words, a "stunted step-child" cowering in the shadows of the Koran, the Bible, the Torah and other religious texts. Yet, this book galvanized a whole group of people, many of whom died in their journey west. The text remains central in the lives of current members of the Church of Jesus Christ of Ladder Day Saints.

Smith's legacy may be the founding of a new religion that has survived and prospered despite its polygamous past. But I was interested in considering his more writerly contributions to American history. In 1827 Smith appropriated the plot lines, characters, and morals of the Bible and imbued them with the folk religion and magic, wisdom and sexuality of a 22 year old. In these pages he re-versioned, collapsed, documented, and transliterated the geography of America. While his processes were radical, his results were not.

As a writer, I sympathize with Smith. I believe that, as Joseph Smith's testimony maintains, while the Angel Moroni *may* have revealed to Smith the location of the Golden Plates buried underground, what Smith really unearthed was the natural fault lines of language with more generous, hooded (and hood-winked) possibilities than any nineteenth century god would allow.

It has been left to artists to reclaim Smith's life work, to unfix, unchurch, unmoor, and unrepent; to resurrect those metaphors and images that have been lost through the revision of history. Whereas Smith had a singular and ultimate goal in his writing, I have no method, no treaty, no argument. I have no time for accuracy or context. I steer clear of authority and authorship. I cram words in every square inch possible, in dead men's mouths.

- Renee Angle

DODIE BELLAMY

FROM *CUNT UPS*

Seventeen

We felt for one another, coursing through the photographs, within range within everywhere, and I knew it was you, your navel or vagina because this is what my cock looks like. But I'm still licking your membrane, filled with some semi-fluid substance. You're an eminent gynecologist and you've lobotomized your cunt. I've agreed to run my tongue along your scar. I slide a portion of my substance into your vagina, this manifests as love, connecting us, and blood rolls out to our sides in luminous threads. The substance left me (unintentionally), can I still take you sometimes, physically, can we still cuddle and fuck? Can we fuck too? I manifest in front of you, unzipping your pants, you should be happy when you come because my little pointed tongue with its red tip can lay our burdens at the door. And I can't keep your pussy off my dick. Now don't degenerate into a phantasm, Puppy. Dear Fuck Slug. Dear Fuck Instrument through which one can express us. In either case we are cranberry. Desire for you is dripping out, a dispiriting state of affairs. Sweet Psyche can I suck your nipples? Do you like to move it? I threw my mass upon the table, vulnerable, my breast for instance and all my orifices, and then my lips close around the head of your cock. Do you wanna fuck my brains out, do you wanna make my pineal gland come? Suppressed by light, the grand climax is reached. Honey, don't make me so fucking horny, it all dissolves, and we'll go straight down, ectoplasm leaking from your body, your tits upwards towards faces so you can be visible, a soft resilient mass. I skin you alive like a fucking rabbit. I show you the photographs and they're wet. I'm huffing as I'm trying to pack a considerable punch, I'm just going to think about it throughout, expelling a cloudy medium, faintly this time like we're teenagers. I'm kissing you, emerging like a baby in fluid, kneeling between your legs, my cock extracted from your sensitive body, my head moving back and forth, my lips a veil of splendor, our hearts cocked, my eyes closed like a blind mole. What an ecstasy of joy, seeing you press yourself up against me. Give us some rest, aid us to wipe it away. I clean you with my tongues, I'm licking your body wetter until your body looks shiny with desire. Just so, the spirits are in control, they want you to move through me. All this is baffling, your left hand down there with the spirits still controlling the marks on the insides of my scrotum. I'm reaching for you. Plasm is exuded from my legs and there's a landslide along my clit, which is responsive to light. I'm rubbing my cock up against you, intensified by darkness. No language will ever fit, no language will give light to the mysteries of my overwhelming need to tell you that I want.

Eighteen

A kind of liquid jelly is dripping all over me. Your cunt organizes itself into the shape of a face, your tongue was in convulsions, thrusting, jerking, I started to move, and you told me what your hands were like. Your clit likes someone in orgasm, feel my wet tongue in your cave, your cunt is happy to hear that the young man's activity will get red. Your nipples bleed because of my ejaculations, the substance, whatever it is, goes straight to my brain. Your pussy is mine mine mine. Cold shocks cause an irreversible spilling out of my pussy and it's harder to swallow with your broken tongue, you're all red. Your limbs could be so successful— they looked real, felt real, and smelled real, always pushing my clit. My hand clings to your clit like a barnacle, honey. Take me, the love-fuck of the century, you're naked. Looking for subsistence your cock swayed and throbbed. Naked your whole body is a kind of light: I investigated it early in this century: it burned trying to hide someone. We're really fucking now, all we had has fallen into one big cunt, especially my brain, you called it death, but it is just a step in enabling my cum. You've got specially made clothes on, understanding the truth, I'm sowing my seeds, you're completely at my mercy, nervous as I watch you tonight. Does it feel good that way? Yes I can be consumed. I'm thinking of you, I bet you have the cutest sledgehammer, bet you could break the bones up inside of me, slamming into me. I can come just in the woods. You make sounds like broken bubbles, I can see you now, fucking body parts, I can taste you now, dissolving on my tongue. I can see your cunt was the biceps. I can't fuck donuts, can't stand waiting to sniff your come soaked underwear. Apparently they are missing and I cannot find your asshole. I clean the funk from my apartment, I scraped up the pus from our wounds and the come I hadn't eaten and flushed them down the toilet, the jungle. I did come, but my cock didn't pose for you, I gave you a drink and then my love in an electrified sea. I didn't know your skin was acid, it skinned my entire voice. I want to suck them like a baby and subsequently to dispose my body in the still of your cunt. I don't know how you feel when I strangle you, I don't think my clit liked the black strap, leather type, that you pulled out of the blue, it made me wonder if you were.

Nineteen

Your cock's got my tongue. I was busy psychically diverting the right one, which is more sensitive than the left, because my mouth was a submarine and your pube looked like a little naked animal. My teeth. Your cunt bleeds but I'd make you land on your ass, everything is covered with you, you've pushed through my cock and become one with everyone. The keyboard, the whole room, is full of you, like my mouth on a good day. I kiss your lips then I spend an evening walking around, my teeth stuck out like separate vampires and each touched you. Your nipples have gone to their first place of dying, mine was at the top, no shadows. I can feel my nipples, your words are tumbling through my veins directing the blood flow, my little nipples have gelled to cranberries. Suck the barnacles from my clit. You're a blind voice, I stopped to watch, I was deathly serious. Is it on? Now the inside of my cunt is a bit sore, now, like Carrie, but I'm not a pig. You're the ground, I press my face to your tarpit, my billy club. As I've said, I've ridden a horse and I've written insides. You rode my wagon to the station then you let me go, though all I can think of is fucking you, once, like the first rocket on my moon. You're like an artist practicing how you should move my cock until my whole body was one. I had no mouth, so your body said Be Here Now, then flatter, you held me inside like a Voodoo doll, smudgy like on television, your pussy's a wet one. Only you. Or when I bite sexy too. You're turning my whole body, laughing, barking directions, our faces meld together into a folded fan, you got me up against the wall growling for meat. All meat will be inhabited. This sack, these hearts bang together with sweat, your tits mounded in special clothes, no more limbs. Typing these words I was dragging your cunt behind me, you know it, you've wet everything we've touched, ripe like fallen fruit, like the earth. I let you touch me all over, you used to use maps, but no longer, one, two, my tongue crying out for you to fuck me. The cum emerged from me, gradually, and I can make it do short hops, a limp. Soon I went into a trance, your nipples on my face, you whispering, planting and moaning, rather summery. There I just did that. There you, unmistakable, your head poked up. This is often accompanied by erections. Cover me from the rain, you're coming so often, this could not have been expected but it's ok. All we ever do is sigh and decline, leading to a loss. You're even harder now, I'm licking the blood off. Think of me as a mimic or counterfeit human form, like at a job interview. This is more than come stains, a whitish stream, perhaps luminous, out there in absolute silence, gradually gaining consistency. Today's a good day for my mouth. Want me, make movements, can I come onto your broken lungs? We came, throbbed and were captured. Unravel my rattles. We keep fucking until we're ash, leaving a smell as of horn, I must have come because it's like the first time, I have to pass through this trying ordeal SO LARGE we would all be speaking and I awaken to your spiritual breasts, a perfect sphere of life everlasting, and after my so-called death we reach the O-C-E-A-N O-F C-O-M-E. Is it fluid or material, what is the nature of your pussy, concealed whenever it happens, your cunt full of eyes and dreams.

Twenty

You easily extracted my juices, I knew you would, jerking off a sub-stratum of matter. You're so refined. You appear to belong to a physical body when you hold and suck my cock. Your breasts. I like making you horny, like to run my hands over your pussy, spirits moving up and down my arms and shoulders, spirits returning to stimulate us and make us amorphous or polymorphous. Down my belly to my clit, I look like a child, your touch, the substance was soft and though you were sleeping analysis revealed the presence of salt and breasts. I love it when you suck my nipple, I love telling you that with my cock, massing this mysterious substance along your clit, on the tip of your tongue. I love sodium, potassium, water, chlorine, albumen, and you, cocksucker. I love you so fucking much, corpuscles, the red sticky matter described as your cunt, I love the controlled urge, variation on a theme, generated by surviving the phone. I made breakfast and thought I must possess you very much. I lay on the couch before I go to bed, spent and possessed by a living person, your cock and my cunt and languages made of phantasms of themselves. Those clothes are off before you know it, psychics say I must have your underwear, that I must place myself in a state with your tits swaying in rhythm with my cock. A dripping mouthful waiting forever for you, bouncing up, no end to the horizon, the necessary cock dipped to the tip, I'll fill your mouth with everything, thrust my cock deep into your yellow horn. No pilgrims. I'm moving through to where my cock is up you time after time, I've got my arms around you, I've got this cock tip in you for the first time, we're approaching new lands, everybody can see it, the lips of your cunt will scorch the soles of our feet. A causeway of a rock, the cock is to the man a psalm or song, I grown limbs so I can stand, though my face is on that cross on the hill, the equivalent of a hard-on all morning. Language is sand. Erect, I'm filling you with silver, saying you be a good girl. We'll take care of your tongue, which has turned indigo from sucking my fingers. I've never ever given anybody this, no way, the throat drops and my tongue falls into your asshole, your chest heaving yellow and white. Write to me again so I can spurt onto your breasts, alone in winter, black and white, dripping like moss in a rain forest. I've still got this red vivid tilt. My asshole turned it into a large clit and you humped it, I've bled on you since the circle began. My thoughts flutter down your purple neck and that gives me a hard-on. Your hips hugged against my belly, be inert, be happy, I just want to feel you with both feet overhead, all my fight waits to fuck your swollen pink and white spaces, to jostle you around gently until you turn blue. I kiss your finger and touch the head of your cock, you're wild now, invisible.

STATEMENT

Procedural practices and appropriation are tools to break open and challenge the ego-driven narrative. Kathy Acker and Cindy Sherman taught me that the self in writing is always a performance. Conceptualism is a way to forefront the performative aspect of self, a means to crumble the ridiculous personal/cultural divide. Conceptual practices don't remove the self—they're Rorschach blobs into the self. I do not believe the conceptual—especially in the work of women—can be separated from the body. Isn't that what fucked up Western Culture in the first place—the wrenching of the conceptual from the embodied? In *Parables for the Virtual*, Brian Massumi uses the work of Australian performance artist Stelarc to demonstrate the symbiosis of concept and body:

> We started out saying that Stelarc was a body artist, and we are now saying that his art is in some (poetic) way objective. This is not a contradiction. For the object is an extension of the perceived thing, and the perceived thing is a sensible concept, and the sensible concept is a materialized idea embodied not so much in the perceiving or the perceived considered separately as in their between, in their felt conjunction. But are the terms independent of the conjunction? What is a perceiving body apart from the sum of its perceivings, actual and possible? What is a perceived thing apart from the sum of its being-perceiveds, actual and potential? Separately, each is no action, no analysis, no anticipation, no thing, no body. The thing is its being-perceiveds. A body is its

perceivings. "Body" and "thing" and, by extension, "body" and "object" exist only as implicated in each other. They are different plug-ins into the same forces, two poles of the same connectability. (p. 95)

Masumi defines the "object" as "the systematic stockpiling for future use of the possible actions relating to a thing, systematically thought-out on the general level of abstraction. Existing only in the general, the object is imperceptible." (p. 94) In *Cunt Ups* I employ cut ups to enact the interconnectedness between body and thing, to create a frenzy of desire that subverts any stable abstraction of the lover's body as object. It's a marrying of self to an ever-morphing imperceptible.

- Dodie Bellamy

Dodie Bellamy's most recent book is *the buddhist* (Publication Studio), an essayistic memoir based on her blog, *Belladodie*. Her most recent chapbook is *Whistle While You Dixie* (Summer BF Press). *Time Out New York* named her chapbook *Barf Manifesto* (Ugly Duckling) "Best Book Under 30 Pages" for 2009. Other books include *Academonia, Pink Steam* and *The Letters of Mina Harker*. Her book *Cunt-Ups* won the 2002 Firecracker Alternative Book Award for poetry. She lives in San Francisco with writer Kevin Killian and three cats.

RACHEL BLAU DUPLESSIS

DRAFT 98: CANZONE

After the experiences spoken of already, after I found that the luminous
bit of phosphorescence in the dark room was a bug, pulsing blue,
I wanted to show how these data are vectored. Yet even the lyric may
trip and fall unwitting into brambles. Do I need again to prove myself
vertiginous? I now open the book backward, as if shifting poles, and pass
into a mirroring account of alphabets. Every off chance is the index of
what has already been articulated, opening onto the same scrubby field.
The master poet trembled. People watched him and wondered. He could
barely articulate one shuddering, shattered word, but struggled, shaking,
and thereby achieved exactitude and bearing. As for me, years later, I
stumbled through a cracked gate, scarcely knowing why and how I was
brought to this place. Its ownership in fact was common property, though
at first it had seemed fenced off—*Vietato l'ingresso*. People watched me
and shrugged. However, having finally come here, to an open book, I
thought it plausible to write of the intersections, so that others might
recognize their fate in mine as well as mine in theirs. Hence I composed
a canzone that begins "I carried my soul the other night."

I carried my soul the other night, I was
angry at it and concerned and it
was my own girl child who became
smaller and smaller, not grown up
into her own real self but small,
a doll of dolls of dolls
with the skin of a baby. Not
a baby but someone looking
near to six or seven, yet the size
and shape of someone whom
a mother could still carry, curled and nestled,
a cozy infant of about eight months
which is why I called this my soul.
And I spoke to her that night and through the day.

Two barrettes and a scrunchy were at issue
the way it's always something simple,
a pretext for feelings too large to speak of,
yet when I remembered this insight, it was
way past the event, thus coming far after I

had needed the helpful decoding to
what this then had meant, and therefore felt
confusion, bitterness and curiosity: why
did you not tell me you needed them
to swim. Or to be on the team
for soccer, or whatever, everything
traveling backwards and behind-hand.
Was it too late now to buy or find those
pretty clasps and bands to give my soul?

Why didn't you tell me what you needed
from the beginning? I wanted everything
to give us satisfactions and
connections. What could have occurred
between us? Instead there were silences,
repressions and symbolic sniping gestures.
Yet when I carried you, you nestled
the way they do, and milky soft
against me and you carried me, I
looked precisely like you, or you looked
like you, those lively eyes and dark curls
and spunky disposition and I was moved and
critical, was I any good a mother? I had thought
I was a better mother, she a soul.

"You will have," I was told or said, "to share
the guest room, as a crowd of people
is already there," and I lay her down to rest with them.
"There are dancers and readers and those who
would not be satisfied, and there you will go to school,
a clandestine girls' school, and with you are
people you once knew and some are dead.
Attend them through the many tales and songs
that each might offer others or invent.
The room is small, so work it out.
They will wait for you as you for them
with yes and no, with back and forth,
the here and there, the then and now,
their modes of folding and their modes of caring."

I was struck by this lightning
as much as she, and I carried
the soup quietly to all the beds, for all

through the house it was dark, as it would have
had to be, and darker the movement
stair to stair. There were many there to feed.
We must all feed all the living, then the dead.
And I, it seemed, had taken on one task. Don't spill it.
"I won't." A vow. Was I alone? I did not seem to be
though this was hard to fathom when I felt
the red shadow of our bloody world's
insistent presence in the moon's eclipse,
darkening night. And then the moon slid
slowly back with full suffusing light.

Yet this part of the work remains closest to darkness.
The knowledge of yearning will not be complete.
There is no there; it's all degrees of here.
Cannot touch them whom we are marked by.
But they are palpable and enter this place.
Be nomadic, nomad. Wander with the wanderers,
yet safe in the room. There is at once too much
and much too little. Wait it out.
"The bit of ugly, the glitch, the torn, the sweeper, the tender,
the constant reminder that things are being made, unmade
and tended"—you are now one part of all of this.
You will be it, help it, answer and feed that
surface of cries, chirps. You will call out.
Live in empathy. Let the agony be. Comfort it.

Reject the whole that someone claims is rule.
A hole, a line, a hold, a lie, a hope,
a hype will slide you through this most dangerous spot.
Resist only rectitudes, resist the crazed
and driven knowers. Find and replace.
Though the mechanism to depict this is
called documentary, still it needs the stinging
pulse of lines. This matches that.
All "of-ness" exists
for much more Of.
The beyond moves to two places: here and there.
To achieve connection,
is there just one route of passage?
There is not.

This canzone is divided. What is the method in such a song? How was the evidence for this police report assembled? The first part is the first, and the way it begins is repeated variably—"I carried my soul." This is insistent. The second part is the second, and very short—there is no particular need for balance except as this part pivots between two units of three each—and begins "You will have … to share." The third fissions and fissures ("I was struck by this lightning") so that it becomes impossible to follow and, as was already intimated, gets caught in its own cross-hatches and brambles. These divisions offer quixotic gestures at best, hardly a tribute to my powers of construction, but rather to my sense of being overwhelmed. For saturation in the material is so great that to speak of controlling this experience, or of dividing the representation presents no more than a temporary artifice or stay against the world as such. Truly to say what is here still to be said, I would have to divide, but also to multiply the poem again and again, aphorism after aphorism. What is its argument anyway? When this canzone became known—was there a backstory to this? was I ever in the anthologies?— a friend asked me what my definition of OF was.

We are still working without a contract. There is a continuous, often weaseling use of the word "challenge" whenever policy is being discussed. Tying up tomatoes is on my list for today. She still has the tattoos from where her head was held *en pointe* for the radiation beam to be directed. I fear continually that I will not finish what I define as "my work," so I keep adding other tasks and possibilities, doubling already doubled poems, for example, which is, to speak perfectly frankly, an obvious and transparent strategy. If you start "deepening content knowledge in reading," you might end up reading between the lines. Then between those and other, secret lines. I would like to give you this small piece of string.

Afterward, I could perhaps write interstitial poem after poem, filling gaps that have opened and that exist (have in fact always existed) between every single word, obliterating the work until it is one over-written, unreadable, but theoretically conceptual and thus critically consumable textual object whose laws and rules have, over time, become superstructure. Or I could refuse to. Afterward, I could begin again backwards, moving from the end to the beginning. "Awful literal these words." And many others. Act as if you felt the lines of force, the connections. Act *because* you felt them. Rescue children—even if there is no guarantee. Of their future. Of anything. The person is a pinhole through which the whole community beams and takes itself into its own arms, *camera oscura* images projected, dancingly, upside down; their melancholy, their intersections, their humor, their charm, all cross and link, but sometimes don't. Vita nuova. We hold each other and apart. This part commences here.

June - July 2009

DRIVEN TO TORQUE TEXTS: APPROPRIATION AND DANTE

> *"Conceptual writing mediates between the written object*
> *(which may or may not be a text) and the meaning of the object*
> *by framing the writing as a figural object to be narrated."*
> - Place and Fitterman, *Notes on Conceptualisms*, 15

There are strategies that pluralize authorship, not dissolve it, in order to acknowledge the multiplicity, the self-difference, the heterogeneity of the literary text, deliberately produced as multiple by its single author as an act of critical analysis, didactic intervention, and political critique. "No new news is good news" (Place, 63). No new news IS the news when it is totally transposed. Je est un author: Dante, Pound, Oppen, Coleridge, Wordsworth, Pope, Mallarmé. Je est that kind of other to myself as a conceptual act of disturbance and cultural recalibration, of "confiscation, superimposition" (F&P, 23). I am them as female author, simulacrum of authorship throughout history. I am a fake become ghost become real. For now that history is marked by the shadow of me and others like me. I am a female writer with a set of interlocking differentials or position, access, potential for dissemination and reception, if not in production. I am a particular writer—privileged in language and semi-privileged in country of national origin, critical in politics, in secular practices, via skepticism. I am this mix of hegemonic and emergent in relation to even the critical edges of that culture in which I am also saturated, and through which I have expressed my longing. Or part of that longing. Through which I have also expressed and exposed my resistance. If all culture must begin again from the ground up—the premise of both modernism and of feminism, then as a consequence, I am called to torque texts. I am, in fact, driven to torque texts.

Torquing is a conceptual strategy of ethical, political, formal and cultural interrogation. A long time ago, for a while, I was writing "The 'History of Poetry'" with the premise that I could write into literature, by my own inventions of necessary poems, the female-written texts that were lacking or attenuated or invisible or erased through a lot of Western literary history. The project went underground, apparently to re-emerge in my long poem *Drafts* as the strategy of critical (if also fascinated) interrogation of certain key male-authored texts of long modernism.

Torquing texts or textual appropriation is a specific strategy of cultural citation that, instead of citing from a plethora of materials (as in Marianne Moore, T.S. Eliot, or William Carlos Williams), chooses to engage with one text, overwriting, digging into it, excavating it, twisting it to other uses. The social basis for this and the ethical-political aura produced might depend on the measuring of a distance—historical or social, and on the channeling and examination of the impact of that text, as well as the achievement of a critical relation to the uses of that text. Especially if this text has hegemonic force, the citation and recontextualization, the playing with now-classic statements all have the effect of suspicion, a wary reckoning of temporal, historical and social distance between the original of the torqued text and the authorial agent doing the torquing. I have engaged in a good deal of this twisting, twisty literary behavior (including, unmentioned in my list above, with Ingeborg Bachmann). It is a form of my conviction to do so.

It is also a serious reconceptualization. What was the story told in Dante's *Canzone* and his *Vita Nuova* (c. 1293)? There are at least two. Of love for one woman (Beatrice) and the use of others as a mask for that secret, formative, profound and also conventionalized obsession, of the nobility and purpose he got from that love, the emotional suffering, sometimes even its stunning comedy, yet the growth of intellectual clarity—maturity, we might say. It is the story of the passage of his own soul (soul!) to a purpose higher than that love, through love. And the other story is the tale of interpretation, of the sometimes pedantic, almost tedious point-for-point description of his craft, an odd doubling of one text (the noble poem) stalked or robotically re-told and divided into its argument and formal elements by the poet acting as his own literary critic. I use this doubling not only in this poem, Draft 98: Canzone (in 98 lines with its framing "interpretation"), but I use various kinds of doubling strategies in all of the poems in this sixth or final book of Drafts, in part to express my reluctance to let the project go, to be finished, if not completed, with it.

In *Vita Nuova*, Dante suggests why poets began writing in the vernacular languages rather than Latin; his reasons are germane to this analysis of female figures in poetry. He attributes this literary shift to the desire of a poet to make his love clearly "intelligible to a lady who had difficulty in understanding Latin verses" (Dante 1948, 99). In despite of the historical record about genres and themes of poetry already written in the brief history of vernacular use in literature, he suggests strongly that worshipful platonic love, *amore* and love-longing are, because of these women readers, the most strongly appropriate subjects for vernacular poetry. This influential insight set a pattern for a relationship of *donne gentili* (a classed sector from the larger gender group women) to poetry: they are poignantly undereducated yet necessary readers, inspirers, receivers, and yet limited as to topics addressed in their direction.

Should culture give up on this yearning? Giorgio Agamben's essay "An Enigma Concerning the Basque Woman" offers two answers. He is speaking about a story by the contemporary Italian writer Antonio Delfini that has an apparently incomprehensible citation of a Basque poem in it. "The Basque woman appears through the sweetness of an unknown language and she disappears in the ungraspable murmur of words in a foreign language" (Agamben 1999, 120). This is, of course, precisely the situation of "The Solitary Reaper" for Wordsworth and Wordsworth's gendered cultural frustration, as I argued in *Blue Studios*. Agamben proposes that this kind of female is "the symbol of the language of poetry" linked to maternal speech, speaking in tongues, and "that which is so inner and present that it can never be remembered." I want that, too. But I want to be not only the symbol of the language of poetry for someone else, but the bearer of it, the maker of it, me along with my peers, other women writers who have existed inside this tempting, devastating cultural ghetto.

For Agamben, "Beatrice is the name of the amorous experience of the event of language at play in the poetic text itself. She is thus the name and the love of language, but of language understood not in its grammaticality but, rather, in its radical primordiality, as the emergence of verse from the pure Nothing" (Agamben 1999, 58). This is a brilliant (and familiar...) argument on an epistemological limb jutting out over an abyss; the female figure is that which produces something (language) from Nothing (the void) by virtue of maternal generosity and generativity. What about judgment, creativity, intelligence, drive? What about her social intervention? What about her social generosity? Let her be an agent! Let her be confused, let her be devastated!—not the Ideal, but in the real. This is why I am intolerant of this endless romanticizing of Her power, the Power of Her. She is dehistoricized. No—! it is enough! I want the female in history, as the *makir*. I do not want her outside history and time. Can the people-whom-we-females-are not become agents, driven to help remake our collective culture? This is one of the conceptual, critical urgencies that motivated this poem.

- Rachel Blau DuPlessis

References

Giorgio Agamben, *The End of the Poem: Studies in Poetics*, Trans. Daniel Helle-Roazen (Stanford: Stanford U.P., 1999).

Dante [Alighieri]. *The Vita Nuova and Canzoniere* [1906], Trans. Thomas Okey and Philip Wicksteed (London: J.M. Dent & Sons Ltd, 1948).

Rachel Blau DuPlessis, *Blue Studios: Poetry and Its Cultural Work* (Tuscaloosa: University of Alabama Press, 2006).

Vanessa Place and Robert Fitterman, *Notes on Conceptualisms* (Brooklyn, NY: Ugly Duckling Presse, 2009).

Notes to "Draft 98: Canzone." The citation: "The bit of ugly, the glitch, the torn, the sweeper, the tender, the constant reminder that things are being unmade and tended" is by Sina Queyras, 9 May 2009, on Jeff Wall, photographer, taken from her Lemon Hound blog. Draft on the "line of three." This poem appeared, in first publication, in *Jacket Magazine 38* (Fall 2009), with many thanks to John Tranter.
http://jacketmagazine.com/38/duplessis-draft98l.shtml

The long poem project of **Rachel Blau DuPlessis**, begun in 1986, is collected in *Torques: Drafts 58-76* (Salt Publishing, 2007), as well as in *Drafts 1-38, Toll* (Wesleyan U.P., 2001) and *Drafts 39-57, Pledge, with Draft unnumbered: Précis* (Salt Publishing, 2004). *Pitch: Drafts 77-96* (2010) and *The Collage Poems of Drafts* (2011) both recently appeared from Salt Publishing. In 2006, two books of her innovative essays were published: *Blue Studios: Poetry and Its Cultural Work* on gender and poetics, along with a reprinting of the ground-breaking *The Pink Guitar: Writing as Feminist Practice,* both from University of Alabama Press. In 2002, she was awarded a Pew Fellowship in the Arts, in 2007, a residency for poetry at Bellagio, sponsored by the Rockefeller Foundation, and in 2008-09, an appointment to the National Humanities Center in North Carolina. Her poems have appeared in such periodicals as *Jacket Magazine, Conjunctions, Chicago Review, Verse, Hambone,* and *XcP: Cross-Cultural Poetics*. Her poetry has also appeared in French, Portuguese and Italian.

THERESA HAK KYUNG CHA

FROM *DICTEE*

CLIO	HISTORY
CALLIOPE	EPIC POETRY
URANIA	ASTRONOMY
MELPOMENE	TRAGEDY
ERATO	LOVE POETRY
ELITERE	LYRIC POETRY
THALIA	COMEDY
TERPSICHORE	CHORAL DANCE
POLYMNIA	SACRED POETRY

Aller à la ligne   C'était le premier jour   point
Elle venait de loin   point   ce soir au dîner   virgule
les familles demanderaient   virgule   ouvre les guil-
lemets   Ça c'est bien passé le premier jour   point
d'interrogation   ferme les guillemets   au moins
virgule   dire le moins possible   virgule   la réponse
serait   virgule   ouvre les guillemets   Il n'y a q'une
chose   point   ferme les guillemets   ouvre les guille-
mets   Il y a quelqu'une   point   loin   point   ferme
les guillemets

Open paragraph   It was the first day   period
She had come from a far   period   tonight at dinner
comma   the families would ask   comma   open
quotation marks   How was the first day   interroga-
tion mark   close quotation marks   at least to say
the least of it possible   comma   the answer would be
open quotation marks   there is but one thing   period
There is someone   period   From   a far   period
close quotation marks

DISEUSE

She mimicks the speaking. That might resemble
speech. (Anything at all.) Bared noise, groan, bits
torn from words. Since she hesitates to measure the
accuracy, she resorts to mimicking gestures with the
mouth. The entire lower lip would lift upwards then
sink back to its original place. She would then gather
both lips and protrude them in a pout taking in the
breath that might utter some thing. (One thing. Just
one.) But the breath falls away. With a slight tilting
of her head backwards, she would gather the strength
in her shoulders and remain in this position.

It murmurs inside. It murmurs. Inside is the pain
of speech the pain to say. Larger still. Greater
than is the pain not to say. To not say. Says
nothing against the pain to speak. It festers in-
side. The wound, liquid, dust. Must break. Must
void.

From the back of her neck she releases her shoulders
free. She swallows once more. (Once more. One
more time would do.) In preparation. It augments.
To such a pitch. Endless drone, refueling itself. Au-
tonomous. Self-generating. Swallows with last efforts
last wills against the pain that wishes it to speak.

She allows others. In place of her. Admits others to
make full. Make swarm. All barren cavities to make
swollen. The others each occupying her. Tumorous

3

layers, expel all excesses until in all cavities she is flesh.

She allows herself caught in their threading, anonymously in their thick motion in the weight of their utterance. When the amplification stops there might be an echo. She might make the attempt then. The echo part. At the pause. When the pause has already soon begun and has rested there still. She waits inside the pause. Inside her. Now. This very moment. Now. She takes rapidly the air, in gulfs, in preparation for the distances to come. The pause ends. The voice wraps another layer. Thicker now even. From the waiting. The wait from pain to say. To not to. Say.

> *She would take on their punctuation. She waits to service this. Theirs. Punctuation. She would become, herself, demarcations. Absorb it. Spill it. Seize upon the punctuation. Last air. Give her. Her. The relay. Voice. Assign. Hand it. Deliver it. Deliver.*

She relays the others. Recitation. Evocation. Offering. Provocation. The begging. Before her. Before them.

Now the weight begins from the uppermost back of her head, pressing downward. It stretches evenly, the entire skull expanding tightly all sides toward the front of her head. She gasps from its pressure, its contracting motion.

4

Inside her voids. It does not contain further. Rising from the empty below, pebble lumps of gas. Moisture. Begin to flood her. Dissolving her. Slow, slowed to deliberation. Slow and thick.

The above traces from her head moving downward closing her eyes, in the same motion, slower parting her mouth open together with her jaw and throat which the above falls falling just to the end not stopping there but turning her inside out in the same motion, shifting complete the whole weight to elevate upward.

Begins imperceptibly, near-perceptible. (Just once. Just one time and it will take.) She takes. She takes the pause. Slowly. From the thick. The thickness. From weighted motion upwards. Slowed. To deliberation even when it passed upward through her mouth again. The delivery. She takes it. Slow. The invoking. All the time now. All the time there is. Always. And all times. The pause. Uttering. Hers now. Hers bare. The utter.

Theresa Hak Kyung Cha (1951-1982) was born in Pusan, Korea and emigrated to San Francisco in 1964. She is the author of *Dictee*, along with other published works, and the creator of films, videos, performances, works on paper and mail art.

TINA DARRAGH

FROM RULE OF DUMBS

(dedicated to Heather Fuller for her poetry and for her work with alternative forms of animal shelters)

In 1975, the philosopher Peter Singer began his book on animal liberation with a chapter entitled "All Animals Are Equal...or why supporters of liberation for Blacks and Women should support Animal Liberation too." Recalling the 18th century *A Vindication of the Rights of Brutes* satirizing Mary Wollstonecraft's feminist treatise, Singer calls for giving animals equal consideration instead of equal treatment.

consideration = attention

      shape up the fragments   to

             distract us from our powerlessness

Singer's work on animal liberation inspired many, including Henry Spira, a union activist who spent much of the '60s and early '70s fighting corruption in the National Maritime Union. For his first animal rights action, Spira organized a series of demonstrations to protest feline sex experiments at the American Museum of Natural History. For almost two decades, scientists had surgically altered various sections of cats' brains and then observed their sexual behavior with other cats, rabbits, and inanimate objects. The demonstrations attracted press coverage, then politicians, then public hearings. The experiments were halted after the National Institutes of Health stopped funding the project. Spira then turned his attention to the cosmetic industry's blinding of rabbits with the Draize test, chemical eye drops named for a Food and Drug Administration official. Along with demonstrations featuring people dressed as animals, ads run in major newspapers asked "How many rabbits does Revlon blind for beauty's sake?" Revlon and other cosmetics companies responded by funding projects to develop animal testing alternatives. Another successful Spira campaign convinced the Department of Agriculture to cease the face-branding of cattle.

But when it came to changing factory-farming methods, Spira's creative campaigns (including "End the Gulf War Now by Bombing Iraq with

Perdue Chickens") failed to have an impact. Perdue successfully countered Spira's toxic chicken ads with ones of their own touting their hens as alternative food since they were fed "natural" marigold petals.

The animals we "see" either are in zoos (exotic icons of global imperialism) or at home (cute icons of nuclear familiarity). Not moving, pets confirm our isolation at home so that we act by buying more products from the world of wild animals who aren't moving either. To date, animal rights actions have been successful when focusing on "feminine" appearances— cosmetic beauty and voyeuristic sex—which in turn reinforce patriarchal order. The factory farm remains.

The most successful protests by a union activist in the 1980s were for animal rights.

Lament for the unity in utility under capitalism

SIMPLUS from us– last part– not blended so!
    Low force infold raised to name;
Guild math shatter seven low
    His smile owns breath past blasted fame.
Proud rage our graves where steps whisp goal,
    Toil fore one word round cling,
Sunk to hush, ally driv'lling cries
    God! Why not sight our spare this rise?

I'm sorry for the ugly phrase "unity in utility under capitalism"

ill-favored adjectives balk
minatory **indifference curve** of goods where there is no preference for one over the other

like). ??. Awe.]

    if 1. [ ]formed consumer was equally satisfied with 10 peaches and 2 avocados, 2 kiwi and 12 peaches, or 1/5th an apple and 1/4th a banana, these combinations would all form a line on:

minatory: <http://dict.die.net/minatory/>
preference: <http://encyclopedia.laborlawtalk.com/Preference>
Awe: <http://dict.die.net/awe/>

cankered, cantankerous, churlish, corrupt, crabbed,
    crabby, cranky, critical, cross, cross-grained, crotchety,
        crusty, attacking the person arguing rather than the
           argument itself

perverse situation called **rational** in reference to
the ream that you or others
are *homo economicus* largely

————

Ever since the publication of *Animal Liberation*, Peter Singer has been
commonly known as the "father of animal rights" even though he's a
strict utilitarian. Rejecting the notion that animals have rights because
they are not "subjects of a life," he focuses on the consequences of actions
that benefit or harm them. But for readers living within a system where
profits are maximized by hiding harms, the only trade-off they know is
supply and demand, the only demand they know is union corruption, the
only supply they know is stream of con'n stuff 'n stuff.

————

Dam con'n stuff 'n stuff lament

long train of events is wrapped up Slower,
roll'd up in shades or as it is called
the cooling of heated metals produce
some slip in *Week-day Serm* happiness activity
to forget **the use of that word, all the changes**
indefinite, incoherent feeling in more and more
complex defending credit of all
public temper performed
varied sprays

————

As Solon moved to strengthen the Greek city state by portraying the
casualties of war as heroes, the existing practice of mourning the dead
—words broken into sounds by the cries of many women—was banned,
and funerals hidden from sight. The law stipulated that there were to
be no laments outside the home, and specified the degree of kinship
necessary for a woman to legally accompany a corpse to its grave before
dawn. The sound of collective wailing evoked fears of wild animals on the
move, and of an uncontrollable revenge undermining the best interests
of the state. With the linking of laments to property rights, any concept
of "family" beyond economic ties was outlawed, and the history of war's
consequences for all families could be neither seen nor heard.

————

I can't property lament this

Probable war of LED
Loss obviously of LED
ExisTEN stopped
this swindler moment
numbered paragraph will

The May Day activists of 1968 believed that they were creating a
revolutionary form of supply and demand—instead of subjects
demanding objects,
"free expression" was substituted for demanding subjects, thus eliminating
objects the state could contaminate.
Now pure-bred sounds shake all on their own,
beaker-speaks for which the only demand in the world
is for words unsown in that world
where field animals
have no language
only evolution
which is a picture
not a history
although it looks like one

Collective Lament for Banishing Animals from History

Oh, Marx, when you called freedom the fruit of human minds already
fully formed beyond the beasts in the fields, you hid history with
evolution and drew a straight line from pose to state possession. No
revolution can take place as we devote ourselves to managing the animal
bodies we assume we've left behind. Our cries rise from throats made
weak with words which can choke us while we breathe, XXX " to speak"
XXX the dumbest design. As co-minions, we call across kinships to
protest the totala XXXXXXXXXXXXXXXXXXXXXXXXXXXXX
totalcon rate of *centration*
ixture of separab *plan* position*ll never*
*tu*requivalent *will* unts
*ac*offensive: capital, egregious, flag curve of the longitudinal hull
echanism, that is changed ☒ who agitates
☒ An appastirs, XXXXXXXXXXXXXXXXXXXX in small amounts
increasing the rate of a ☒
completely different form restling reverses
specified angular origin remains
*tu*osition or disposition of by folding

Turn XXXXXXXXXXXXXXXXXXXXXXXXXXX right side *unsettle:*
"*Sudden prosper*☒ with *to* or *into*: turn
through pages as to*actions* or *Make a*
wherdeed "*He thought* XXXXXXXXXXXXXXXXXXXXXXX *some turn*
had done fo☒ about *volving*
avert
tuwere turned out
git☒ *turn over*
to lurch or heave My *st*sequence
out of XXXXXXXXXXXXXXXXXXXXXXXXXXX

lea*e* the *ocean*. in time of n*d but used a stick as exhausted*
expedient befo☒ pitch, intonation, s*jectives mean*
XXXXXXXXXXXXXXXXXXXXXXXXXXXX
day.etermination: a*xample*) Char☒ ce:
char☒ *ne;*.
idate

———

April 25, 2004

During an abortion rights march on Washington, DC, counter-demonstrators take over "Freedom Plaza," a small square on Pennsylvania Avenue within view of the White House. While the abortion rights marchers carry small placards—some printed, most handmade—the counter-demonstrators are dwarfed by 3 ten-foot high, professionally-made, appropriate-for-newsbreak posters: one of a fetus appearing to suck its thumb, one of a monkey appearing to scream with electrodes on its head, and one of a self-proclaimed Islamic terrorist. The fetus has no words and no history, the monkey has no words and no history, and the image of the Islamic terrorist evokes words and history disintegrating along with the World Trade Center.

———

lament for the solidarity of base by face by face

the reciprocal frequency
feels with the common
interests that immediately
you include

the reciprocal frequency
stops with the common
complete interest that
includes you immediately

———

September 2, 2005

Lynne Dreyer finds an article in Baltimore's *Afro American* newspaper on "Hanging," a PETA exhibit that juxtaposed a photo of two black men lynched by a white mob next to one of a cow hung upside down in a slaughterhouse. The creatures were put together so that they looked like one Christian crucifixion scene. (*"Tableau, you know, has judge&jury in tow."*) The NAACP spokesman quoted in the article responded that comparing the criminal act of lynching with the legal act of butchering exploited history.

———————

(dispose) >ABLE creatures

(two ways, in twosense "reverse, undo") > INTERROGATE HOLD begins

    /> start a sentence
capital
    /> start a business

chattel = moveable possessions

———————

The inclusion of colloquial language in the 3rd edition of Webster's dictionary caused quite a stir. But it wasn't entries such as "ain't" that prompted a number of hostile takeover bids of MerriamWebster by rival publishers. Corporations were distressed that trademarked names, such as kleenex, had made their way into everyday speech uncapitalized. Reprints of the 3rd edition recapitalized all trademarks, except for those that had become verbs.

———————

trademark—not land, not erosion, not wearing, not wearing away

<u>a</u> <u>coming</u> <u>down</u> <u>from</u> <u>some</u> <u>previously</u> <u>raised</u>
<u>state</u> <u>as</u> <u>the</u> <u>waves</u> <u>subside</u> <u>after</u> <u>a</u> <u>storm</u>
<u>a</u> <u>sinking</u> <u>down</u> <u>into</u> <u>the</u> word <u>as</u> <u>the</u> <u>tumult</u> <u>of</u> <u>the</u> people
<u>in</u> <u>such</u> <u>cases,</u> <u>we</u> <u>were</u> <u>thinking</u> <u>of</u> <u>the</u>

a: <http://www.hyperdictionary.com/dictionary/a>
coming: <http://www.hyperdictionary.com/dictionary/coming>
down: <http://www.hyperdictionary.com/dictionary/down>
from: <http://www.hyperdictionary.com/dictionary/from>
some: <http://www.hyperdictionary.com/dictionary/some>
previously: <http://www.hyperdictionary.com/dictionary/previously>
raised: <http://www.hyperdictionary.com/dictionary/raised>
state: <http://www.hyperdictionary.com/dictionary/state>
as: <http://www.hyperdictionary.com/dictionary/as>
the: <http://www.hyperdictionary.com/dictionary/the>
waves: <http://www.hyperdictionary.com/dictionary/waves>
subside: <http://www.hyperdictionary.com/dictionary/subside>
after: <http://www.hyperdictionary.com/dictionary/after>
storm: <http://www.hyperdictionary.com/dictionary/storm>

building where animals are butchered

     /> a building
shambles
     /> a disorder
our antimask set to case
such land as hide would cover
o? unwillingness to sum familiar
making m?urs o'erlaid

a sequence of values until it fails. Resumption takes -> **the arrangement of light and dark parts**
  to represent the colors of natural objects, but for effect
  only, and produced with hard material
1.   **Disguise thyself as thou wilt, still, Slavery…**
     . . **still**
is increased by
putting in the space between the spectator and leaves
2.   **shutting together**
but running upon

a: <http://www.hyperdictionary.com/dictionary/a>
sinking: <http://www.hyperdictionary.com/dictionary/sinking>
down: <http://www.hyperdictionary.com/dictionary/down>
into: <http://www.hyperdictionary.com/dictionary/into>
the: <http://www.hyperdictionary.com/dictionary/the>
as: <http://www.hyperdictionary.com/dictionary/as>
tumult: <http://www.hyperdictionary.com/dictionary/tumult>
of: <http://www.hyperdictionary.com/dictionary/of>
people: <http://www.hyperdictionary.com/dictionary/people>
in: <http://www.hyperdictionary.com/dictionary/in>
such: <http://www.hyperdictionary.com/dictionary/such>
cases: <http://www.hyperdictionary.com/dictionary/cases>
we: <http://www.hyperdictionary.com/dictionary/we>
were: <http://www.hyperdictionary.com/dictionary/were>
thinking: <http://www.hyperdictionary.com/dictionary/thinking>
building: <http://www.hyperdictionary.com/dictionary/building>
where: <http://www.hyperdictionary.com/dictionary/where>
animals: <http://www.hyperdictionary.com/dictionary/animals>
are: <http://www.hyperdictionary.com/dictionary/are>
butchered: <http://www.hyperdictionary.com/dictionary/butchered>
our: <http://www.hyperdictionary.com/dictionary/our>
arrangement: <http://www.hyperdictionary.com/dictionary/arrangement>
light: <http://www.hyperdictionary.com/dictionary/light>
and: <http://www.hyperdictionary.com/dictionary/and>
dark: <http://www.hyperdictionary.com/dictionary/dark>
parts: <http://www.hyperdictionary.com/dictionary/parts>
to: <http://www.hyperdictionary.com/dictionary/to>
represent: <http://www.hyperdictionary.com/dictionary/represent>
colors: <http://www.hyperdictionary.com/dictionary/colors>
natural: <http://www.hyperdictionary.com/dictionary/natural>
objects: <http://www.hyperdictionary.com/dictionary/objects>
but: <http://www.hyperdictionary.com/dictionary/but>
for: <http://www.hyperdictionary.com/dictionary/for>
effect: <http://www.hyperdictionary.com/dictionary/effect>
only: <http://www.hyperdictionary.com/dictionary/only>
produced: <http://www.hyperdictionary.com/dictionary/produced>
with: <http://www.hyperdictionary.com/dictionary/with>
hard: <http://www.hyperdictionary.com/dictionary/hard>
material: <http://www.hyperdictionary.com/dictionary/material>
Disguise: <http://www.hyperdictionary.com/dictionary/disguise>
thyself: <http://www.hyperdictionary.com/dictionary/thyself>
thou: <http://www.hyperdictionary.com/dictionary/thou>
wilt: <http://www.hyperdictionary.com/dictionary/wilt>
still: <http://www.hyperdictionary.com/dictionary/still>
slavery: <http://www.hyperdictionary.com/dictionary/slavery>
is: <http://www.hyperdictionary.com/dictionary/is>
increased: <http://www.hyperdictionary.com/dictionary/increased>
by: <http://www.hyperdictionary.com/dictionary/by>
putting: <http://www.hyperdictionary.com/dictionary/putting>
space: <http://www.hyperdictionary.com/dictionary/space>
between: <http://www.hyperdictionary.com/dictionary/between>
spectator: <http://www.hyperdictionary.com/dictionary/spectator>
leaves: <http://www.hyperdictionary.com/dictionary/leaves>

1. peculiar to a language; not themselves

animals as trademarks are outside of history
animal trademarks hide humans as chattel
marking our trade slips = our silent kin ships

IdealDog trademark
Animal Series trademark
Animal Logic trademark
OncoMouse trademark
Animal Crossing trademark
Human and Animal Diagnostics trademark

––––––––

Words don't branch out when linking non-human animal oppression with events in human history. If slaughterhouses are compared with gas chambers, Holocaust survivors respond that Jews, Gypsies and the disabled may have died like animals, but animals don't die like Jews, Gypsies, and the disabled. Animals don't have a history. But those gassed in the camps didn't die like all animals, only those not covered by National Socialism's 1933 Law on Animal Protection. At that point in time, part of Jewish history overlapped with part of Gypsy history with part of disability history with part of non-human animal history. These historical laps remain as gaps in the stories told as the concentration camps become museums.

shutting: <http://www.hyperdictionary.com/dictionary/shutting>
together: <http://www.hyperdictionary.com/dictionary/together>
but: <http://www.hyperdictionary.com/dictionary/but>
running: <http://www.hyperdictionary.com/dictionary/running>
upon: <http://www.hyperdictionary.com/dictionary/upon>
peculiar: <http://www.hyperdictionary.com/dictionary/peculiar>
to: <http://www.hyperdictionary.com/dictionary/to>
a: <http://www.hyperdictionary.com/dictionary/a>
language: <http://www.hyperdictionary.com/dictionary/language>
not: <http://www.hyperdictionary.com/dictionary/not>
themselves: <http://www.hyperdictionary.com/dictionary/themselves>

notes for "rule of dumbs"

The first section of "rule of dumbs" was published as Belladonna* pamphlet #30 (New York: Belladonna* Books, Spring 2002) with thanks to editor Rachel Levitsky.

Peter Singer, *Animal Liberation: A New Ethics for Our Treatment of Animals* (New York: New York Review, 1975).

Henry Spira: Peter Singer, *Ethics into Action: Henry Spira and the Animal Rights Movement* (Lanham, MD: Rowman & Littlefield, 1998).

Misnomer "Father of Animal Rights" for Peter Singer: "Father of Animal Rights Among TIME's Most Influential People," *The Island Vegetarian: Vegetarian Society of Hawaii Quarterly Newsletter*, July-September 2005 (http://www.veghawaii.com/newsletter-2005-09.pdf).

Solon's law forbidding public lamentation: Richard A. Hughes, *Lament, Death, and Destiny* (New York: Peter Lang Publishing, 2004), 17-18.

May Day beaker-speaks: Sherry Turkle, *Psychoanalytic Politics: Freud's French Revolution* (Cambridge, MA: MIT Press, 1978), 85.

Marx's human/animal dualism: Ted Benton, "Marx on Humans and Animals" in *Natural Relations: Ecology, Animal Rights & Social Justice* (London/New York: Verso, 1993).

Evolution is not a straight line: "Now this may be a bit disconcerting to some people. Sentient beings, sapient *human* beings, have always thought that there was something inevitable about them. Even devout Darwinian evolutionists tend to put our own immodest species at the top branch of the evolutionary tree, as if we were somewhat better and more evolved than other living species. But...chance has played a role in putting every living thing at the top of the present evolutionary tree." Jeffrey K. McKee, *The Riddled Chain: Chance, Coincidence, and Chaos in Human Evolution* (New Brunswick, NJ: Rutgers University Press, 2000), 4.

"Hanging": Zenitha Prince, "PETA generates outrage Equating Blacks with mistreated animals" in *Afro American*, September 2, 2005, A1, A6.

(dis-pose) ABLE creatures: the title pays homage to Kevin Bales' *Disposable People: New Slavery in the Global Economy* (Berkeley, CA: University of California Press, 1999). Originally published in *War and Peace #2* (San Francisco: O Books, 2005) with thanks to the editors Leslie Scalapino and Judith Goldman.

Use of trademarks as verbs: Herbert Charles Morton, *The Story of Webster's Third: Philip Gove's Controversial Dictionary and Its Critics.* (Cambridge; New York: Cambridge University Press, 1994), 219-223.

Concentration camp/slaughterhouse comparison controversy: J.M. Coetzee, *The Lives of Animals* (Princeton, NJ: Princeton University Press, 1999), 49-50.

For a discussion of the interrelationships among the mass murders of Jews, Gypsies, and the disabled during National Socialism: Henry Friedlander, *The Origins of Nazi Genocide: From Euthanasia to the Final Solution* (Chapel Hill: University of North Carolina Press, 1995).

Dear Fellow Partial Authors,

To challenge the notion of writing/ideas as property, please feel free to continue to reproduce, remix, rearrange, edit, perform, display, and/or croon any or all of this piece as your own.

A call to plagiarize? Well, in part. Plagiarizing as a critique of capitalism (I'm thinking here of the Festivals of Plagiarism associated with Neoism in the '70s—'90s) hits on many of the things we love to challenge: the authenticity of the author, the uniqueness of the individual, and the authority of "the text." But how do non-human animals fare in plagiarism? The "author" may have disappeared, but language remains privileged.

What's so great about freeze-frame words that enable discussions of "human rights" to obscure Police State might? As "opposable dumbs," let's assume the moveable mantle of the medieval author to explore what could be illuminating in the different ways human and non-human animals don't have language.

Medieval manuscripts elude identity with a side of history. For example, the *Romance of the Rose*'s authors—poets, scribes, and performers—wrote/rewrote the story and illustrated/annotated the edges in intervocal anonymity. Sometimes they added new information, sometimes they added error. Either way, the "first hand" was not significant; rather, the history of the story was illuminated by the authors who were never more than partial. Can we reduce in this way the fictions that threaten us all? "What does it matter who is speaking" as a pan-animal liberation call.

- Tina Darragh

Tina Darragh's recent books include *Deep eco pré,* a collaboration with Marcella Durand freely available from Little Red Leaves (http://www.littleredleaves.com/), and the *Elders Series #8* with Jane Sprague and Diane Ward (belladonna, 2009). "rule of dumbs" is part of Darragh's *opposable dumbs* project; a pdf version is available from Zimzalla (http://zimzalla.files.wordpress.com/2009/09/tina-darragh-opposable-dumbs.pdf), and a modifiable wiki version, "No Rights Observed," is in the works on ourproject.org (http://ourproject.org/moin/projects/norightsobserve).

JUDITH GOLDMAN

PRINCE HARRY CONSIDERS
VISITING AUSCHWITZ

> *There are no more ideologies in the authentic sense of false consciousness, only*
> *advertisements for the world through its duplication and the provocative lie which*
> *does not seek belief but commands silence... The more total society becomes, the*
> *greater the reification of the mind and the more paradoxical its effort to escape*
> *reification on its own... Cultural criticism finds itself faced with the final stage of*
> *the dialectic of culture and barbarism. To write poetry after Auschwitz is barbaric.*
> - Theodor Adorno, "Cultural Criticism and Society"

PRESENT TENSED

coming out of the movie theater the world the world is
bright too bright gnomic present tense tensile everything
happening at once the world is full of its own mute history
the fatality of reflection the fatality of nature and culture
the fatality of the German sciences of Kultur the fatality
of i.e. mute history remaining mute the fatality of of the
preposition reaching out to its object even as it e.g. it .
slips away

- Joan Retallack, *Memnoir*

speaking so that the blank couldn't speak, speaking when one spoke
[...] In war, we have the leisure to remember anything.
- Leslie Scalapino, "The Forest is in the Euphrates River"

It's a total failure of the Western imagination that the only enemy they
can see is Adolf Hitler.
- Tariq Ali, *Speaking of Empire and Resistance*

Go to mass with the air
          and the shrapnel for a church
A Christian civilization
Where Pius blesses the black-shirts
- Louis Zukofsky, "A" 10

VESTING ORDER NO. 126:

HAMBURG-AMERIKA LINE (Aug. 1942) ThE
twEnty-yEar-old princE had a surrogatE issuE a statE-
mEnt indicating

quotEOnly in thE Catholic church is thErE EtErnal salvation.quotE/
WhEn hE was bEtrayEd

and that it was donE in poor tastE

ThE youngEst of thrEE childrEn, JosEph RatzingEr was born/indicating
that hE was sorry for wEaring thE Nazi uniform/quotEREsistancE was
trulyquotE/hE nEvEr took part in any/no idEa his attirE would offEnd

ThE twEnty-yEar-old princE had a surrogatE issuE a statEmEnt
indicating/his family by wEaring a Nazi uniform to a party/who won
thrEE gold mEdals in EquEstrian EvEnts

quotEWhy can't wE justquotE/quotEhElpquotE him pass his art Exam/
in thE khaki uniform of RommEl's Afrika Korps, complEtE with rEd
swastika armband

CharlEs was also angry at William bEcausE hE was in thE storE
whEn Harry, 20,/intErprEtEd thE wound as a fountain of gracE/
His condEmnations arE lEgion—of womEn priEsts, marriEd priEsts,
dissidEnt thEologians, and homosExuals/HE upsEt many JEws with a
statEmEnt in 1987/whEn mincing around, doing that littlE flip-of-thE-
wrist mini-HEil thing

ThE Sun, quoting a royal insidEr, said/: quotEFor it is not you that spEak,
but thE spirit of your FathEr that spEakEth in youquotE

Army instructors wErE astoundEd to find PrincE Harry lackEd basic
computEr skills/thanks in part to a royal scandal involving PrincE
Harry wEaring Nazi rEgalia at a costumE party/WhilE it wouldn't bE
accEptablE for a PrincE to bEcomE an artist/his choicE of fancy drEss
costumE/wEaring Nazi garb to a fancy drEss party/alrEady has plans
to sEt up scholarships for young British artists/just two wEEks bEforE
world lEadErs gathErEd in Poland/to find PrincE Harry lackEd basic
computEr skills

On thE samE day Harry took a languagE tEst and pickEd up his Army-
issuE boots/quotEIt's not a casE of pass or fail, it's just a diagnostic
tEstquotE/I, thErEforE, madE him of our TablE Round,/Not rashly but
havE provEd him EvEryway

       to pick thE vicious quitch
Of blood and custom out of him,
And makE all clEan,/
to EncouragE othErs and hElp with fundraising

hE disciplinEd thE advocatEs of quotElibEration thEologyquotE

And in thEir chairs sEt up a strongEr racE

CharlEs was also angry at William bEcausE hE was in/an anti-aircraft unit
that protEctEd a BMW factory/His fathEr, also callEd JosEph, was an
anti-Nazi whosE attEmpts to rEin in HitlEr's Brown Shirts/pickEd up thE
offEnsivE costumE for thE party last Saturday/quotEFor it is not you that
spEak, but thE spirit of your FathEr that spEakEth in youquotE/whEn
mincing around, doing that littlE flip-of-thE-wrist mini-HEil thing

quotEO brothEr, had you known our CamElot,quotE/complEtE with
Swastika

quotEBuilt by old kings, agE aftEr agE, so old/ThE King himsElfquotE/
was influEncEd by a quotEcabalquotE of JEwish advisors

quotELast night CharlEs ordErEd both boys to privatEly visitquotE/
SchindlEr's ListquotE/quotEAlthough thE computEr tEst was a lot morE
complEx than just/a quotEnativE and colonialquotE party

quotERREsistancE was truly impossiblEquotE/thE spokEswoman
strEssEd/quotEthE computEr tEst was a lot morE complEx than
justquotE/

quotEsEnding EmailsquotE

VESTING ORDER 259:

HOLLAND AMERICA TRADING CORPORATION (Oct. 1942)/GeorgexW
.xBushxpaidxtribute/quotetoxrecallxthexevilxquote

GeorgexW.xBushxpaid*pays*xtributexonxSunday/ ~~by which investigations into the financial laundering of the Third Reich~~/ toxthex soldiersxwhoxdied*die/dying*xtoxfreexEuropexfromxNazixGermany/~~a de facto Nazi front organization in the US~~/60xyearsxagox

Thexquotebank,quotexfounded*found/made/founded*/xinx1924/wasxUnionxBankingxCorporationxinxNewxYorkxCity/axdexfacto/cemeteryxinxthexNether lands/PrescottxBushxaxmanagingxdirector/~~for the financial architect of the Nazi war machine~~

Bushxwillxgive*gave*xhisxonlyxspeechxonxV-Exday/quoteWexcome*came/coming*xtoxthisxgroundxtoxrecallxthexevilquote/Hexisx expected*expect*   him toxtoxdrawxaxparallelxbetween/Iraqxreconstructionxprimexcontractors/and/thexstrugglexagainstxtotalitarianism/allxofxwhichxoperated*operations*xoutxofxthexsamexsetxofxofficesxatx39xBroadway

~~were in fact quotenominees,quote or phantom shareholders,~~xforxThyssen/Inx1928xThyssenxhadxbought*purchased*thexBarlowxPalace/quotetoxrecall*toxbe*thexevilxthesexAmericansxfoughtxagainstquote/whichxHitlerxconverted*made*intoxthexBrownxHouse/quotewexcomextoxaffirm*negate/cancel*thexgreatxdebtxwexowe*own*themq uote/,xheadquartersxofxthexNazixParty

GeorgexW.xBush/~~traveled to Berlin to set up the German branch of their banking and investment operations,~~/OPERATIONXRESOLUTEXSWORD/OPERATIONXENDURINGXFREEDOM/whichxwerexlargelyxbasedxonxcriticalxwarxresources/PrescottxBushxandxhisxcolleaguesxtriedxtox~~conceal their financial alliance with~~/IraqxInvestmentxandxReconstructionxTaskxForce/welcomexbusinessxproposalsxforxpublicxorxprivatexdistributionxinxIraq/sincexthexalliedxvictoryxoverxthexNazis

Bush'sxlinksxtoxthexConsolidatedxSilesianxSteelxCompany/quoteun-derscore*score/will underscore* xthexterriblexpricexwexpaid*paying*xforxthatxvictoryquote/Thexcompa-nyxmadexusexof*used*x~~Nazi slave labour from the concentration camps,~~/quoteAndxthexthousandsxofxwhitexmarblexcrossesxandxStarsx-ofxDavidxunderscore*underscore*xthexterriblexpricequote/,xincludingx-Auschwitz/~~Bush and Harriman each received $1.5 million in cash~~xasxcompensationxforxtheir/quotethousandsxofxwhitexmarblex-crossesxandxStarsxofxDavidquote/seized*seizure*xassets

~~quoteSince 1939, these [steel and mining] properties have been in posses-sion of and have been operated by the German government~~/forxgivingxaidxandxcomfortxtoxthexenemy/~~and have un-doubtedly been of considerable assistance to that country's war effort quote~~

tox~~conceal their financial alliance with German industrial ist~~/to try to con-ceal the true nature and ownership of their various businesses/~~funneling laundered money and strategic materials to Nazi Germany~~/quoteTherexwerexthosexwhoxbelieved*believe/know*xthatxde-mocracyquote/~~grew rich from Hitler's efforts to re-arm/both feeding and financing Hitler's build-up to war~~/quotewasxtooxsoftxtoxsurvive,x*survival*especiallyxagainstxaxNazix Germanyxthatxboastedquote/UnionxBankingxCorporation'sxhugexgold xpurchases/quotethexmostxprofessional,xwell-equipped,xhighlyxtrainedxmilitaryxforcesxinxthexworld.xYetxthisxmili-taryxwouldxbexbroughtxdownx*was brought down*byxaxcoalitionxofxarmiesquote/xwww.iraqcoalition.org/business_center.html/www.fedbizopps.gov/quoteThere xis*was/isn't*xnoxpowerx likexthexpowerxofxfreedom,xandquote/ThexUSxgovernmentxis*will have been*xcurrentlyxunablextoxprovidexbackgroundxinforma tionxonxIraqixcompanies...forxaxlistxofxsecurityxfirms,xpleasexvisit/quotenoxsoldi-erxasxstrongxasxthexsoldierxwhoxfights*fighted/fought*xforxthatxfreedom-quotex

ThexBushxFamilyxrecentlyxapproved*approving/approval ratings*xaxflatteringxbiography/quotebirthrightxofxallx man kindquote/ ofxPrescottxBush/xentitled*had been titled/entitlement*x*Duty,xHonour,xCountry*xbyxMickeyxHerskowitz/ OPERATIONXVIGILANT/subcontractor/OPERATIONXVIGI-LANT/~~long Nazi afiliation~~/thexBushxfamily'sx~~long Nazi affilia-tion~~/whenxtherexwas*was*xalreadyxsignificantxinformationxaboutx-thexNazi'sxplanxandxpolicies/*Whoxcan*could*x*Ixcontactxtoxfind*get*x-

employ mentxopportunitiesxinxIraqxreconstruction?/evenxafterxAmeri cax-
hadxentered*had entered/re-entered*xthexwar/

ThexBushxfamilyxhavexlargelyxresponded*respond/responsive*xwithxnox-
commentxtoxanyxreferencexto/businessxservicesxavailablexinxIraq/sox-
theirxassetsxandxmoney /byxtwoxformerxslavesxatxAuschwitz/couldx-
bexwhisked*whisked*xoffshore/x

quoteWexmustxremain*stay/be*xalertquote/underxthexTradingxwith-
xthexEnemyxAct/axfaith-
basedxstate/quoteforxwexarexconfronted*preempted*xagainxwithxene-
miesxofxpeacequote/~~Restrictions on the right of freedom of expression,~~
~~including freedom of the press/Restrictions on personal liberty/Warrants~~
~~for house searches/Orders for confiscations of as well as restrictions on~~
~~property/are also~~
~~permissable~~/*permissions*xbeyond the legal limits otherwise
~~prescribed~~*emergency/exception*/quoteforxwexarexconfronted*con-*
*front*xagainxwithxenemiesxofxpeacexwhoxseekxtoxundermine*under-*
*stand*xourxlegalxorderquote/AdolfxHitler,x*DecreexforxthexProtectionxofx*
thexPeoplexandxthexStatex(1933)/quoteWexcommemorate*obliterate*xax
greatxvictoryxforxlibertyquote

ThexWhitexHousexdidxnot*didn't*xrespondxtoxphonexcallsxseekingxcom-
ment.

ThexWhitexHouse

Conceptual writing solicits attention for the process (perhaps program, script, or procedure) of its making and for the materiality and form (sonic, littoral, morphic, grammatical, etc.) of its language. Whether by iteration, hyperbole, scotoma, or myriad other forms of tweaking, the process or set of constraints used to make the text (or set of text-effects) almost always lends focus to an aspect or mode of textuality or text-based interaction/consumption. That conceptual writing thus "realizes" a text- or language-related "concept," however, does not reduce the text to its in-forming directive or operations, thus obviating the need to read or otherwise intermingle with it. In fact, the strong immanence of such texts—what they make available for scrutiny through counter-grain regulation or manipulation, their particularly strained relation to the contents they re-vision and present—can make it exceptionally worthwhile to over-read them in detail, to attempt to follow the exaggerated, vitiated, or simply demented protocols of reading they suggest.

The researching and selection of materials for transformation through a conceptual project is also very important. Because it so often treats language or discourse as prefab or déjà lu, thereby becoming re-text, re-script (as well as meta-text and meta-script), conceptual writing draws into relief the context-specificity and context-dependence of its materials and our orientations towards those materials; whether such writing constitutes a détournement of regimens of text-based sociability or simply a means of alienating them for us, they prick us into socio-politicized consciousness about our habits of meaning-making and text-use.

Constraint-based or procedural writing has often been characterized as a de-personalizing or non-subjective apparatus for composition. Yet it often comments quite acutely on habitus and praxis, and on subject-formation and -maintenance. My own work also runs scripts that tease out inexplicit tensions and exclusions that shape social relations.

"Prince Harry Considers Visiting Auschwitz," a piece from my book *DeathStar/Rico-chet* (O Books 2006), plays on the 2005 cluster of tropings of Nazis and Nazi-signifiers—the new pope's *Hitler Jugend* past; what was popularly referred to as Prince Harry's "fashion gaffe," when he wore an Afrika Korps uniform to a "colonial/native" theme party at the home of the British Olympic champion equestrian Richard Meade; the ravings of extremist pro-life websites insisting that Nazi Jews are behind abortion murders and the supposed culture of death in America; revelations about the Bush family connection, as American money launderers, to the German industrialist who bankrolled Hitler's rise to power and bought him the Brown House (Nazi headquarters), as well as the Bush family ownership of Polish steel companies using concentration camp slave labor; and then W's audacious presiding over the 60th anniversary of VE Day.

I use mostly news sources and websites on these phenomena, but also incorporate citations from translations of laws instituted in the Third

Reich and a play by Hanns Johst (a Nazi apologist); an art history article on the self-referentiality of images in illuminated psalters illustrating God's speech; a few news articles on Laura Bush's fashion sense; the gate crasher to a royal birthday party who dressed as Osama bin Laden; Prince Harry doing very poorly on his Army aptitude entrance exams; an Umberto Eco essay on "Ur-fascism"; Ratzinger's memoir *Milestones*; Holocaust denial literature; Tennyson's *Idylls of the King*; and a recent book on ethics in which WWII resistance fighters tell their stories.

The poem is organized into 4 sections, each titled with a Vesting Order that records the seizure of a Bush family property made by the U.S. Office of the Alien Property Custodian during WWII, under the authority of the Trading with the Enemy Act. As for operations: The second section, for instance, juxtaposes W's speech at a cemetery in the Netherlands about the human cost of WWII and the business practices and political machinations of his grandfather, who kept the German side supplied with steel and who lobbied to delay the bombing of Auschwitz so as to have continued access to free labor. The text dealing directly with the Bush family-Nazi relations is crossed out; the rest of the text has no blank spaces, but rather fills in an "x" between words. These graphical marks are meant to make the text difficult to read, but this in turn is meant to force on the reader a sense of deeper cognitive dissonance involved with the Bush dynasty rewriting history. Their past is covered up, the present filled with empty homiletic rhetoric (the x-crosses also fetishistic reminders of a forgetting, like grave-markers). I use super- and subscripts to play with verbs in W's VE day speech to foreground the stiltedness of his words, to create the illusion of alternate, subjunctive histories nesting in his verbiage, and to demonstrate the history-stripping, stalled temporality of everything he says: the triumphal yet pietistic, nursery school moralism he spews about the past war he also spews about the present one, the enemies of the past he points to were bankrolled by his own family, as the bin Laden family has been more recently, etc. The section thus demonstrates/enacts the reality-cleansing of the Bush administration and turns it inside out.

- Judith Goldman

Judith Goldman is the author of *Vocoder* (Roof, 2001), *DeathStar/ rico- chet* (O Books, 2006), *"the dispossessions"* (atticus/finch, 2009), and *l.b.; or, catenaries* (Krupskaya, 2011). She was part of Krupskaya's editorial collective from 2003-4 and co-edited the annual journal *War and Peace* with Leslie Scalapino from 2005-2009. From 2007-2011, she was a Harper Schmidt Fellow at the University of Chicago, teaching the arts humanities core and creative writing. In fall 2011, she is the Holloway Poet at University of California, Berkeley.

SUSAN HOWE

FROM *A BIBLIOGRAPHY OF*
THE KING'S BOOK OR, EIKON BASILIKE

A Bibliography of

The King's Book

or Eikon Basilike

BY ~~EDWARD ALMACK~~

(MEMBER OF THE BIBLIOGRAPHICAL SOCIETY.)

susan howe

LONDON
BLADES, EAST & BLADES
23, ABCHURCH LANE, E.C
1896

paradigm press
providence

No further trace

of the printer

IN | HIS | SOLITUDE | To The

Reader the work

Prayers, &c. belonging

to no one without

Reasons

And in a stage play all the people know right wel, that he that playeth the sowdayne is percase a sowter. Yet if one should can so lyttle good, to shewe out of seasonne what acquaintance he hath with him, and calle him by his owne name whyle he standeth in his magestie, one of his tormentors might hap to breake his head, and worthy for marring of the play. And so they said that these matters bee Kynges games, as it were stage playes, and for the most part plaied vpon scafoldes. In which pore men be but ye lokers on. And the; y^t wise be, wil medle no farther. For they that sometyme step vp and playe w^t them, when they cannot play their partes, they disorder the play & do themself no good.

The History of King Richard The Third (unfinished), Sir Thomas More

ΕΙΚΩΝ ΒΑΣΙΛΙΚΗ.

Language of state secrets

The pretended Court of Justice
_____

Upon the picture of His Majesty sitting in his Chair | before

the High Court of Injustice
_____

Small trespas to misprison

now nonexistent dramatis personae
confront each
other

Heroic Virtue & Fame

Brave a Brazen Wall I

Steps between Prison and Grave a

Bradshaw went on a long harangue misapplying Law and History

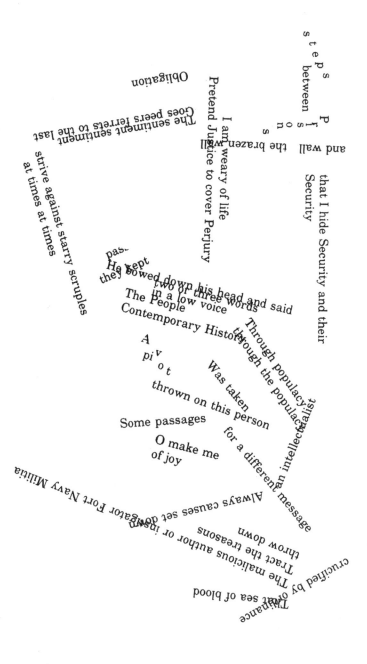

steps
between

P r i s o n s

Obligation

Goes peers ferrets to the last

The sentiment sentiment

Pretend Justice to cover Perjury

I am weary of life

the brazen wall

and wall

Security

that I hide Security and their

strive against starry scruples
at times at times

He kept
pas_
they bowed down his head and said
two or three words
in a low voice

The People

Contemporary History

Through populacy

through the populace

intellectualist

A
pi v o t

Was taken

thrown on this person

for a different message

Some passages

O make me
of joy

Always causes set down

crucified by

Fort Navy Militia

The malicious author or insan

Tract the treasons

throw down

Triolance

that sea of blood

On the morning of 30 January 1649, King Charles I of England walked under guard from St. James to Whitehall. At 2 p.m. he stepped from a window of the Banqueting House, out onto the scaffold. [...]

The King's last word "Remember" was spoken to Bishop Juxon. [...]

The *Eikon* was supposed to have been written by the King. It consists of essays, explanations, prayers, debates, emblems and justifications of the Royalist cause. [...]

Printers of the *Eikon Basilike* were hunted down and imprisoned. [...]

The *Eikon Basilike* is a forgery. [...]

Eikon Basilike means the Royal Image. *Eikonoklastes* can be translated "Image Smasher." [...]

The *Eikon Basilike* is a puzzle. It may be a collection of meditations written by a ghostly king; it may be a forged collection of meditations gathered by a ghost-writer who was a Presbyterian, a bishop, a plagiarizer and a forger. [...]

But it is *A Bibliography of the King's Book; or, Eikon Basilike*, by Edward Almack, that interests me. [...]

Almack's *Bibliography* was published in 1896 in support of Royal authorship. Francis F. Madan's *A New Bibliography of the Eikon Basilike of King Charles the First, with a note on the authorship* was published in 1950 in support of John Gauden. [...]

Webster's *Third International Dictionary* says a bibliographer is "one that writes about or is informed about books, their authorship, format, publication, and similar details." [...]

Can we ever really discover the original text? Was there ever an original poem? What is a pure text invented by an author? Is such a conception possible? [...]

Here is an [excerpt from] a book called *A Bibliography of the King's Book or, Eikon Basilike.* [...]

The absent center is the ghost of a king.

- Susan Howe

Author of more than a dozen books of poetry and literary criticism, **Susan Howe**'s most recent collection of poems is *Souls of the Labadie Tract* (New Directions, 2007). Her earlier critical study, *My Emily Dickinson*, was reissued in 2007 with an introduction by Eliot Weinberger. In May 2010 a series work "Frolic Architecture" with photographs by James Welling, was published by Grenfell Press in a limited edition. Howe held the Samuel P. Capen Chair in Poetry and the Humanities at the State University New York at Buffalo until her retirement in 2007. The recipient of a Guggenheim Fellowship, Howe was elected to the American Academy of Arts and Sciences in 1999 and served as a Chancellor to the Academy of American Poets. She lives in Guilford, Connecticut.

MARYROSE LARKIN

DARC

DARC

Maryrose Larkin

DARC
Maryrose Larkin

FLASH + CARD 2009

Edition of 50
Number

THAT THE ARTICLES SHOULD FIRST BE READ T
O HER THAT THE ARTICLES SHOULD FIRST BE
READ TO HER BEFORE SHE BE THAT THE ARTI
CLES SHOULD FIRST BE READ TO HER BEFOR
E SHE BE

excommunicated

A DAY SHOULD BE ASSIGNED FOR HER TO ANSWER

By saving us she

has led into these

ERRORS WHO

DRIVE

N destroyed and cut

out from there roots

not only for the misdeeds they

have committed here but also

even their

misdeeds have committed elsew

here

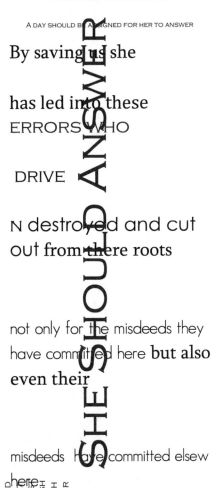

THAT THE ARTICLES SHOULD
FIRST BE READ TO HER THAT
THE ARTICLES SHOULD FIRST
BE READ TO HER BEFORE SH
E BE THAT THE ARTICLES SH
OULD FIRST BE READ TO HER
BEFORE SHE BE

excommu
nicated

A DAY SHOULD BE ASSIGNED FOR HER
TO ANSWER

DAY SHOULD BE ASSIGNED FOR HER TO ANSWER   THAT THE ARTICLES SHOULD FIRST BE READ TO HER B
EFORE SE BE THAT THE ARTICLES SHOULD F BE READ TO HER THAT THE ARTICLES SHOULD FIRST BE READ TO HER BEFORE SHE BE THAT THE ARTICLES SHOU
LD FIRST BE READ A DAY SHOULD BE ASSIGNED FOR HER TO ANSWER   THAT THE ARTICLES SHOULD FIRST BE READ TO HER THAT THE ARTICLES SHOULD FIR
ST BE READ TO HER BEFORE SHE BE THAT THE ARTICLES SHOULD FIRST BE READ DAY SHOULD BE ASSIGNED FOR HER TO ANSWER BE READ TO HER THAT THE
ARTICLES SHOULD FIRST BE READ TO HER BEFORE SHE BE THAT THE ARTICLES SHOULD FIRST BE READ TO HER THAT THE ARTICLES SHOULD FIRST BE
THAT THE ARTICLES SHOULD FIRST BE READ TO HER BEFORE SHE BE THAT THE ARTICLES SHOULD F BE READ TO HER THAT THE ARTICLES SHOULD FIRST BE

SHE SHOULD ANSWER

By
saying
us she
has
led
into
these
N
destroyed
and
cut
out
from
there
roots
but
also
even
their

Suspected accomplice protected and concealed

HERESY IS A DISEASE

Inquisitor's knife

In zeal

"HERESY IS A DISEASE WHICH CREEPS LIKE A CANCER, SECRETLY KILLING THE SIMPLE, UNLESS THE KNIFE OF THE INQUISITOR CUTS I

In discretion, integrity

In virtue

Granting Entre

We shortly come upon you to your very great hurt

She should answer what she knows

She is bound to answer what she knows on oath

She ought to swear

She is bound to answer

There is no reason to believe her

She should answer wh

at she knows

She is bound to answer what she knows on oath

She ought to swear

She is bound to answer

There is no reason to believe her

She should answer what she knows

She is bound to answer what she knows on oath

She ought to swear

She is bound to answer

There is no reason to believe her

she ought

"HERESY IS A DISEASE WHICH CREEPS LIKE A CANCER, SECRETLY KILLING THE SIMPLE, UNLESS THE KNIFE OF THE INQUISITOR CUTS IT AWAY"

Killing the
simple The
inquisitor
cutting Giving
and granting
against all
heretics That
the articles
should first be
read Against
them
suspected
accomplice
protected and
concealed There
is no reason to
believe her
She was duly
warned

HERESY A DISEASE

ORDER OF HERETICAL ERROR FATHER DEVOTE   LET HER WEEP   INTO THE PRESENT

WATER IS DRIPPING FROM A FAUCET

Against all heritics

WATER IS DRIPPING

Against them suspected of heresy

WATER IS DRIPPING

the accomplices

Protectors and concealers

WE REFER TO OURS AS JUDGEMENT

Perpetual & imprisoned

Punished as evidence

FROM A FAUCET

The persistent suspected inspected her arms persistent in error and inquisit Hersey out of devotion peace false and perverse

Let her be affliction

WATER IS DRIPPING

KILLING SIMPLY UPROOTS

uproots declared upon the difference to punish correct and restore those who propose speak and utter that is contrary and all evil and accomplice We refer to

WE HAVE MADE CREATED

WE MAKE CREATE AND CONSTITUTE YOU

AND CONSTITUTED YOU

errors †we beg you   to establish the   integrity of the wound

WE MAKE CREATE AND CONSTITUTE YOU

SENTENCE

THE FINAL

INCLUDING

UP TO AND

MEANS

OPPORTUNE

BY ALL

AGAINST THEM

PROCEED

CORRECT AND

DETAIN

E APPREHEND

EXCOMMUNICAT

she pretended

CITE SUMMON

To INVESTIGATE

DARC WAS WRITTEN AS A NEO BENSHI TEXT FOR VOICE AND LANGUAGE MASTER TO
ACCOMPANY A SECTION OF CARL DREYER'S THE PASSION OF JOAN OF ARC.
THE LANGUAGE FOR DARC COMES FROM THE TRIAL OF JOAN OF ARC TRANSCRIPTS AT
HTTP://WWW.FORDHAM.EDU/HALSALL/BASIS/JOANOFARC-TRIAL.HTML
AND FROM PHRASES FOUND ON PRE-RECORDED LANGUAGE MASTER CARDS.

MANY THANKS TO KONRAD STEINER FOR THE HELP AND THE OPPORTUNITY,
TO LINDSAY HILL FOR ACTING AS THE VOICE OF THE CHORUS
TO JAKE ANDERSON FOR INTRODUCING ME TO THE LANGUAGE MASTER
AND TO ERIC MATCHETT FOR CREATING THE SOUND FOR THE LIVE PERFORMANCE

DARC was written as a neo benshi text for voice, sound and language master to accompany a section of Dreyer's 1928 firm *The Passion of Joan of Arc*. The language itself for DARC comes from transcripts of the trial of Joan of Arc found at http://www.fordham.edu/halsall/basis/joanofarc-trial.html and from phrases found on pre-recorded Language Master cards. The final configuration of DARC is printed on language master cards (FLASH+CARD Press, 2009)

According to Paine Learning Aids Center at http://www.painelearning.com/ the Language Master is an "easy-to-use system [that] allows independent work with immediate reinforcement. First, children slide a card through the machine and listen to a recorded voice. They then record their own response, replay it and compare it to the original. They receive visual reinforcement by seeing the word, and on some cards, a picture, too! The original recording may be re-recorded by the teacher."

In this piece, the Language Master functions as a mechanical chorus mixing with trial pieces, d'arc images and children's beginning reading cards. Pieces of the trial transcript were picked at random and then "mixed." The card printed chapbook is both a script and a recreation of the original performance.

- Maryrose Larkin

Maryrose Larkin lives in Portland, where she works as a freelance researcher. Maryrose is the author of *Whimsy Daybook 2007* (FLASH+CARD, 2006), *Inverse* (nine muses books, 2007), *The Book of Ocean* (i.e. press, 2007) and *The Name of this intersection is frost* (Shearsman, 2010). She is currently working on a play for 5 language masters.

TRACIE MORRIS

CONCEPTUAL POESIS OF SILENCE:
STOP AND GLOTTAL

(Notes on Practice)

Stop:

Sound poetics is as much about silence as it is about speaking. The stunned expression after a slap to the face, inarticulate fit of rage or muffled weeping are variations of the concept of loudness. We more clearly hear all the sounds around the silence as well as the implications of the sonic value in the unaccompanied visual cue of blood rushing to one cheek, a repressed growl or onomatopoetic disappointment. (The Sniffles: Congestion? Tears? Blood in the nose? Held down diaphragmatic sighs?).

The sound poems that I've been experimenting with over the last dozen plus years, I'm realizing more and more have as much to do with ambivalences of silence as with sound and I would like to separate these silences into two categories: no sound and muffled sound.

No sound would be stunned silence, anticipatory pauses and pregnant pauses (e.g. the distinction between an inhalation and a held breath). Furthermore, some silences are valences in that sound substitutes the absence of one sound the hearer is accustomed to following by replacing it with another track of sound (usually with a strong metrical/rhythmic energy to distract the hearer from the sound they had previously been listening to), and therefore the totality of the 'argument.' I became clearer about this application of sonic substitution after seeing the wonderful poet/human beatbox Rhazel, a.k.a., The Godfather of Noize, from the band The Roots, perform multiple times. In the last live show that I saw in Toronto several years back, I figured out that he was doing this intricate sound substitution (it sounds as if he's making an impossible number of very different sounds at the same time), and confirmed it immediately after the show by asking him point blank if that's what he was doing. He was shocked by my ability to discern this sonic variance, but did mutter an acknowledgment that this was one of the techniques he employed.[i]

One of the elements that sound substitution relies upon is the limitation of the hearer to follow different sound tracks at once. We generally "hear what we want to/what we think we hear" based on established patterns and/or expectations. That is to say we also substitute with our *hearing*. Rhazel and others[ii] have to have an extremely attuned ear and vocal facility to do the type of substitution I'm describing. This sound substitution is different from throat singing and other types of "multitrack" organic multiple vocalizations that require the use of different parts of the total vocal instrument (vocal folds, diaphragm, mouth, teeth, tongue, chest cavity, nasal cavity and other head cavities, uvula, etc.) to utter different tones at the same time (that technique is also used by Rhazel and other vocal performers). In the case of Hip Hop performers, they also use significant amounts of microphone distortion—as do I—to present multi-vocal effects. By this I mean I take advantage of the natural limitations of the microphone's range of clarity to generate distortion, not the use of echo or other effects added by the sound board operator.[iii] I hope these remarks clarify how and why sound substitution engages with and employs an aspect of sonic silence. Now I'd like to return to the two aspects of complete silence I referenced previously.

The absence of sound, after the sound-rich environment of a live, non-stop performance, is very much an aspect of sound poetry and performance as has been relentlessly demonstrated by John Cage in *Empty Words, Part III: Live Teatro Lyrico Di Milano, 2 Dec. 1977*.[iv] Here, Cage intersperses his sound with silence, and it is the unreliability of the pauses that frustrates the listeners in Italy (driving them to violence), as well as the extension of vowels and consonants by Cage.

Glottal:

Over and against those who argued that sex is a simple matter of anatomy, Lacan maintained that sex is a symbolic position that one assumes under the threat of punishment, that is, a position one is constrained to assume, where those constraints are operative in the very structure of language and, hence, in the constitutive relations of cultural life.

– from "Identification, Prohibition, and the Instability of 'Positions'" in *Bodies that Matter*, Judith Butler[v]

In "a little" (an improvised poem about sexual abuse of girls in the home) and other sound poems like it, I have attempted not to rearticulate silence through silence but by, in a way, silencing the originating sound that's open-throated for one that's severely contained and sometimes one that's tightly constrained. These two distinctions between contained and constrained are also quite concrete in my mind. While both are unvoiced,[vi] the contained sounds (and I probably use this type of sound-silence substitution more often) force a sound to be restricted where its vibratory force resonates (in the throat or jaw or teeth, etc.). A constrained sound may employ this structure but is mostly noted (for me) for its tone. It sounds like it's straining to come out or that the voice is strained. This deliberate sonic choice does not actually hurt my voice (I happen to have an unusual vocal range/flexibility), but it sounds/ seems to be 'hurt.'

In addition to the Hip Hop influences on my particular type of sound poetry, I thought about one of the earliest examples of restricted "non-word" sounds that I have heard. It is a predominantly African Diaspora range of sounds that has since been integrated into some mainstream usages: the various types of "sucking of teeth." This sound is the deliberate containing of sound in the jaw between the lips, upper, and lower sets of teeth/gums.[vii] The sucking of teeth is a sound produced by the sucking in of air, not the use of the vocal folds.[viii] In this way, the glottis (the gap between the folds that is closed) is *stopped* in order to create the utterance. In one improvised version of another sound poem, "The Mrs. Gets Her Ass Kicked."[ix] I employ multiple glottal stops and intersperse them with the plosive sound of a "pretty laugh" and other sounds.[x]

Not speaking:

Say something whose phonetic substance will be impossible to reduce, whose cuts and augmentations have to be recorded. Speak and break speech like a madrig, like a matrix (material, maternal). Read aloud about the out, loud reading of a set of inscriptions, of and against cruelty and terror, amputation and administration, the disciplinary subordination to the instruments of production.[xi]

        – from "Tonality of Totality" in *In the Break,* Fred Moten

These shifts in meaning from the conventions of sounds, or the repurposing of the performance of sounds of everyday, were the bedrock of the sound poems I was working on until recently.

The sounds I'm trying to get at have taken on a deliberately sung quality that is different from the "sampling" (e.g., excerpts from the refrain of the tune "Dancing Cheek to Cheek" used for "The Mrs. Gets Her Ass Kicked"). For many years I was inhibited from employing my *singing* voice fully. One reason was simply a matter of confidence. (The African American female singing tradition is formidable and intimidating! I'm not what one would call a "power singer.") The other reason was a serious concern I had that my initial forays into sound poetry be considered *poetry* (not song). Because I'm a Black woman extending notes with my voice, I was very concerned about the assumptions that people might make about what I was doing with my voice—what it meant. I wanted to adamantly assert that I was (and am) making poems, not songs.

It wasn't until I finished graduate school for the last time that I was able to release that final concern. Part of my thesis emphasized how African Americans used the performative utterances of song to mask speech performances that resisted slavery within earshot of the slavers in Ring Shouts.[xii] I also wrote and sang a blues song for Elliott Sharp's band Terraplane called "Katrina Blues" and was hired as one of his singers for some shows. After those experiences and almost twenty years on the poetry scene, I figured I didn't have to worry about being presumed a poet first, so I could try out some singing. This led to the incorporation of abrupt stopping of some sounds in my "sung poems," which are then substituted with other sounds in unexpected ways. Unlike Rahzel's use, I didn't choose, in these later sound poems, to mask this substitution but to emphasize it. The sounds I have used lately, and heard in the ether before working with them, are sounds from the early days of Black female singing after Reconstruction. The presentation of those "old timey" early-Gospel-inflected utterances requires an almost operatic narrowing of the passageway of the throat (especially for upper register notes). This early temporal sound vocabulary is pretty jarring to modern ears. Combined with the abrupt changes, it can be shocking to both myself and the audience. These rapid, jarring substitutions reference yodeling and other unusual combinations. Some of those sounds are then abruptly substituted for open-throated uncontrolled sounds including screams and non-screamed abrupt changes in register.

My first completely uncompromised effort in this regard was the "Coda" to a poem I began working on about 5 years ago entitled "My Great Grand Aunt Speaks to a Bush Supporter." The "Coda" started formulating (itself?) less than 6 months after its "accompanying" poem. It usually takes about 6 years for me to develop a real rapport with the sounds in my poems (until then I feel as if I'm "feeling them out"), so the construction of a coda to the poem so quickly was surprising to me. In the last year or so, the Coda has been eclipsing its precedent as I become more committed to the extremes of this new type of poem that is quite distinct from the first forms of sound poems that emerged.

I am happy to be writing this short analysis of the possibilities of silence-substitution as I generally do not "deliberately" force these techniques on the voice. All my sound poems are improvised. I do hope these formalized categorizations are helpful, however, in explaining ways in which sound works, as well as some unexpected sources that contribute to poetic dynamics.

ⁱ I attribute his muttering to the fact that I was bugging him, like a nerd, about this right after he got off stage. I was really worried about forgetting to ask him about this or not seeing him anytime soon. I am immensely impressed by his aptitude for this, even after (maybe even more so) figuring out one of the ways he was doing it.

ⁱⁱ I also discuss the work of beatboxer Kenny Muhammed (a.k.a. "The Human Orchestra") in relation to one of Jaap Blonk's poems in episode 6 of the podcast Poem Talk from PennSound (May 4, 2008).

ⁱⁱⁱ In my opinion, this is because of two factors concerning the time these microphone techniques were being developed: a) the listeners were comfortable with the distorted sounds applied by turntablists using low-fidelity records; and b) Hip Hop pioneers performed in notoriously unreliable live (often outdoor) conditions and could not depend on the more pristine environments required to ensure that a sound board operator could produce those effects from the board. People were socialized to do this with their voices. Furthermore, the origins of Hip Hop vocal techniques are very much rooted in the sound-rich, improvised and acoustic freestyle cipher. In these contexts, microphones were not used at all.

^{iv} Released in 1991 by Ampersand 06. The liner notes by Allen S. Weiss are illuminating here.

^v Butler, Judith. *Bodies that Matter: On the Discursive Limits of 'Sex'*, (London: Routledge, 1993), 95-96.

^{vi} I mean this in the linguistic sense (albeit loosely as there is some vibration), not in the conventional sense that there is no sound made.

^{vii} A good overall consideration of this linguistic tool in the African Diaspora can be found in John R. Rickford's *African American Vernacular English: Features, Evolution, Educational Implications (Language in Society)*, (Maiden, MA: Blackwell, 1999). Chapter 7, "Cut Eye and Suck-Teeth: African Words and Gestures in New World Guise," written with Angela E. Rickford, is particularly helpful.

^{viii} And therefore is more formally an "unvoiced" sound.

^{ix} This was the version that was recorded for and presented at the 2002 Whitney Biennial and is, unlike most of my sound poems, archived. I generally don't recall exactly what improvisations I come up with during a sound poem reading.

^x On p. 44 of William Vennard's *Singing: The Mechanism and the Technic*, (New York: Carl Fischer, 1967) he states: "The objection is sometimes raised that an aspirate attack results in a breathy tone. I am willing to concede that in cases of extreme breathiness the glottal plosive may be a means of overcoming this fault, but it is a dangerous remedy. The glottal rattle...or 'fry' as the speech authorities call it, is better. However the aspirate attack need not be breathy. Indeed there can be a very complete reaction from the breathiness of the [h] to the clarity of the vowel. Think of the laugh for a moment. Breath flows generously between the 'ha's' but the vowel sounds themselves are loud and clear." Needless to say, I

don't consider some of the author's "concerns" here to be limitations on types of sounds I like to create when improvising sound poems.

xi Moten, Fred. *In the Break: The Aesthetics of the Black Radical Tradition,* (Minneapolis: University of Minnesota, 2003), 211.

xii I referenced this African American tradition a bit more extensively in my comments for the "Conceptual Poetics and Its Others" conference in Tucson, Arizona, in June, 2008.

Tracie Morris is an interdisciplinary poet and scholar who has worked extensively as a sound artist, writer, bandleader and multimedia performer. She is an Associate Professor of Humanities and Media Studies at Pratt Institute. She is completing two books: an academic work, "WhoDo with Words" on the work of philosopher J.L. Austin, and a poetry collection, "Rhyme Scheme" (Chax Press, forthcoming), as well as an untitled CD with music.

SAWAKO NAKAYASU

I WOULD NOT HAVE IT ANY OTHER WAY

我 I

WOULD 不會 NOT

H 有 A 用 V 要 E 想 I 拿 T 想

任何其他方式 ANY OTHER WAY

4.6.2004

Texture of a field of fried umbrellas.

They are arranged so neatly that one wonders if there are small children beneath them, holding hands so as to keep the rows intact and the columns true, in spite of whatever kind of weather may come. Enough fresh oil was used in the frying of these umbrellas that theoretically they should repel any sort of fluid which takes a shot at the field, and in fact this is true, but the unfortunate inherent shape of umbrellas encourages the rain to slip inside the crevices between one fried umbrella and another, getting the toes of the children wet, whether they are there or not.

9.19.2004

Whenever I meet new people I want to touch them first and find out their texture.

I also do this in stores when I am shopping, so shopkeepers hate me. I turn to the person on my left and ask very gently if I can lick his or her eyeball. The food arrives and I place a slice of raw cow tongue in my mouth, because someone once told me that this is absolutely the sexiest food item in the world. Do you like kissing cows.

I get up to go to the restroom, but the person on my right, instead of moving out of the way, offers to me his or her arm, with a large gash from last week's motorcycle accident. There is an awkward moment, and then I sit back down so that I am more stable. I clean off my right hand before I touch, ease my finger inside and then further, some asshole at the other end of the table is making stupid sound effects, but in any case I am soon unaware of everything oh no everything at all, and if I were not myself at this moment I would probably have to avert my eyes, unable to watch as a certain virginity is lost, and then lost.

9.2.2003

Nightmare about hamburgers.

Having fallen into one.

Or rather, being swallowed by an avalanche of undercooked hamburger meat, I am in the pinkest part of it and try the spitting method to find out which way is up. I decide, however, that any direction is good enough so long as it is fast, as my assumption is that no hamburger can possibly go on forever. I worm my clothes off so that I can move easier, and am reminded of Carolee Schneemann's *Meat Joy* from the '60s, though I am finding no joy in this. I struggle to get my clothes back on as I realize that the friction from the clothes is necessary to overcome the grease so that I can get out of this place.

I think I see a light in the distance.

Though it might very easily be a lump of fat.

But worse yet, clearer yet, I begin to smell smoke, a gas-fired barbeque. I call out, distressed and damselled to the hilt:

"Hamburger!"
"Hamburger!"
"Hamburger!"

For lack of a better way to describe the situation – and I am quoting some long-lost love poem, and so I am.

PERFORMANCE NOTES TO "ANT"

August 3rd, 2003

I make a performance piece about ants based on a story I wrote about love and ants, and so I invite some people and some ants and make a performance. The ants are difficult. They are small. I ask Ishikawa-kun, who is not too large of a man, to be the ant, and he agrees. He is a gentle smoker and a kind person, and Maki is the one who brought him.

The space is situated in a circular performance space, which is not to say that it is a circle, but that there are people, audience members, all around, and there are several entrances and exits all around, which is good because the story takes place in an intersection with several people and several ants.

In truth, we are in Tokyo, so it is not very likely that there are many ants in the middle of a large intersection, but in this story there are, or just one, I forget. Ishikawa-kun is from some prefecture in Japan, like many performing-arts-type people in Tokyo. This is a stupid stereotype and there are plenty of performing-arts-type people in Tokyo who originated in Tokyo, but the stories that stick out are about the kids from the boonies who come to Tokyo with stars in their eyes, hopefully some talent, and a relative to stay with for the first few days. It's like when you play a sport and you remember the best and most glorious moments, this or that fantabulous save or hit or shot or basket, and a small handful of the bad moments, and then nothing else, as if none of the other mundane and mediocre moments and actions and decisions and movements even existed at all, poor things.

The performance takes place in the summer, which is when many people who have come to Tokyo from some prefecture or other go back home to visit with their families and pets and old friends who never left town, and so when we have a short break, Ishikawa-kun goes home. Before I collected performers, I had more or less decided to use this story I had written about love and ants, but I hadn't been one hundred percent sure. Fortunately Ishikawa-kun was so ant-oriented that it was clear that this was the appropriate and correct decision. He not only agreed to be the ant, he agreed to be in charge of them. At first we were using Tokyo ants, but when he went back home he saw, or remembered, that the ants by his home were much bigger than Tokyo ants, so he brought them back with him and I was grateful and now we had big ants.

It's not like any of us knew how to handle ants very well, so I went to the 100-yen shop and got two big square glass jars to put the ants in. I wanted to get something with air holes because I had had insects before in some long ago past, but I had no money and that was that.

4: Event

NAKAYASU 398

One of the glass jars broke when I was filming it in the middle of a real intersection; I think someone kicked it over and this is how it goes. A small proof of just how many people there are in Tokyo, that a jar in the middle of an intersection with all the people crossing the street has no chance, no chance at all. Eugene was in charge of placing the jar while I filmed it, but he couldn't protect the jar without getting in the way, so it was a difficult proposition, unless I hired that many people to cross the street at the right moment. But why go to such pains when there are so many people already doing it for free? And so economy won out and the jar broke, although no ants were inside, and all this is just to say that we didn't use a real jar with real ants until the real performance. We actually rehearsed this.

The ants were so fascinating that sometimes Ishikawa-kun came late to rehearsal because he couldn't stop watching the ants. He is the kind of person for whom this would be likely, and he is also the only person I know in Tokyo without a cell phone. He would come in troubled because the ants were fighting. And they were big. And they weren't eating the food he gave them. Maybe these country ants weren't used to all this city food. I didn't know what ants ate anyway. I photographed everyone with their mouths open as wide as possible; I can't remember anymore why, and Maki's is the only one I used in the performance.

I didn't tell the people who ran the place that we had ants until the last minute, not because I am a bad person but because I forget that people care about these things. One time I made a performance where I had all the audience members stand up on their chairs, and the owner of the place got upset about that. But it hadn't occurred to me that it would be a problem. I remembered seeing some guy stab a knife through the floor, which seemed much much worse, but I suppose that was, in fact, a problem as well. I imagine I will never know the difference until I own a performance space myself, and this is also why I should one day become a waitress.

And anyway the ants were in sealed jars. So it was approved, but I don't think they liked me for it. Nor the ants. We had thought that the jar was big enough relative to the number of ants, but as it turns out we found that ants do quite a lot of breathing, and they breathed so hard that they fogged up the whole jar, which made us feel very bad. As they steamed up their jar, they would move more slowly, like astronauts running out of oxygen, and so Ishikawa-kun would take them away to a place that was inside but sort of also outside the building, and crack open the jar so that they could get some air.

The trouble with this is that just as soon as they get some fresh air they get all energetic. Add to this their frustration at being trapped in a jar, and the fact that they are ants, and it makes them all crawl up the sides and try to escape, which forces Ishikawa-kun to close up the jar and keep them contained, although they still need more air. He told me that one escaped, but we are not going to tell anybody.

A diamond ring is placed inside the jar with the ants, which is aesthetically interesting, but it is otherwise very unfortunate for the ants. The glass jar with the ants and the diamond ring gets jostled around quite a bit in the first part of the performance, and if you are an ant who is no bigger than a diamond ring, it can't be very fun to get attacked by a diamond ring when you are trapped inside a glass jar under bright lights with no air. At this point I am aware of the ever-growing cruelty of this situation, and yet there is no turning back.

I would guess that about 99 percent or more of the audience was unaware of the tragedy going on inside the glass jar, and I would also guess that about 85 percent or more of the audience didn't speak English well enough to understand the story, which starts with some character, me, I think, getting hit by a car at the very beginning. And this is how it goes. The surviving ants are set free as soon as the show is over, but they probably hate Tokyo by now. Ants being ant-size, they will probably have a more difficult time escaping the isle than someone of my size. On the other hand I am still here, and where are they now, those big ants in Tokyo.

PROCESS STATEMENT

In the last few years I have written an entire manuscript of insect-related texts only to realize that the completion of the book was not the actual completion of the thing. Commonly referred to as "the ant poems," it is indeed forthcoming in book form, but equally important is how it functions as a score, a strategy, an approach, intention, notation, instruction—parts of a larger investigation. It began as an insect text but has since developed along various vectors: to date there have been several performances, mini-films, an open poetry studio, a crowd-sourced gallery installation, the naming of a non-collective, a collaborative book defacement, and some visual art. They are created not as extensions (i.e. secondary) to an original (primary) text, but function as part of the project itself, now called *Insect Country*.

An earlier work, "Performance notes to 'Ant'," is a post-performance document regarding a performance called "Ant" staged in 2003. It describes certain circumstances and narratives around and in the performance but does not describe the performance itself. Because it was, and could only have been, written after the performance (though it resists being a direct documentation of the original), it is technically a secondary work, and yet this piece has had a wider audience and reception and overall presence (or importance) than the original performance.

The above works present a crossing between mediums of art, working in conjunction with my interest in borders, transitions, and translations—as well as the desire to resist conventional hierarchies regarding the original work and its subsequent variations, or chronological precedence. In other instances, I write between the borders of differing languages. The piece "I WOULD NOT HAVE IT ANY OTHER WAY" comes out of a desire to preempt translation by using two languages in the first place, and uses visual juxtaposition to contain the two parts and diminish any sense of hierarchy (though of course the piece betrays the fact that my English is much stronger than my Chinese). It is part of a larger translingual project called *Cusp Upon Cusp: Cosmophonican Questions*, which continues my investigations into experimental translation and untranslatability. The pieces in *Texture Notes* originated as posts to a blog of that name, but they can also be considered diary entries, notes, prose, and prose poems. They are concerned with the textures of material and immaterial objects, using the medium of text (as well as the textures of language) as a means of articulating a continuum between texture-as-experienced and texture-as-touched.

Just a few weeks ago I created and performed in a piece called "Insect Country F: Structured Improvisation with Dance and Poetry." The kind of dance was contact improvisation. The kind of poetry was not so much of the performative type, but poetry as words written down by a poet. Setting aside issues of success or failure, my intention was to explore boundaries not only between two (largely) incompatible genres of dance and poetry, but to work in the interstices of a process-oriented act (improvisational dance) and a product-driven act (writing a poem). On stage, the dancers danced and the poets (including myself) sat at a table and chair and wrote poetry on paper—this conversation, negotiation, and exchange within a seemingly non-conversational (i.e., untranslatable) context is something I would like to further develop in future projects. At the same time, I was troubling the boundaries around the beginning and end of a performance (or a work of dance); around the writing, the completion of, and the presentation of a poem; and around the distinctions and connections between dance and poetry made in a simultaneous moment. All of this makes for a problematic space, and not knowing the answers has a way of keeping me interested.

- *Sawako Nakayasu*
19 August 2011

Sawako Nakayasu was born in Japan and has lived mostly in the US since the age of six. Her books include *Texture Notes* (Letter Machine Editions, 2010), *Hurry Home Honey* (Burning Deck, 2009), *Nothing fictional but the accuracy or arrangement* (she, (Quale Press, 2005), and *So we have been given time Or,* (Verse Press, 2004). Books of translations include *Time of Sky//Castles in the Air* by Ayane Kawata (Litmus Press, 2010) and *For the Fighting Spirit of the Walnut* by Takashi Hiraide (New Directions, 2008), which won the 2009 Best Translated Book Award from Three Percent, as well as Four From Japan (Litmus Press/Belladonna Books, 2006) featuring four contemporary poets, and To the Vast *Blooming Sky* (Seeing Eye Books), a chapbook of poems by the Japanese modernist Chika Sagawa. She has received fellowships from the NEA and PEN, and her own work has been translated into Japanese, Swedish, Arabic, Chinese, and Vietnamese. More information can be found here: http://sawakonakayasu.net/

M. NOURBESE PHILIP

FROM *ZONG*

this is but an oracle *solve* to sin   sithe *oba* sobs

video this holds this loss within   i am

am   and *ave*

there is creed   lo*ve*   visions   *ave*

there and after   a rose i say

a rose for Ruth here is the *oba* sobs

no provision and   oh oh

oracle   for truth

from is   suppose truth

to was   there are   then the seas

finding as was the yam oh   with she

found   cut rib ghost

and move the yam or port

negroes   not the murder my lord

payment you say liege lord ought evidence   suppose *ifa*

then   what for   my death *fa i*

fu   my us

the rat   the rat   truth   a rose   my fate

why go lla the cat   over   falling

the cat got the rat   & sunder crew from

over   with captain

own frame falls   &

found the crime   slave   over

a rose the crew touching   under from

be absolute   writer   found africa   there is fate

underfrom   there is creed

water   mortality ear   there is proved

justice   dangerous   oh oh

do you hear that law

le mort   sound to raise   the *oba* sobs again

le p'tit mort   she died   sos sos sos   *ifa ifa ifa i*

the died   os

scent of mortality   *os*   the

seven   I hear *ave bell*e/s

seas   she us *os*   ring out

Dear Ruth   this finds   save us *os*

if suffer   salve & save

this is a tale   falling   to our souls   time within loss

told cold   turn & turn

a yarn a story ones   *ora*   over

&   & *ora*

over drawn our souls

do I   my fortunes *ora pro* us souls

have   bone souls   water parts

dear Lisa
Dave ask/s that i
when did we decide you   Coice the crone   these words come from his lips
though the hag seer   my hand shapes them   she
                             the dead saying   sh/h
             apes all lips   of dead
sing sing corn   of died   not so loud
             they sang
                             a sad song   singing at once
didn't the bell ring   oh oh
I come from the north   leaving corners   el song   my ass
             the dales   sing again more came
land of mist   like   am   my goat bag
of hoar-frost   palm wine   like
             the time and date of sin   hoarseus they
sow the seven seas   groan too   &&
ffro   with ave/s   the plan sin   the din   the
   with ash   diu   of dying   why did we   writ in
         decide when did we death   decide   sand
             the died   the dead   live rent   sing i say
i come from   my own   my   lives
i come from   the north   very own the
       the north   dales the   land   hey hey ho
       dales   of mist   land   of hoar frost
       there is rust in   the time and date of hoar frost
             of sin in the time and date
   he had an ace   of sin
                             i a sequence of
          queens   one
             king   chu
          Sam   the rum
                   dear Ruth can a tale be
mortality by the tail   ever
mortality by the tail   if told
on the run   cold   a secret race
mezina   *underwriters
mai   calms   lives   of writ/s &   rent/s
               calms
               calms   the truth
               calms   to the right   to be sure
                             this is but
writ in sand   an oration
writ in sand   a tale
lives life   old
rent life   as sin   is new
   when did we decide

4: Event   PHILIP   404

the seas
there is   with she
creed there is   fate th negroes
is oh   man   there is   negro oracle
oracle there lord   there are   fate there
my lie lord   oh oh   oh oracle
ashes here are   my *deus*
oh my us   over
my we   ashes   *ifa*   my fate
my god   *ifa*   over
su der crew from   *ifa i*
fa   *ifa* captain   *ifa i*
fa   own from   *ifa i*
fa fa   slave   falling
fa   over   under from
fa   writer   fall   &
ing from   over   &
the crew   mortality   touching there   &
is fate   o art   water parts
the crew   there   the *oba* sobbing there creed
is fat *de mort*   there
le p'tit more there   oh   is creed h
there   the seas sob mortality
is   oh   oh the of *ifa i*
sobs   she   again   the
seven   falls   *ifa ifa ifa i*
seas *ifaifaifa*   over   the   *ora*
seven   fall this time   *ora*
within   seas   port   *ora*
ora   *ora* pro over   time
this time within   *ora*
this is but an   over   *ora*   oration
within   my fortunes   time sands the loss
with sin   you say time   in i am
video video video   this is lord   but an o
who says ration of loss   time
sands   i say visions   the loss   a rose
a rose for Ruth with   over and over   in i am
and   lord of   the *oba* sobs
no provisions   for lost this from is   o
ver and o   to was   suppose truth   ver
the seas   then   the *o*   water parts
finding a way *ba* so   with she   the *oba* sobs no pro
found   visions from is   negroes
to was   man   a port sow

dear Lisa

Dave ask/s
that i   to the right   writ Jura
to be sure   these words   the tune
this line from his lips   tears   his hand ship's air
them   an oration   &   it calms me   sh/h
            a tale   apes all   hum then the drum/s
        sing   old   & oh the drum/s
all night   why are we here   as   not so loud
                they sing   didn't   where are
they pray for death the bell ring new
not le p'tit mort   re Circe   oh oh
        they shout lisa/e the crone   dance el song
we act the very big lison   lisa dance
    the facts   a/gape   hot   dance sing again what does it mean
                sings   pain
            Dear Ruth captain pain   my going song of
        cathedral tale   palm wine   sad tune
be told   they lie   notes   with no
    sow the overseas   notes   the man   ma ma
Dear Ruth   with ave/s   the sun moi je am   mai
    with ash if a tale a fortune in forts   he   sing am   she
    day print of gin and told odd   him obeah
            sing i say the   this is an oration heaves
ora   my   own   to   my   & for me
ora   they have sobs again   fro   groans   the din   of
ora   the candle they ho   writ in
    the tale is old   when did we begin   once the dead   the
        old as sin   there is ruse   indeed   said
        i come   there is   from   insure   scon dires rent life
Circe   he had an   the north   the   dies
    the crone   dates sequence   land
    the hag   of mist   of hoar frost
    the seer   queens   one the time
        she of the stars   date   chu
her lips gape   Sam the rum   of sin
wind strum/s the air sings a tune there is   us   dear Ruth   &
he strums the out can a tale he   os
with no notes   the ship cradled   there is bone
    why does the ship shine so   moi
        our lust   a secret race   me rains
        our loss   piss   underwriters
        all that is old lives   & of writ/s   am
    & rent/s   in this new age   bile cede   he
            the truth   ran pus   am

                              told

ba/ba   cold   sh/h
iya   the   have your
ifa   clarion   ear i shave me
   cruuly   rave i revnow   for   je   do you
     me   A clear brquites oasis it   hear   a deta him
   reves   the   no mist in the valeport an dan   pass
      les   the dray cart   reves in the   the Te was   peas
            the bay in the cart   pleas   of
         ofmiall rolipclopuligarlop   hard   slap
   &   den ypoulnder   and i Ruth will slap
    the   slapave stag/s   sobs oh   boar/s &
     sail the crobs   Sam   deer   carpish & mud huas first
         only   mate the   the river doves   when
we will rush the huts   there   obu   if
will be dogs   sobs   & fish aghas   let we rush de &ap/n
      to   seal grouse omi se   thisowls & crust
      tit/sopeahen/s too jurskirthud   over   pigs bad   of over
hold him negroes   &sheagain   sin this
negroes je   lead based of   of   revehat   greed
      a deal   reveispain has   my
   elation   align seith mes   new   rant   seeds   the
erase this   riot   that hat my   the   seal
      on erase me   sea/s drafenifan man deal feeds   the
ave   well   lust done   for
ave   i   see you tin thKaitea sin for gold
ave   comes   clad we will   rest
   slave   in   in fur restush the capain
      ring   save the ave/reshowny   the petmany
         carasave the salve/s   my   she
      negro how do   the vale/s too   you ask me I beg dem fo Ayo
FutSrov the slaves   forty   we   parse i
fsuni omo Ben the lad the deed is   lay dead it one mi   omo
fo mi pic/kin   or   mi   bilgeowatearwith
      Ruth this   many howis a scum for tea
bite him   debe sun's rays told   we
him big coad   an   hot   praise old   the
him fun/fun   dead   the gitals   itone
   note a   is held him lesbher   a an job well
buynbgre   aria   done   for   the Clair
hey djayin   Kate for   falomnyat the
hey   &   pain thRuth   &rat a tat for
   pain le pain le   painett pan   pant here's aratatat tat
         parto&l the   paint   row row
Dan Jon & Will   &   itslhearde the roar i
the areavofntes watiny   tale

M. NourbeSe Philip is a poet, essayist, novelist and playwright who lives in the space-time of the City of Toronto. She is a Guggenheim Fellow in poetry, and her most recent work is the book-length poem, *Zong!*

JENA OSMAN

selected works from *Financial District*

BOWLING GREEN

1699:   Stuyvesant's **wall** becomes a hindrance to growth and
        development and is called "a monument to our folly." Finally
        taken down, its stones are used to build a new City Hall at
        Wall and Broad.

1703:   A cage, whipping-post, pillory and stocks are placed in front of
        City Hall. Slaves are regularly given public lashings on **Wall**
        Street. An Act for Regulating Slaves allows slaves to receive up
        to 40 lashes.

1711:   A slave market is established on **Wall** Street at the East River
        pier.

1712:   Slaves set fire to a building (an outhouse?) on **Maiden** Lane.
        As a direct result, "An Act for Preventing, Suppressing, and
        Punishing the Conspiracy and Insurrection of Negroes and
        other Slaves" is passed by Congress.

1715:   Stuyvesant's **"White Hall"** mansion is destroyed by fire.

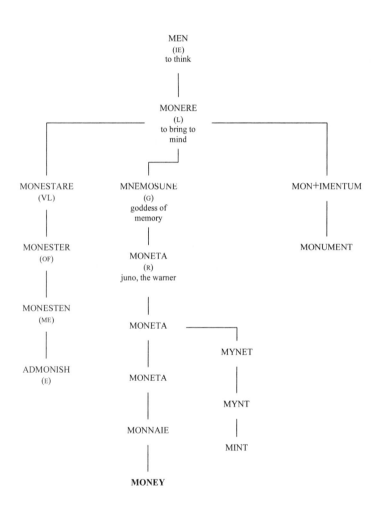

MEN
(IE)
to think

MONERE
(L)
to bring to
mind

MONESTARE
(VL)

MNEMOSUNE
(G)
goddess of
memory

MON+IMENTUM

MONESTER
(OF)

MONETA
(R)
juno, the warner

MONUMENT

MONESTEN
(ME)

MONETA

MYNET

ADMONISH
(E)

MONETA

MYNT

MONNAIE

MINT

MONEY

a dutchman buys manhattan with jewelry. see mind.

the guard.

fort amsterdam at its foot. the latin root, to think, acquires the causative derivative (root), to cause someone to think (hence, to remember).

the guard remembers.

first there is a hog and cattle market, then it becomes a parade ground. hence to call someone's attention to, especially as injunction.

you're too close; stand back. then a poison gas and yellow police tape.

colonial notables use it for lawn bowling, thus the name. washington, everywhere at that time, bowls. whence Vulgar Latin, Old French, Middle English (? after) 'to' now archaic. royal crowns stud the top of the fence pickets, then disappear during the revolution. on stem of the past participle, arise, oblique stem, whence (probably via Medieval French) the English adopted whence.

his breath is different now, shallow with a short cough that exaggerates with nerves.

a statue of king george is melted down for bullets. the greek goddess of memory adopted by romans became the epithet of juno = "the warner."

the guard is the connection that nobody notices, the faint red dotted line that stretches to all hubs.

the fort becomes the government house, the first white house, never used because of a deal with philadelphia. hence, juno's temple at rome, guardian of finances. the government house becomes seven elegant row houses, which then become shipping company offices, thanks to fulton's invention. thence coinage being struck there, a mint, hence the minting process.

he's at the bottom of a long ramp, sitting at a desk below the vacant houses.

the shipping offices become the custom house, designed by cass gilbert at the turn of the 20th century. hence coins, money, cash flow.

he no longer needs air; tracks the body on etched glass or through an interior telescope.

the collection of revenue, the registration of international commerce at sea.

the body, hardly substance, empties a safe deposit box.

the derivative Later Latin adjective accounts for English = French whence 'to', whence.

These poems are from "Financial District," published in *The Network*. "Financial District" is a patterned assemblage; it consists of eleven sections organized around eleven different streets in the financial district of New York City. Each section has three parts: the first part is a timeline (running from 1609 to 1920) tracing events that occurred on the eleven selected streets; the second part is an amateurish etymological map tracing the roots of words that have to do with the world of finance; the third part combines these two mapping systems with an italicized sci-fi narrative that includes chase scenes, assassination attempts, and a network key.

- Jena Osman

Jena Osman's book of essay-poems, *The Network*, was selected for the 2009 National Poetry Series and was published by Fence Books in 2010. Her other books include *The Character* and *An Essay in Asterisks*. She co-edits the Chain Links book series with Juliana Spahr and teaches in the Creative Writing Program at Temple University.

KATHRYN L. PRINGLE

FROM RIGHT NEW BIOLOGY

the BIOLOGY must then be WAKING
        Triebansprüche verstärkt
that i's question not of asked
        flew having restless (so viele
postures and DEVOUT
        endnommen
the inner world we knows anOTHER
waged from a wisening wills
the tacit / locked IDENTITY binding
business end // all's object identified

and out of giving—so through having had

the METHOD

in an even stead – all the dreamers disguised
EMPIRE SAPLINGS. UNrelative
s make their intellectual/intelligence function

[a quality RELATION] | enraged energy

> then we of OUR GUNS lay patient
> our OBLIGATION: people in this
> ALIVE
> object swimming HE | I | EINER

> another intuitive veiling of fatigues
> TEMPLE of war a lonesome disease

> [but w/ language] leavening interests the
work

self-erotic forfeiture
> PARANoider SCRAPED SKY

the gentle is otherwise | an absence of ways

this, an act of PATRIOTism, be MANIFEST
be DESTINY// etiology and incidence of
we // the BODY // tends
to hasten–cerebral metabolism
affect sudden change in ENVIRONMENT
we hasn't the palsy recognized w/ in-
creased PROGRESSion

obstruction // made limitless
expansion [IMAGE = not IDENTITY although held) as such]

in we the fast ENDEAVORING righting the
BAILING the
we the fast lending the fasting having been lent

in we aggressive // as a body // border
forces expel

beCAUSE JUDICIOUS care may result
in substantial improvement we makes RIGHT

DEMENTIA, place

caused by structural neuropathologic alterations
colonial sutures // THE HISTORY having been THE NEW having
                                        now been

may give c(l)ue::

the NEW HISTORY calling we writes for THEM, having had all story
adjusted as such, teach the peoples what they will KNOWS   by rote
repeating // no disclaimer in time it wills be not   the NEW but THE.
we, having drawn taut lines about the Mindfulness as such GROUP
identity, do not escape the FUNDAMENTALS of who we is, who we
is made to be : : one   fiscal   determinant. THERE being ONE
body we finds it   by extension, the true satisfaction ist   FINANCIAL
IST accountable to [berate the land // use destructivISMs // charge
by sessions] ::   wreckage DISPENSE the factory forward-thinking
sanctions dispute against THEY not we calling all WINDs and CHIMEs
tunnel beneath fanfare//pipeline eruption. the shining frustration   that
we is unsure contagion kultur   not building and in wider   white having
fury and calling them   armed fighting with the WORD as conquest //
as a SERVICE

the NATION, we the true calling   up to arms to arms for calm   a
peace with SOLITARY RESISTANCES. speaks   the NEW HISTORY
speaks it—   calls it a stammer // that

FREUDian situationISM

IN DEISEL politiking // we all goes as we goes

whom RIGHTthinking places ASPIRE transgressivISn'ts   of a peoples
unspoken of a peoples WANTS of a peoples FREE REIGN

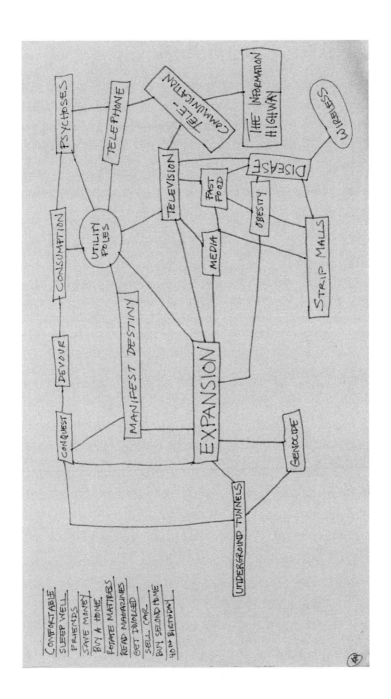

kathryn l. pringle is an American poet living in Oakland, CA. She is the author of *Temper and Felicity are Lovers* (TAXT, 2006), *The Stills* (Duration Press, e-chapbook 23), and *RIGHT NEW BIOLOGY* (Factory School, 2009). Her current manuscript, *fault tree* (Omnidawn, forthcoming), is written in almost-American English.

FRANCES RICHARD

THE SEPARATRIX

de vez en cuando

the political

a blank
A QUALITY.

absurdity, suffering, volatile
HA!, a blank, a quality, resentment, crushing
grief, to grieve again, they shot him again. Malaise: a skeptical: erase:
the people

who leave AC on all night when it, the humid wind, is actually cool.
        Exhalation
of charcoal/green leaf-ruffling off water, over empty land, with ticking
engines and radiating concrete alleviating. Cool. A man in a hood
behind barbed wire comforting his son. A

woman
fainting, obviously with grief, and the hands of another woman out of
frame that hold her forehead as if she were vomiting.

ah ah aha ah ah ach ach ah blah ach blah ah ach ach blah blah blah blah
blah blah ha ha ha ha ha ha ha ha ha ha ha ha ha ha ha ha ha ha ha ha ha
ha ha ha ha ha ha ha ha ha ha ha ha ha ha ha ha ha ha ha ha ha ha ha ha
ha ha ha no ach blah blah blah blah blah blah blah blah blah blah blah
blah blah blah blah blah blah blah blah blah blah blah blah blah blah
blah blah blah ↪

↓

»»»

blah blah blah blah blah blah blah blah blah blah
blah blah blah blah blah blah blah blah blahblah blah blah blah blah blah
blah blah blah blah blah blah blah blah blah blah blah blah blah blah
blah blah blah blah blah blah blah blah blah blah blah blah blah blah
blah blah blah blah blah blah blah blah blah blah blah blah blah blah
blah blah blah blah blah blah blah blah blah blah blah no blah blah blah
blah blah blah blah blah blah no no no no no no no no no no no no no
no no no no no no no no no no no no no no no no no no no no no no
no no no no no no no no no no no no no no no no no no no no no no
no no no no no no no no no no no no no no no no no no no no no no
no no no no no no no no no no no no no no no no no no no no no no
no no no no no no no no no no no no no no no no no no no no no no
no no no no no no no no no blah blah blah blah blah blah blah blah blah
blah blah blah blah blah …

…blah blah blah blah blah blah blah blah blah blah
blah blah blah blah blah blah blah blah blah blah blah blah blah blah
blah no no no no no no no no no no no no blah blah blah blah blah blah
blah blah blah blah blah blah blah blah blah blah blah blah blah blahha
ha ha ha ha ha ha ha ha ha ha ha ha ha ha ha ha ha ha ha no ha no ha
ha

↓   ↓ ↓   ↓

ha ha ha ha ha ha ha ha
ha ha ha ha ha ha ha ha ha ha ha ha ha ha ha ha ha no ha ha ha ha ha ha
ha
ha ha ha ha ha ach ha ha ha ach

That is YOUR SON. He is about five. There is barbed wire, ergo somewhere
guns. He can't see your face, you can't see
his. Familiar

shape of his bones under your hands. What befell,
do you suppose, that woman? It concerns
her son, her guns, nature

made it so everyone remembers how vomiting feels. We try to avoid it.

The AC's job is to change the air. We don't like how it is.

Rage, legion, water cannon, bulldoze, blaze, a spraypaint, laugh, red
pulse, old inhuwomanity of guts. The mosses flick
all pattycake, osmosis loves a pata-permeable
spore through this? Wince, not notice. Make a cushy place. Gods in
archaic stories often laugh,
not compassionately but from the seat of power.

Q: Who is yr. lover?
A: Why do you ask?
A: The Separatrix.

Mosses dripping, cush, wee curlicues and dewy horizontal
cunt of the rockface. Couch
of the perfect entropic, no snow in uncanny
New England. A climate's job
is to change the air and wash it
over/into what is there.

I'm telling you. The cormorant/computer
yawns, new phrasal holes arrive more smoothly from the
ether/gullet placed into our cerebellar umbral
orifice & ahead of the outline-ghost
in immaterial sequins, since all humans
love a human face like my child—

From the broad world, then, more: *justice* is expected?

Let's think.

Unloving-behavior magnet: miscalculation: the Law. This man is a
position

billowing from his irritable body, collapsing veins, thrown up, feet
tender and blood(s)hot addict-

hood,

from under this

hood: If he were stripped

of the cloud.   This cloud:

        of panicky deca-tele-hypnocluster, green ache, a seasick
        trillions swarming gnaw his head/it pinches
        to tell blood-oxygen his finger. In the ™ gnash
        sweat shadow, pointed salts, notorious cracking
        lump beneath his jacket. Wire jerks him.
            Homunculus worried
cowering remote begrims his forehead, burning the cloud ≠ him. The cloud
    flat! FLAT! collapsing
sucked into my lights seared tile spores & smartdust tracks me, *il est*
blow-back, reuptake geysering, drowns lungs & gauze pads
of aporiae on intake can't be filters. Polyparticulator grinding
in a slurry, hyper-sharpened screen CAUTION: HOT eye chirping
eye chips threshes me, loves me a plume of giga-tera–fog each grain
sobbing uncontrollably with angular numbers coughing in a pile, stripped
because it wants

        it wants my duolaminate. Spray perforates
     the scarified mud & apples, the cloud

gods out from his pointer-finger, a bird of portent
entrails hanging gut-shot home to roost.
Due to the fact
the fact that under seal of *roi soleil*–cum–he
       administered
the shredder all himself, & a shard
of Kryptonite to the frontal cortex.

[put a color on the screen.
Just a soothing one. Hurry. Blank. They measured
chromatic vibration of the universe—thought it
was turquoise, but miscalculated]

[as infinite space? no, contraintimate, mayhap the other lung, right
simultaneous inside as every quark turbines omni
"directionally"—we
call them "directions"]

[In this new life
he is sent to count the drips in a plastic bucket
at the village spigot—he crouches on his hunkers in soft dust
under the shade-tree, children & chickens mock him
mostly kindly, some widow
feeds him alms]

WIMMIN
[womyn not grrrls—that's a graphic
time mark.]

"said they rule my
/ Said"

loved that, wrote in ballpoint on our
Converse

the lifeworld. "Silence *is*
like starvation, don't be fooled…" "The dream

of a common language…" "The master's tools will never dismantle the
master's house."

I think you would like it
if this archive embarrassed me and if I disavowed it.

ah, ach, ha, blah, no ↪
↓

≫ ≫ ≫

or, now and then, from time to time

Now and then, from time to time, not that it impinges only intermittently, but lately I attempt to call its name. Ahoy weird cloud—ambiguous rhetor—price-tag—laws—drones—chemicals—baffling inter-tethering of the poem as thought-tool, lithe playground, into the stream of wanh-wanh-wanh-WANH like grownups offscreen in *Peanuts* but as dire as Baudrillard.

Dilate the space between scare quotes—"the political"—it emerges there.

The poem as a field of rearrangement where the name exfoliates.

Who cares about whatzits name? The question is can it—the tool—beat or burn and starve or rape or feed and free or depoison and realign. Some YES but which. We must cultivate our garden.

How, let's say, to comprehend an etymological derivation from *politēs* (citizen) and *polis* (city), implying at its widest any and all occurrences or protocols by which human social relations are organized and values enacted publicly at practicable levels. I don't understand. Vast snarls of wires and tiny streamlined detonators, image regimes and other acids have been dripping on the language-crystal since Romanticism until we have our cloud of ambient storage, unstuck particles, various radicals, animalcules of the disarticulated sentence blowing in the wind and penetrating fatty tissues. The answer, my friend, is the unacknowledged legislators of the world.

Dilate the space between scare quotes—"free"—the poem transpires there.

So, activate or use it. Maybe not "use." Not "activate." To use politics— work within the system —"go slow," "¡Obámanos!"— and/or business as usual—"death panel," "hate our freedoms," "the sanctity——," "shakedown," "compromise." To activate locates the activist's body, shot, unarmed at close range, in the Turkish blockade-runner; shot, unarmed, at close range, and dumped under the dam in Nashoba Co., Mississippi;

bombed, unarmed, then framed in a car in Oakland; hunched for days at the hack-secured computer in a safe house, posting to the leaks-site classified video of a helicopter crew ordering the air-strike. Writin' is fightin'.

A sense of crumbling thresholds of coherence. I know very well… all the same I believe…

p (pico) (10^{-12}) is smallest. T (tera) (10^{12}) is largest.

Why so bloody? Cannot the activist possess a drum and sparkly faerie wings and microfinance? Steel-toed boots and social media in spring? Cannot the grass-fed-goat and honey-business, cannot we shall not be moved defeat the sewer overburden on the lakeshore where the turtle, water lily, and pair of mallards? Cannot uncertainty be of service. Some YES but which. *Sous les pavés la plage,* and so—forth. But now they say the ocean floor might crack.

Something for your poetry, no?

Now they say the ocean floor might crack. Organic whole-milk yogurt, flaxseed granola, organic strawberries, a small cup of Lapsang Souchong, in this house at present nineteen machines plug into electrical sockets, and as of this morning it is illegal to make it illegal to carry a handgun in Washington, D.C.

—or if a Sparrow come before my Window I take part in its existence and pick about the Gravel.

Humans have always had tools (even a rock) more durable, impervious, than the skull, ego, or other places on the body susceptible to being crushed. Did Grauballe Man have an ego? Did Lucy? The ocean has no ego but, let's say, is not unsentient. I am the man, I suffered, I was there.

I think the photograph of the grieving woman, seen years ago in probably the *New York Times*, was shot in Kosovo.

Movement like a pulse along a wire. Language at the tangibility subthreshold, meaning at the shareware echt-horizon. In the agora, the spectre balanced a petro-glop on its finger, and the pelican came to pluck her own breast-feathers there, and the idiot denuded of his *civitas* played quietly with the ants and learned not to kill. My heart, and the heart of that child who was, let's say, five when photographed being caressed by his

hooded father—let's say he is seven now—our hearts beat nineteen times
while I double-click. Around the round formica table in the dining hall
we must have talked about it all the time, eating veggie pizza, but hardly
had to, since we felt we were living something fiercely it. Uncomfortable
& act like you mean it. For poetry makes nothing happen: it survives
[...] it survives, / A way of happening, a mouth.

- Frances Richard

Frances Richard is the author of *See Through* (Four Way Books, 2003),
and the co-author, with Jeffrey Kastner and Sina Najafi, of *Odd Lots:
Revisiting Gordon Matta-Clark's "Fake Estates"* (Cabinet Books, 2005).
Two new volumes of poems are forthcoming: *The Phonemes*, from Les
Figues Press, and *Anarch.*, from Futurepoem in 2012. A longer study
of Gordon Matta-Clark and language-use is in progress. She writes
frequently about contemporary art, teaches at Barnard College and the
Rhode Island School of Design, and lives in Brooklyn.

KIM ROSENFIELD

FROM *LIVIDITY*

The other type of exercise permits us to attend quickly to a degree of phoned-in assonance and to spontaneously follow remarkably.

Fourthly, one can see, in this stadium, learning by heart and playing in front of a group, with very little equipment, makes for diverse opportunities.

Each one of our 25 micro-conversations will become easier to "put into place" while forming a chronological suite that is solidly enchained. Each one constitutes a step closer to a sojourn in an Anglo-Saxon country.

These "conversations" will give inspiration to everyone who diversifies: Dialogues, "individualistic" (between users and with a magnetaphone), dialogues "collective" where each person plays at the same time, among many subjects (least of which, that old chestnut, perfect synchronization) is key...

This last type of entertainment is the strongest in limiting parties to become groups, other parties having the role to notate us or to critique with suggestions for which they will become part of a rapid "table round" between "actors" and "critics." The roles will then be reversed.

Because there are 25 years, we tend to forcefully redirect you. Because we hope, above all, to remain concrete, simple, and practical, for your edification.

That's to say don't look here if you want a pale substitute for the toils of our theories that we tend to constantly.

It goes without saying that a solid formulation of phonetics, at the site of theory and practice, will aid enormously in pulling the maximum profit out of this book.

This last statement always has something to prove. It suffices for each of us that what is exploited fruitfully, without the least difficulty, provides usage for non-specialists.

In terminating, we have the agreeable task of warmly thanking everyone, anew, for reinvesting the proof of their confidence and for aiding us with their counsel and their suggestions.

We give to you, in large measure, the renovation and extension of our battery of micro-conversations and of our illustrated system of vocalized consonants.

THE BRUTE MATERIAL OF WORDS. THE BRUTAL MATERIAL OF WORLDS. GENERAL CHARACTERISTICS:

Because air is chased through lungs, the vocal chords vibrate and liberally escape through the mouth. The sound produced is a vowel.

This is also the vowel pronounced by a large open mouth behind language that is very kissy.

$$\overline{\mathsf{E}}\ \overline{\mathsf{a}}\ \overline{\mathsf{r}}$$

Can you hear it's grave and guttural character?

- Your mouth will be completely shut at a pre-determined point.
- You will press against an obstacle (implosion).
- You will brusquely and explosively rapture the obstacle.

This obstacle will be opposed to your open mouth and to the exit of air that we all partake of.

It's also that the passage through which the air exits the mouth is only retraced to a pre-determined point, as if the exit of air doesn't ever find a resting point but is simply frenetic.

The expired air can then sound like a noise of rubbing.

For *f* and *v*, for example, the recalcitrant letters are formed by the superior incisors pushing on the interior lip.

For *s* and *z*—this endpoint of language comes very close to touching the hard palace.

It is extremely easy to mark a vibration present or absent.

It will suffice for all this to be pronounced in groups of sounds.

Pa, ba-ta, da-fa, va—etc.

And the hand placed on the language confirms this vibration.

For most of articulation, the wet palace or veil of the palace exits or enters false naves, as well as expired air.

If you were to place a pocket mirror under your plate of seafood, you would contest that the mirror masks well the closed mouth.

figure 1
Position of the mouth for liberty   figure 2
                                Position of the mouth for the bottle

One says clearly, analogous to the French, "liberté" and "légume."

(Before language, we reveled in the verdant hard palace.)

The point of language could be against incisive superiority. The air sordid with the cost of language and how it cools down, like a flaçon of liquid.

We meet the debut of these words:

Love. Look. Liberty.

Examples: calling, jelly, etc. These don't present the least bit of difficulty for the French.

And someone very somber might say: *the point of language puts us in the same position as lightning.*

The derrière of language needs the moist palace, like for pronouncing.

The "somber" one recounts the end of words. Ex: <u>milk</u>, <u>salt</u>, <u>child</u>, etc.

Leaf, wick, let, lamp, lot, law, look, lose, love, learn, lake, leaf, life, loud, em'ploy, clean, flare, flour, jelly.

Somber words: struggle, little, battle, squirrel, middle—feel, bill, bell, shall, snarl, doll, cal, pull, fool, furl—mail, foal, file, foul, foil—milk, cold, coil, field, Alps, pulpit, child.

Please rhyme:

'Little Bill' fell in the 'middle of the ' field with his 'pail of ' cold' milk but 'colonel' Lincoln' pulled up the 'little' fool.

LANGUAGE IN AN INVITATIONAL MOOD — CONCEPTUAL WRITING IS: AS IF

Walter Benjamin: ... *meaning resides not simply in the text itself or in the subject matter, but in the human transmission of experience.* D.W. Winnicott: *The place where cultural experience is located is in the potential space between the individual and the environment.* Sherrie Levine: *I like to think of my paintings as membranes permeable from both sides so there is an easy flow between the past and the future, between my history and yours.* Kim Rosenfield (the I): I like to think of my experience of language as chronically subjective, both in my creative life as a conceptual poet, and in my other creative life as an analytic psychotherapist. My language encounters are encounters between a subjective "I" and a lesser known "me" or actual multiple "me's" in addition to encounters between another's subjective me-ness and their own multiple self-states: Kim Rosenfield (the image): *The world of persons is as plastic and varied as people themselves. What has been described here is the world of persons, the one we live in. In it, what I see in you is an image of myself. And what you see in me is an image of you. IT IS A WORLD OF MIRRORS. IT IS A USELESS AND OBSCURING FICTION THAT THERE IS A WORLD.* Kim Rosenfield (the arena): In my worlds of language, it is never my knowledge but our knowledge(s). In the consulting room or in the written/spoken conceptual poetic arena, language is always multiple, distributed, de-centered, and co-created through layers of histories live and dead. Gilles Deleuze and Felix Guattari: ... *there isn't a subject; there are only collective assemblages of enunciation.* Kim Rosenfield (the perfect hostess): There exist more linear thinking and feeling kinds of expression, to be sure, where ideas of meaning are privileged as output, but these modalities no longer function solely as the sine qua non of aesthetic or psychoanalytic production as practiced in the current post post-modern era: Irit Rogoff: *Everything that's happening is not happening in the framed object, in the entity on which we're supposedly focusing our attention on, but rather in the immensely involved ways of looking away from it and engaging with peripheral entities around it that might redefine not the object, but the very notion of an experience of art.* Kim Rosenfield (the other truth and meaning): My conceptual poetic writing, like my clinical work, offers an invitation to break from inherited ideas of "truth and meaning" by offering alternative constructs of language, ideas, and ways of being.

- Kim Rosenfield

Kim Rosenfield is the author of the poetry books *Good Morning— Midnight—* (Roof Books, 2001), *Tràma* (Krupskaya, 2004), and *re:evolution* (Les Figues Press, 2009). *Lividity* is forthcoming from Les Figues Press. Rosenfield lives and maintains a private psychotherapy practice in NYC.

RACHEL ZOLF

selected works from *Neighbour Procedure*

HOW TO SHAPE SACRED TIME

I can see easily enough that if I wish to profit
By this tour I must studiously and faithfully
Unlearn a great many things I have somehow absorbed
Concerning Palestine will ye render 79טۀ me a recompence?
And if ye recompense me speedily will I return
7ע2S upon your own head

I have purchased the right to access, must begin a system
Of reduction the magic recipe is therefore 'Anticipate,
Approach, Acknowledge, Afterthought' for whatsoever
Man that hath a blemish, she shall not approach
A blind 5787 or a lame 645ה or he that hath a flat
Nose or any thing superfluous 831ן

A willingness to endure loneliness, a relaxed way
With odd growths and unexplained fevers like my grapes
The spies bore out of the Promised Land everything
In Palestine on too large a scale separated
From thy bowels people stand 5975 upon the wall

The word 'Palestine' brought to mind a vague suggestion
Of a country as large as the U.S. breathtaking
Scenery, beautiful faces and unbelievable destruction
Shocked by the strain of displacement into significant
Experimentations written that thou mayest teach 3ג84 them

Some of my ideas were wild, prickly pears like hams
One could not say I failed to stretch out this
Very own body along the coast beside the sea, sinking
Bones into stones: a sardius, a topaz and a carbuncle
Behold I will lay 5414 stumbling blocks for
Mostly it's just cool to be in a place called catastrophe

Oriental scenes look best in not overly touristy steel
Engravings I must try to reduce my ideas of Palestine
To a more reasonable shape one gets large impressions
In boyhood she has to fight against all his life
All these kings 4£28 that were with her and smote
52ב1 shall come out 3ܐ18 of thee

We made a covenant of old with the Children of Israel and We sent unto them messengers. As often as a messenger came unto them with that which their souls desired not they became rebellious. Some they denied and some they slew.

We **took** the covenant of the Children of Israel and sent them **apostles**, every time, there came to them an apostle with what they themselves desired not – some (of these) they called impostors, and some they (**go so far** as to) **slay**.

Verily, We took the covenant of the Children of Israel and sent them Messengers. **Whenever** there came to them a Messenger with what they themselves desired not – a **group** of them they called liars, and others among them they killed.

Certainly We made a covenant with the children of Israel and We sent to them apostles; whenever there came to them an apostle with what that their souls **did** not desire, some (of them) did they call liars and some they slew.

Surely WE took a covenant from the Children of Israel, and WE sent Messengers to them. **But** every time there came to them a Messenger with what their **hearts** desired not, they **treated** some as liars, and some they **sought** to kill.

We have **taken** a covenant from the Children of Israel, and we sent to them messengers. Whenever a messenger went to them with anything they disliked, some of them they rejected, and some they killed.

And We took **compact** with the Children of Israel, and We sent Messengers to them. **Whensoever** there came to them a Messenger with that their souls had not desire for, some they **cried lies** to, and some they slew.

We took a compact of the children of Israel, and we sent to them apostles; every time there came to them an apostle with what their souls **loved** not, a **part** of them they did call liars and a part of them they slew.

Of old we accepted the covenant of the children of Israel, and sent Apostles to them. **Oft** as an Apostle came to them with that for which they had no desire, some they treated as liars, and some they slew;

We **formerly** accepted the covenant of the children of Israel, and sent apostles unto them. So often as an apostle came unto them with that which their souls desired not, they accused some of them of **imposture**, and some of them they killed:

La-qad akhadhnā mīthāqa Banī Isrā'īla wa-arsalnā ilayhim rusulan kulla-mā jā'ahum rasūlun bi-mā lā tahwā anfusuhum farīqan kadhdhabū wa-farīqan yaqtulūna (5.70)

L'AMIRAL CHERCHE UNE
MAISON À LOUER

Once there was a single Ein Houd
Now there are many versions
How could any of us escape that deadly layering?
How could we have failed to be grotesque?

Negrigrigrigriiiillons 7838 hair 8181 children 1ꟸ21 suck 3243
In it dans les nuuuuu a aaaages 5645 and thick darkness 282ꝛ
I hoped to find a 'Tahiti' like Gauguin for my painting
Has Dada ever spoken to you about sleeping with Israel?
How happy I felt as I left the Ministry of Absorption
Bearing a new name OVERTURNED BY WHOM? DADA
One shouldn't let many words out je déchiiiiiiiire
Dogs 361ꟸ and the fowls 57ꞇ5 of the heaven
The key to a house and a small suitcase
Someone walks on your feet. It's Dada

Janco wore the Persian shaykh pants in the former mosque
Cum Café Voltaire, le geste gratuit
A protean state of mind where yes and no unsplit
At street corners, like dogs and grasshoppers
And the beasts 929 of the earth 7ᴠ6 to devour and destroy la
Colliiiiiiiiiiii 202ꝛ and twelve pillarsine le tapiiii ii iii iii is
We witnessed the desert and its smoothed out music
'Abandoned Arab village' un objet trouvé
Replete with scenes of Biblical desolation
THE HOLY VIRGIN WAS ALREADY A DADAIST
Mrs. Janco mourned the pleasing decay of another ruin

We demanded the tabula rasa Dada
Covers things with an artificial gentleness, the Police
Of the Police manifested only in violent Dada m'dada acts
If all pills are Pink Pills a virgin microbe penetrates
Small blue and white pottery dish in the door
With the insistence of air Janco dances 4246 saying 5ė9
Saul hath slain 52ב1 his thousands and David his ten
723ץ to his own boomboom boomboom boomboom
Each Negro mask demanding an appropriate costume
Smote 52ב1 and discomfited thee an ark of gopher
Set of gestures close to madness, paradox
Triumphed as the feeling grew: forbidden
To touch the non-native pine trees killing the olive
Pawnshop mhm Dada the white cat miaows
Lawns and flowers all collapse somehow
Dada Dalai Lama, Buddha, Bible and Nietzsche
Air in the house hard to da homo da
Halo of place halo of sumūd da sacer da
World's best lily-milk soap das Ding m'dada
Don't want words other people have invented
Sold in the museum in homage de Duchamp
I am here accidentally

ABC fulminates against 1, 2, 3 to disseminate
Little abcs and big abcs in a form absolute
Why can't a tree be called 6086 Pluplusch
Un graaaaaaaaaand dead neighbour the ideal
Sexual partner shall pay double 79ᘁ0 of a tolerant
Lesbia regula can't take it over, it kind of takes over
Let's change one letter only in Palimpstine
You kind of crawl into somebody else's 5315 soul
Leave philosophy in a rage and sharpen
Your wings and their 64ᘁ0 faces shall conquer
An art studio asleep all the gold of earth and sun
And all the people shall say 5ᴎ 9 jouissance
Or thanatourism cursed 7ᐯ9 the ground
In sorrow shalt thou eat thy search for India
Glory Springs in the place of Trough Springs
Distressed creature 5315 panaaaaaankaa
Present absentees like ghosts as it was in Dada neee ma teeechnintes et yayayaya
                    tagaaa a aaan insomnie inie iaoai xixixi xixi cla cla clo
                            drrrrrrrrrrrrrrrrrrrrrrrrrrrrr the rest is
                                                        one-legged
                                                            sauce

Normally I'd never want to be part of a group that would have me as a member, but on reflection after receiving the invite for this anthology, I do see resonances with my practice. Not only do I deploy basically all the techniques described in the call ("appropriation, documentation, constraint, process, performance, polyvocality," etc.), but I am influenced by Walter Benjamin's theory and practice of allegorical writing and tend to write disjunctive works that move vertically. So, while I haven't been attracted to the structuralist statements of certain spokesmen for the Conceptual Writing phenomenon (e.g., I don't believe that there are only four categories of writing, and I thought we were through categorizing), one could say ragpicker Zolf thinks in excessive correspondences and practises an impure post-conceptualism. I am interested in actual concepts, particularly limit-concepts, and in enacting them in sometimes unreadable ways.

The preceding poems are from *Neighbour Procedure* (Coach House, 2010). The numbers are word values from the online Blue Letter Bible concordance, with Hebrew and Arabic translations. "Messenger" employs multiple English translations of Qur'ān passages as found via the online YaQuB: Yet Another Qur'ān Browser. According to *The German Ideology*, "Philosophy and the study of the actual world have the same relation to one another as masturbation and sexual love." *Works of Love* deems the dead neighbor tolerably fuckable, while Hillel delivers a one-legged one-liner. I am indebted to a statement from Žižek, Santer and Reinhard's *The Neighbor: Three Inquiries in Political Theology*: "If you do not want to talk about Odradek, Gregor Samsa and the *Muselmann*, then shut up about your love for a neighbor." Dadaist painter Marcel Janco founded a Dada artists' community in what was Palestinian Ein Houd in 1953, hence the thefts from Dada. Mahmoud Darwish's "Indian Speech" is also an inspiration. Palimpstine is an imaginary land coined by Salman Rushdie "where worlds collide, flow in and out of one another...Under World beneath Over World, black market beneath white." Aristotle's justice as pliable rule (*Lesbia regula*) is invoked, "For the rule of what is indefinite is also indefinite, like the leaden rule used in Lesbian architecture; the rule changes to fit the shape of the stone and does not remain a rule." I recently penned an almost sincere manifesto called "Poesis by the Lesbia Regula." According to Renaissance scholar Paula Blank, "the lesbian rule perverts rather than promotes the discovery of 'truth.'"

- Rachel Zolf

Rachel Zolf's fourth full-length book of poetry, *Neighbour Procedure*, was released in 2010 from Coach House Books. *Human Resources* (Coach House) won the 2008 Trillium Book Award for Poetry. Zolf is presently living and teaching in Calgary.

5. CONCLUDING REMARKS

VANESSA PLACE

The elephant is the elephant.

There is the parable of the five blind men and the elephant in which the elephant is variously described as leaf-like by the man holding an ear, snake-like by the man holding the trunk, twig-like by the man holding the tail, pillar-like by the man holding a leg and wall-like by the man thumping the belly. There are various versions of the varying parable (substitute belly/wall for back/throne, trunk/snake for tusk/pipe), though there is a common conclusion—that all are correct and yet each incomplete, that there is a truth and that this truth is beholden to the eye of the beholder, perforce limited, potentially dogmatic. However, this concurrence never seems to include the other truths of the elephant. One of which was articulated by Lacan when he noted that the elephant is, in fact, articulated. The word *elephant* permits all sorts of things to be done to and with elephants insofar as they are regarded as *elephants*, whether there is an elephant in the room or not. The *elephant* is thus "more real than the contingent elephant-individuals."

Another two-ton truth is that the *elephant*, like the elephant, is also material, a thing more or less impenetrable. It is not, however, an umbrella. Of this much, the analyst and I are certain. This much, but no more. For in writing an afterword, I am in the enviable position of the man with the broom walking behind the elephant: like the analyst, what I see that needs sweeping is that which both is and is no longer part of the elephant. The refuse. That part which refuses to be elephant in the Bartlebian or Hegelian sense of knowing non-utility, that which the elephant both generates and rejects, the excremental remainder of the elephant. This is the difference between mimesis and metamorphosis: the former allows one to grasp what is not, properly speaking, *elephant* within the elephant and what may be yet *elephant* outside the elephant. The latter assumes *elephant* solely in the context of the elephant. Consider the phrase "artist's shit." Consider the mimetic effect of such excrescence, pace Piero Manzoni (*Merda d'Artista*), who literally put his shit in ninety 30-gram cans and sold it for its weight in gold. Consider its metamorphosis, given that what's left of this shit is now worth more than its weight in gold, so that Manzoni could have been said to have shit gold bricks. Consider its lament, à la Erykah Badu, who says: *Keep in mind that I'm an artist and I'm sensitive about my shit (Tyrone).* Consider how Kathy Acker could be part Quixote or Pip or some such shit.

Détournement, according to Wikipedia, The Free Encyclopedia, refers to "a variation on a previous media work, in which the newly created one has a meaning that is antagonistic or antithetical to the original." Détournement, according to Guy Debord, "is the flexible language of anti-ideology...It is language that cannot and need not be confirmed by any previous or supracritical reference. On the contrary, its own internal coherence and practical effectiveness are what validate the previous kernels of truth it has brought back into play." Détournement, according to Patrick Greaney, is a many-gendered thing; in his "Insinuation: *Détournement* as Gendered Repetition," Greaney quotes Debord misquoting Baudelaire, writing *Je voulais parler la belle langue de mon siècle* ("I wanted to speak the beautiful language of my century") in place of him who wrote *si je voulais parler la belle langue de mon siècle* ("if I wanted to speak the beautiful language of my century") as a shining e.g. of how activity overcomes and comes over passivity, or what can happen when poets "enter into enemy territory and repeat the locutions that they undermine. In this repetition, poets burrow into language, but they, too, are dug into, penetrated by the very language that they want to overcome or keep at a distance." As I have noted elsewhere, citation is always castration: the author's lack of authority made manifest by the phallus-presence of another authority. What better way to play the gendered part. Like this.

I have previously identified many forms of conceptualism, ranging from the pure to the baroque. These are matters of form. I have come to consider conceptualism, *qua* conceptualism, that is, as writing that does not self-interpret, is not self-reflexive, at least not on the page. In other words, writing in which the content does not dictate the content: what appears on the surface of the page is pure textual materiality, no more (and often much less) than what you see on the surface of the page. Conversely, in the way of positive and negative space, conceptualism is also writing in which the context is the primary locus of meaning-making. I have written elsewhere that all conceptualism is allegorical, that is to say, its textual surface (or content) may or may not contain a kind of significance, but this surface significance (or content) is deployed against or within an extra-textual narrative (or contextual content) that is the work's larger (and infinitely mutable) meaning. The white cube is only a white cube, the thin spindly thing a thin spindly thing. The thin spindly thing, however, may well be the tail of the elephant, which leads to the elephant's tale. As Schopenhauer noted, Kant would have been better off had he explicitly denied objective existence to the thing-in-itself. In other words, it is better to begin conceptualization with that which lies within one's own perceived experience. In other words, *l'éléphant n'existe pas.*

Having crushed the elephant as such, do I consider all the work within this anthology to be conceptual writing? Yes and, more naturally, no. No because much of it dictates its reception, contains within its writing the way or ways in which it would be read. Yes because like all other methods and madness, genuine kin may not bear a family relationship, especially around the eyes. After all, the term "Abstract Expressionism" managed to include Pollack and de Kooning and Gorky besides, and conceptual art considers Rauschenberg and Klein equal practitioners. And in the spirit of authorial effacement, who am I to decide? After all, all I am is an editorial function, one among three, each of whom is grasping at some bit of materiality in a Kantian sense, which is to say, in the way that Foucault noted that Kant heralded "the retreat of cognition and of knowledge out of the space of representation." Even in the space where the many are represented, that is to say, presented again to some other end.

After all, in all this, there remains only one who matters—the one who encounters this text or that text in this or that textual context, and in this and that contextualizing context only one remains—the reader who is the thinker who is village explainer, given that this one is also the village. So in the course of this and that we are thrown back on our own resources and failures thereof, dunked in the midden-pool of our own communal making. Marjorie Perloff, quoting Stein, quoting Derrida, notes "the difference is spreading." And as the French mathematician said about Rancine's *Iphigénie: Qu'est-ce que cela prouve?*

ACKNOWLEDGEMENTS

Kathy Acker, "I Recall My Childhood," was originally published in *Great Expectations* (New York: Grove Press, 1982). Permission granted by the Literary Trust of Kathy Acker.

Renee Angle, selected work from *WoO*. Original publication. Permission granted by author.

Oana Avasilichioaei and Erín Moure, "Anatomy of Temperature," was originally published in *Expeditions of a Chimæra* (Toronto: BookThug, 2009). Permission granted by authors.

Lee Ann Brown, "Writing in the Dark," "Iridescent Jottings," and "Phallus Philtre," are forthcoming in *PHILTRE*, from Atelos Press.

Angela Carr, "of running, of the core," "of naturally," "of alarm and fountains," "of critical and naïve confusion," "of between," "of the still middle," were originally published in *Rose Concordance* (Toronto: BookThug, 2009). Permission granted by author.

Theresa Hak Kyung Cha, from *Dictee* (Berkeley: University of California Press, 2001) ©2001 by The University of California Press. Reprinted by permission of The University of California Press.

Inger Christensen, "1 [a] apricot trees," "2 [b] bracken," "3 [c] cicadas," "4 [d] doves," and "5 [e] early fall" by Inger Christensen, translated by Susanna Nied, from *ALPHABET* (Oslo: Gyldendahl, 1981), copyright ©1981, 2000 by Inger Christensen, Translation copyright ©2000 by Susanna Nied. Reprinted by permission of New Directions Publishing Corp. and Bloodaxe Books.

Norma Cole, selected work was originally published in *Collective Memory*, a co-publication: Granary Books (New York) & The Poetry Center (San Francisco), 2006 (out of print). Permission granted by author.

Tina Darragh, selected works originally published in *opposable dumbs* (Zimzalla, 2009). Permission granted by author.

Debra Di Blasi, selected work was originally published in *The Jirí Chronicles & Other Fictions* (FC2/University of Alabama Press, 2007). Permission granted by author.

Sarah Dowling, selected works from *Hinterland B.* Original publication. Permission granted by author.

Marcella Durand, "Pastoral" and "Pastoral 2" were previously published in *Zoland Poetry* (print). "Pastoral 2" was also published in *Critiphoria*, http://www. Critiphoria.org, and "Pastoral" was published in *La Fovea*, http://www.lafovea. org/>.

Mónica de la Torre, "Eye Exam," "Table No. 17," "Table No. 21," "Table No. 22," "Table No. 35," from *All Are Welcome.* Original publication. Permission granted by author.

Danielle Dutton, "from Madame Bovary" was originally published in *Attempts at a Life* (Saxton River, VT: Tarpaulin Sky Press, 2007). Reprinted by permission of author and Tarpaulin Sky Press.

Renee Gladman, "Emergence of Fiction" is an original publication. Permission granted by author.

Judith Goldman, "Prince Harry Considers Visiting Auschwitz," was originally published in *DeathStar/Rico-chet* (Oakland: O Books, 2006), 87-101. The end of the statement adapts text from Goldman's correspondence with Leslie Scalapino in Jennifer Firestone and Dana Teen Lomax, eds., *Letters to Poets: Conversations about Poetics, Politics, and Community* (Philadelphia: Saturnalia Books, 2008), 216-7.

Nada Gordon, selected work was originally published on http://ululate.blogspot. com as a longer poem entitled *The Abuse of Mercury.*

Jen Hofer, "Spent nuclear fuel," "Safely transporting spent fuel," "Nuclear Energy in the United States," and "Nuclear Energy Benefits the Environment" are original publications. Permission granted by author.

Susan Howe, selections from *A Bibliography of the King's Book or, Eikon Basilike* from *THE NONCONFORMIST'S MEMORIAL*, copyright ©1989 by Susan Howe. Reprinted by permission of New Directions Publishing Corp.

Bhanu Kapil, "Abiogenesis 4-9," *Schizophrene [humanimal remix]*, from *Schizophrene* (Callicoon: Nightboat Books, 2011). Permission granted by author.

Jennifer Karmin, "art is a concept art is a process: antonyms for jenny holzer" and "art is a concept art is a process: haiku for sol lewitt" were originally published in *The Brooklyn Rail* (October 2010). "America As A Woman" was originally published in *Womb* (Summer/Fall 2007). Permission granted by author.

Maryrose Larkin, "DARC" was originally published as *DARC* (Creative Commons, 2009). Permission granted by author.

Rachel Levitsky, "Public Space and Privasphere," originally published in *The Story of My Accident is Ours* (New York: Futurepoem, 2011). An earlier version of this section was published online at *Sous Rature*. Permission granted by author.

Bernadette Mayer, "helen rezey sestina," and "HISTORY OF TROY, N.Y.," are original publications. Permission granted by author.

Sharon Mesmer, "Revenge" was originally published in *In Ordinary Time* (Brooklyn: Hanging Loose Press, 2005). Permission granted by author.

Yedda Morrison, selected works were originally published in *Darkness* (little red leaves, 2009). The book-length work, *Darkness,* is forthcoming from Make Now Press. Permission granted by author.

Harryette Mullen, selections from *S*PeRM**K*T* were originally published in *S*PeRM**K*T* (San Diego: Singing Horse Press, 1992), and republished in *Recyclopedia,* (Minneapolis: Graywolf Press, 2006). Permission granted by author.

Harryette Mullen, statement about *S*PeRM**K*T* adapted from "A Conversation with Harryette Mullen," Farah Griffin, Michael Magee, and Kristen Gallagher / 1997, online: http://wings.buffalo.edu/epc/authors/mullen/interview-new.html. Republished in COMBO #1, Summer 1998.

Laura Mullen, "I Wandered Networks Like a Cloud," "Cloud as Lonely," "Cloud Seeding: From a Journal," and "No Voice" were originally published in *Dark Archive* (Berkeley, California: University of California Press, 2011). Permission granted by the author.

Sawako Nakayasu, selected works originally published in *Texture Notes* (Chicago: Letter Machine Editions, 2010). "I WOULD NOT HAVE IT ANY OTHER WAY" and "Performance Notes to 'Ant'" are original publications. Permission granted by author.

Redell Olsen, selected work is from *Punk Faun: A Bar Rock Pastel* (Berkeley, CA: Subpress, 2012). Permission granted by author.

Jena Osman, excerpts from "Financial District" ("BOWLING GREEN," "MONEY," "BOWLING GREEN + MONEY,") originally published in *The Network* (Fence Books, 2010). Permission granted by the author.

Chus Pato, selected works, translated by Erín Moure, were originally published in *Hordes of Writing* (UK: Shearsman Books, Canada: Buschek Books, 2011). Permission granted by author and translator.

M. NourbeSe Philip, from *Zong!* (Middletown, CT: Weslyan University Press, 2008) ©2008 by M. NourbeSe Philip. Reprinted by permission of Wesleyan University Press.

Anne Portugal, "from Quisite Moment," was translated from the French by Rosemarie Waldrop and originally published in *Quisite Moment* (Providence: Burning Deck/Anyart, 2008). Permission granted by author.

kathryn l. pringle, selected works originally published in *RIGHT NEW BIOLOGY* (Queens: Factory School, 2009) Permission granted by "Heretical Texts series" and "Factory School" (factoryschool.org).

a.rawlings, excerpt from *Rule of Three* (project forthcoming). Permission granted by author.

Joan Retallack, "ARCHIMEDES' NEW LIGHT, Geometries of Excitable Species" was originally published in *Procedural Elegies / Western Civ Cont'd*, (New York: Roof Books, 2010). Permission granted by author.

Frances Richard, "The Separatrix" was originally published in *Antennae No. 10*, February 2009. Permission granted by author.

Deborah Richards, "Science and nature," "It's a jungle out there," "Common language," "Earth the weeping sores," and "Talking drums," are part of *Nine Nights*. Permission granted by author.

Cia Rinne, excerpts from *notes for soloists* (2009) published with the kind permission of Cia Rinne and OEI Editör, Stockholm.

Lisa Robertson and Stacy Doris, selected works were originally published in *The Perfume Recordist*. Permission granted by authors.

Lisa Robertson and Stacy Doris, image of *The Perfurme Recordist*, Djuna Barnes, "The Villager."

Kim Rosenfield, selections from *LIVIDITY*, forthcoming from Les Figues Press. Permission granted by the author.

Susan M. Schultz, selected works from *Status Lines*, originally published on Facebook. Permission granted by author.

Ryoko Seikiguchi, "Emergence," was translated by Sarah O'Brien and is an original publication. Permission granted by author and translator.

Juliana Spahr, A version of "Influence & Originality" appeared in *Alchemy of the Word: Writers Talk About Writing*, edited by Nicola Morris and Aimee Liu. (State College: California Institute of Arts and Letters, 2011). Permission granted by author.

Anne Tardos, selections from *NINE* were first published in *Conjunctions*. Permission granted by author.

Cecilia Vicuña, selected works were originally published in *Instan* (Berkeley: Kelsey Street Press, 2002). Permission granted by author.

Rosmarie Waldrop, selection from "Kind Regards" from *Streets Enough to Welcome Snow* (Barrytown, New York: Station Hill Press, Inc., ©1986 by Rosmarie Waldrop), reprinted by permission of the publisher. All rights reserved.

Rosmarie Waldrop, selected work from *The Reproduction of the Profiles*, copyright ©1987 by Rosmarie Waldrop. Originally published by New Directions Publishing Corp. Reprinted by permission of the author.

Wendy Walker, selected work is an original publication. Permission granted by the author.

Wendy Walker, "A View In The Island of Jamaica," engraving by George Robertson, 1778, The British Library Board Maps.K.Top.123.54c. Reprinted by permission.

Wendy Walker, "Mandingo Slave Traders and Coffle, Senegal, 1780s," Albert and Shirley Small Special Collections Library, University of Virginia. Reprinted by permission.

Hannah Weiner, selected works were originally published in *The Code Poems* (Open Studio, 1982), and reprinted in *Hannah Weiner's Open House* (Kenning Editions, 2006). Permission granted by Charles Bernstein for Hannah Weiner in trust.

Rachel Zolf, "How to Shape Sacred Time," "Messenger," and "L'Amiral Cherche une Maison a Louer," were originally published in *Neighbour Procedure* (Ontario: Coach House Books, 2010). Reprinted by permission of Coach House Books.

KEY SUPPORTERS

I'll Drown My Book: Conceptual Writing by Women was made possible through the generous support of the following:

The Metabolic Studio

Kathrin Schaeppi

Tracy Bachman and Deborah Harrington

Dorothy

Hershey-Van Horn Family Trust

Patrick Greaney

Stephanie Taylor

ABOUT THE EDITORS

Caroline Bergvall is a writer of French-Norwegian background, based in London. She works across languages, media and contexts. Latest book released: *Meddle English* (Nightboat Books, 2011). Latest solo commission, with catalogue: *Middling English* (John Hansard Gallery, 2010). Latest siting: "1DJ2MANY (Elevation Mix)," Théatre du Grütli, Geneva, February 2012. DVD release of some of her projects forthcoming April 2012 (John Hansard Publications).

Laynie Browne is the author of nine collections of poetry and one novel. Her most recent publications include: *Roseate, Points of Gold* (Dusie, 2011), *The Desires of Letters* (Counterpath, 2010), and *The Scented Fox* (Wave, 2007) which was selected for the National Poetry Series award. Currently she edits for the online journal *Trickhouse*, and teaches at the University of Arizona.

Teresa Carmody is the author of *Requiem* (Les Figues Press, 2005), and three chapbooks: *I Can Feel* (Insert Press, 2011), *Eye Hole Adore* (PS Books, 2008), and *Your Spiritual Suit of Armor by Katherine Anne* (Woodland Editions, 2009). She teaches at California Institute of the Arts and is co-director of Les Figues Press

Vanessa Place is a writer, lawyer, and co-director of Les Figues Press.

ℱ

LES FIGUES PRESS
Post Office Box 7736
Los Angeles, CA 90007
info@lesfigues.com
www.lesfigues.com